Taking Literature and Language
Learning Online

Also Available from Bloomsbury

Video Enhanced Observation for Language Teaching, edited by Paul Seedhouse
Digital Games and Language Learning, edited by Mark Peterson,
Kasumi Yamazaki and Michael Thomas
Posthumanism and the Digital University, Lesley Gourlay
Teacher Education in Computer-Assisted Language Learning,
Euline Cutrim Schmid
Autonomous Language Learning with Technology, Chun Lai
Language Teacher Education and Technology, edited by Jeong-Bae Son
and Scott Windeatt

Taking Literature and Language Learning Online

New Perspectives on Teaching, Research and Technology

Edited by
Sandra Stadler-Heer and Amos Paran

BLOOMSBURY ACADEMIC
LONDON • NEW YORK • OXFORD • NEW DELHI • SYDNEY

BLOOMSBURY ACADEMIC
Bloomsbury Publishing Plc
50 Bedford Square, London, WC1B 3DP, UK
1385 Broadway, New York, NY 10018, USA
29 Earlsfort Terrace, Dublin 2, Ireland

BLOOMSBURY, BLOOMSBURY ACADEMIC and the Diana logo are
trademarks of Bloomsbury Publishing Plc

First published in Great Britain 2023

A catalogue record for this book is available from the British Library.

A catalog record for this book is available from the Library of Congress.

ISBN: HB: 978-1-3502-6852-4
ePDF: 978-1-3502-6853-1
eBook: 978-1-3502-6854-8

Typeset by Newgen KnowledgeWorks Pvt. Ltd., Chennai, India

To find out more about our authors and books visit www.bloomsbury.com
and sign up for our newsletters.

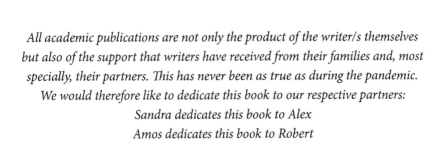

All academic publications are not only the product of the writer/s themselves but also of the support that writers have received from their families and, most specially, their partners. This has never been as true as during the pandemic. We would therefore like to dedicate this book to our respective partners:
Sandra dedicates this book to Alex
Amos dedicates this book to Robert

Contents

Figures

Tables

Contributors

Fatma Abubaker is Associate Tutor at the School of Education, University of Glasgow, UK, where she teaches in the MSc TESOL programme. She obtained her PhD in educational studies from the University of Glasgow, with particular focus on teaching literature in the language classroom and developing creativity. Her research focuses on developing programmes and multimodal pedagogies that integrate media, literature and short fiction using response-based and arts-based approaches. Her research interests include using literature in ELT, reader-response theory, curriculum design, reading in EFL/ESL and using digital technologies in EFL classrooms.

Hana A. El-Badri is Assistant Professor in the Faculty of Languages, Department of Literature at the University of Benghazi, Libya. She obtained her PhD in educational studies from the University of Aberdeen, UK. She teaches a range of literature courses, including American literature and literary stylistics. Her research interests focus on teaching literature to EFL learners, using interactive reading in ELT, language assessment and cultural and intercultural communication. Her recent research focuses on issues related to assessing online learning and learner autonomy using student self-assessment.

Gail Ellis is an independent teacher educator and adviser who has been working with picturebooks since 1989. Her main interests include children's rights, picturebooks in primary ELT, young learner ELT management and inclusive practices. Her recent publications include *Teaching English to Pre-primary Children*, with Sandie Mourão (2020); *Teaching Children How to Learn*, with Nayr Ibrahim (2015); and *Tell It Again!*, with Jean Brewster (2014). She is a co-founder of PEPELT (https://pepelt21.com/) and a member of the editorial review board for the open-access *Children's Literature in English Language Education Journal* (https://clelejournal.org/).

Christine Gardemann is interim professor at the University of Marburg since October 2022. She was a Research Assistant at the Department of English Didactics at Hamburg University, Germany, where she worked on her PhD at the nexus of literature teaching and teacher identity. After having taught German, English and media for several years at a secondary school in Hamburg, she is now working as a Postdoctoral Research Fellow at Bielefeld University, Germany. Her current research projects focus on the learner perspective in EFL classrooms, for example, by reflecting on democracy learning as a basis for EFL teaching, and exploring ways to support teachers in dealing with linguistic and motivational heterogeneity.

Ingrid Gessner is Hochschulprofessorin for English and American studies at the University College of Teacher Education Vorarlberg in Feldkirch, Austria. She is the author of *Collective Memory as Catharsis? The Vietnam Veterans Memorial in Public Controversy* (2000) and of the award-winning books *From Sites of Memory to Cybersights: (Re)Framing Japanese American Experiences* (2007) and *Yellow Fever Years: An Epidemiology of Nineteenth-Century Literature and Culture* (2016). She co-edited special issues on *Iconographies of the Calamitous in American Visual Culture* (2013), *Commemorating World War II* (2015), *Material Culture Studies* (2019) and *Digital Pedagogy* (2020). Further publications include articles on 9/11, feminism and gender studies, eco-photography and questions of transnationalism.

Geoff Hall is Professor of Applied Linguistics, University of Nottingham Ningbo China and Professor II at Nord University, Norway, where his duties primarily include research leadership and supervision of postgraduate students. His research interests are literature and language teaching and learning in first language and foreign language contexts. With extensive experience in English and education teaching and teacher training in East and South East Asia, he brings valued additional perspectives to European contexts. His most widely cited publication is *Literature in Language Education* (2015), and he has authored many other invited contributions to international handbooks and professional events.

Annett Kaminski is a Teacher Educator at the University of Koblenz-Landau in Germany with more than twenty years of teaching experience. She holds a teacher qualification for secondary school and a PhD in applied linguistics. Currently, she teaches EFL classes and a course on teaching English to young learners and conducts seminars on children's literature for students on the primary education degree scheme at the university campus in Landau. Her research focuses on early English language learning in classroom settings. She is particularly interested in learner response to multimodal features, story-based EFL teaching and reflective teaching practice in teacher education.

Verena Laschinger works at the University of Erfurt, Germany. From 2005 to 2010 she was employed as an Assistant Professor of American Literature and Culture at Fatih University Istanbul, Turkey. She holds a PhD from Ludwig-Maximilians-University Munich, Germany. Her research interests include American urban literature and photography. She is also a founding member of the European Study Group of Nineteenth-Century American Women's Literature.

Christian Ludwig is currently Visiting Professor at the Freie Universität Berlin, Germany. His teaching and research focus on literature, graphic novels, digital media and plurilingual approaches to learning English as a foreign language. He is one of the organizers of the symposium series titled 'Taboos in Foreign Language Education'. Together with Elizabeth Shipley, he is co-editor of the two-volume work *Mapping the Imaginative: Teaching Fantasy and Science Fiction in the EFL Classroom* (2020).

Pedro Malard Monteiro has a PhD in English and creative writing from SUNY-Albany in the United States. He is a professor of English at Universidade Federal de Uberlandia, Brazil, where he teaches literature, English as a foreign language and creative writing. He has been involved in Simply Stories since 2018 when he spent his sabbatical at Newcastle.

Sandie Mourão (PhD) is Research Fellow at Nova University Lisbon, Portugal, with over thirty years of experience as a teacher, teacher educator and materials writer in English language education. Her main research interests are early language learning, picturebooks, intercultural citizenship education, classroom assessment practices and teacher research. Her recent publications include *Teaching English to Pre-primary Children*, with Gail Ellis (2020), and, as co-editor, *Fractures and Disruptions in Children's Literature* (2017) and *Early Years Second Language Education* (2015). She is coordinator of the Erasmus+ project ICEPELL (https://icepell.eu/) and co-founder of PEPELT https://pepelt21.com/.

Amos Paran is Professor of TESOL at the UCL Institute of Education, London, UK. He started his career teaching EFL in secondary schools in Israel before moving to the UK. He has worked with teachers in many international contexts, including visiting appointments at the Universities of Tübingen and Szeged. Amos is a tutor on the free MOOC, *Teaching EFL/ESL Reading: A Task-Based Approach* and is co-convenor of the AILA research network, *Literature in Language Learning and Teaching*. Publications include *Literature in Language Teaching and Learning* (2006) and *Testing the Untestable in Language Education* (2010).

Jennifer Schumm Fauster is Senior Lecturer in the English Studies Department at the University of Graz, Austria. She teaches courses in language teaching, English for specific purposes and English language teaching research and methodology. In addition, she is a teacher trainer at the Pädagogischen Hochschulen (the University Colleges of Teacher Education) in Austria. Her main areas of research are using young adult literature in the language classroom, intercultural communication and writing in the L2 context.

Elizabeth Shipley teaches EFL, literature and culture at the Pädagogische Hochschule Karlsruhe, Germany. Her recent research focuses on fantasy and science fiction, creative writing, gender and cultural studies. Together with Christian Ludwig, she is co-editor of the two-volume work *Mapping the Imaginative: Teaching Fantasy and Science Fiction in the EFL Classroom* (2020).

Sandra Stadler-Heer is Senior Lecturer of TESOL at the Department of Linguistics and Literature, Catholic University of Eichstätt-Ingolstadt, Germany. She is co-convenor of the AILA Literature in Language Learning and Teaching Research Network. Her research focuses on professional teacher competences, teaching foreign languages online and teaching literature.

Theresa Summer is Associate Professor of Teaching English as a Foreign Language at the University of Bamberg, Germany. She was an English and music teacher at secondary schools for several years and is co-editor of the journal *Englisch 5–10*. Her research interests include pop culture and songs in ELT, grammar education, global education, ecomusicology and taboos in critical foreign language education.

Engelbert Thaler is Professor of TESOL at the University of Augsburg, Germany. He is an expert on methodology in foreign language teaching with more than 680 academic publications in this field of research. He is the editor of the textbook series *Access* and *PRAXIS Fremdsprachenunterricht*. His research foci lie with teacher training, the development of textbooks and improving the quality of teaching modern media, literature and intercultural learning. He is a highly active speaker at conferences and heavily involved in the professional development of in-service teachers.

Margaret Wilkinson is a prose, stage, screen and radio writer. Her special interest is dramatic structure. She has been Degree Programme Director for the MA and PGC in Creative Writing at Newcastle University where she continues to teach dramatic structure for both script and prose writers.

Martha Young-Scholten is Professor of Second Language Acquisition at Newcastle University, UK. She investigates the second language acquisition of morphosyntax and phonology by adults with and without literacy in their home language and the development of second language reading by those without native language literacy. With Margaret Wilkinson, she started and co-directs the Simply Cracking Good Stories project.

Acknowledgements

We would like to thank Petra Kirchhoff, our co-convenor of the AILA Literature and Language Learning and Teaching Research Network, for her invaluable comments on the first draft of the introduction to this collection. As the co-founder of the research network, Petra's insights into the developments of teaching literature have shaped the operations of the network over the past four years, and she was also the co-organizer of the symposium which gave rise to this publication.

We would also like to express our gratitude to all the unseen contributors to the chapters in this volume: the anonymized participants in the studies, school students, pre-service teachers, colleagues and attendees of presentations at conferences. Without their participation, these projects would not have come alive and turned out the way they did. It is a privilege to tell their stories in this volume.

Introduction

Amos Paran and Sandra Stadler-Heer

'That's how people live, Milt' – Michael Antonious again, still kindly, gently –
'by telling stories. What's the first thing a kid says when he learns how to talk?
"Tell me a story." That's how we understand who we are, where we come from.
Stories are everything'.

– Jeffrey Eugenides, *Middlesex*, p. 179

This is a time when we need art more than ever. We need art to remind us why
life is worth living. We need art to reawaken our sense of the wonder of being,
to remind us of our freedom and to highlight the things in our cultures that
enable us to withstand the dreaded visage of death.

– Ben Okri, *Financial Times*, 20 March 2020

As the two quotes above remind us, literary and artistic creation is a basic
human activity and indeed a basic human need. Jeffrey Eugenides reminds us
also that stories and storytelling are inextricably linked with the people who
surround us; the listener or the reader is inextricably linked to the storyteller and
the author. And human beings are storytelling animals, as Jonathan Gottschall
(2012) points out in his eponymous book. Ben Okri's more recent comment
came as a reaction to the cancellations and shutdowns that accompanied the
arrival of the Covid-19 pandemic in the UK in March 2020 and was a sentiment
echoed during the first wave of the Covid-19 pandemic in 2020 over and over
again by writers, musicians, theatre directors and artists in all media.

The centrality of literary creation to human lives means that it comes as no
surprise that literature has 'been' online ever since there has been an online,
virtual world. Published nearly a quarter of a century ago, *Literature and the
Internet* (Browner, Pulsford and Sears 2000) lists hundreds of websites devoted

to literature, highlighting ways in which literary scholars, literature students and teachers of literature could use the internet for research, study and teaching already then. Going even further back, it is salutary to remember that the Gutenberg Project started in 1971 (Hart 1992), in an era when computers had barely impinged on the consciousness of most readers. Indeed, one could argue that with publications such as introductions to online literature production (e.g. Hammond 2016) as well as handbooks on electronic literature (e.g. Tabbi 2020) this is a maturing field. In the same way, language learning has been conducted online, in one way or another, ever since there was an 'online' (see Kern (2021) for a history of digital literacies) as has language teacher education. The intersection between language learning, literature and online environments has also been explored (see e.g. Short, Busse and Plummer 2007; Lima 2013; Kirchhoff 2019; Naji, Subramaniam and White 2019).

And yet, as much as we were used to conducting great parts of our educational and literary lives in online environments, in March 2020 we were taken online in a more profound way than we had been able to envisage. Whereas online interactions had previously been optional and, for some of us, occasional, there was now no choice. Anything that was not online had to be moved online. Everything optional became compulsory. Most aspects of our lives were now conducted online in ways that had been unthinkable previously.

The response to the move online in foreign language education has been charted in a number of journal special issues (e.g. *ELT Journal; Foreign Language Annals; System; TESOL Journal*), and much of this research is surveyed in a systematic review by Moorhouse and Kohnke (2021). The collection we present here focuses on one specific aspect of this move – the intersection between literature, language teaching and language teacher education, during and through the move to online publishing and teaching.

The Origins, Scope and Reach of This Collection

The chapters in this volume originated in a half-day online symposium held on 23 October 2020 and organized by the Literature in Language Learning and Teaching Research Network of the International Association of Applied Linguistics (AILA LiLLT ReN, https://lilltresearch.net). The focus of the AILA LiLLT ReN in general is on promoting research into literature in language teaching, highlighting learning designs, discussions and implications for both research and teaching. The focus of the symposium (and of the chapters in this volume) was the response to the wholesale move online, and on presenting and debating the formation of new digital and interactional practices (rather than providing suggestions on the methodology of teaching literature online, though some chapters do make methodological suggestions). In its specific focus this volume joins previous recent research-oriented collections that have focused on specific areas of literature in foreign and second language teaching and learning, such as primary and secondary educational settings (Bland 2018), multimodality (Dominguez-Romero, Bobkina and Stefanova 2018) or spoken language and speaking skills (Jones 2019). The contributors to the collection come from literary studies, language teaching and language teacher education backgrounds in Austria, Brazil, France, Germany, Lybia, Portugal and the UK. Although the majority of the chapters originate in Europe, and only two specifically deal with contexts outside Europe, many contributions deal with literature and literature teaching available online and accessible globally, transcending national boundaries.

The Chapters in This Volume: An Overview

Members of the AILA LiLLT ReN come from various research traditions, and this variety in approaches – both research approaches and writing approaches – is reflected in this collection. Rather than imposing an identical structure on all chapters, authors were invited to contribute within their own disciplinary discourses as far as possible, though all were asked to comment on implications of their work for future research. Coupled with the different contexts of teaching and the different learners contributors work with, this has resulted in a volume where the four sections and individual chapters are different in their outline and in the technology- and research-based insights into how literature and languages can be taught online.

Part 1, 'Literary Responses in Times of Crisis', focuses on literary outputs stimulated by the pandemic as well as by past pandemics. In 'Literary Narratives as Recordings of the Pandemic Present', Ingrid Gessner investigates the *New York Times Decameron Project* stories as a literary alternative to the official news narratives, interviews, autobiographical reconstructions and proposed monuments, arguing that the twenty-nine short stories are more than factual recordings of the present and are figurative time capsules that defy (easy) closure. Engelbert Thaler presents a carefully selected historical list of what he calls 'pandemic literature' in a chapter entitled 'Pandemic Literature: What It Is, Why It Should Be Taught and How', and outlines concrete approaches to including pandemic fiction in online and hybrid teaching and learning scenarios. Like Okri in the quote at the start of this introduction, Thaler widens our frame of reference by connecting literature with other artistic creations such as museum exhibitions as well as references to important literature in other languages. Presenting an overview of teaching literature in a foreign language, he also highlights the ways in which dealing with pandemic literature provides insights into the human condition. Taken together, Gessner and Thaler present a textual basis that is available to us for researching and teaching about and in crises.

Part 2, 'Researching and Teaching Literature for/to Young Learners', includes two chapters examining the pedagogy of engaging learners with literature online, both looking at picturebooks. In a chapter entitled 'Identifying Quality in Asynchronous, Pre-recorded Picturebook Read-Alouds for Children Learning English as a Foreign Language', Gail Ellis and Sandie Mourão investigate some of the affordances of 'Read-Aloud Talk' in asynchronous picturebook read-alouds, focusing on issues of quality and ways of identifying quality. Based on previous typologies and their own initial analysis of existing read-alouds, they construct and present a typology for analysing read-alouds based on their inductive micro-analysis of read-alouds in their own project. In her contribution, 'Digital Picturebooks in Times of Crisis: From Picturebooks about Covid-19 to Developing Critical Environmental Literacies', Theresa Summer discusses and explores the pedagogical potential and teaching options of a digital picturebook as an eco-artefact for English language education and particularly for developing critical environmental literacies, providing a task sequence for working with digital eco-picturebooks, but in fact applicable and extendable to other types of picturebooks as well.

Part 3, 'Researching and Teaching Literature in Online Teacher Education', looks at the affordances of various technologies for teaching online and the way they interact with literature and language learning when the focus is on educating teachers to work with literature. In her aptly named chapter, 'Exploring the Educational Potential of Literature in English Language Teaching: Continuity and Change in Digital Literature Teaching', Christine Gardemann extends her previous work on perceptions of teaching literature in secondary school EFL classrooms and suggests ways in which teachers might be able to transfer their understanding of teaching literature into a digital setting without having to completely reinvent their professional identity. In 'Conducting Story-Based Activities in Times of Social Distancing' Annett Kaminski reminds us that many of the issues we are confronting have been part of the debate on open, distance and online education for many years, and offers detailed insights into the views of future primary school teachers in Germany on the way in which their courses moved online and the challenges these courses faced. Kaminski highlights issues involved in working with story-based activities – some of which rely on physical proximity – at a time when such proximity is the victim of social distancing. Kaminski's chapter also offers insights into the ways in which online teaching develops from one iteration to the next.

Part 4, 'Tools and Concepts for Teaching Literature Online', brings together chapters from a very wide range of contexts, presenting tools and concepts in teaching literature online and describing concrete ways of facing the challenges of implementing new forms of teaching with literature, actively training learners and pre-service teachers in collaborative literary analysis, collaborative literary response and collaborative literary creation. Jennifer Schumm Fauster, in 'Implementing a Collaborative Reading Project Online: Solutions for a Pedagogically Meaningful Virtual Workshop', discusses solutions to transferring an established face-to-face course format to an online environment, looking at a collaborative reading project involving student-teachers and secondary school learners working together. Fatma Abubaker and Hana El-Badri, in their chapter on 'Digital Storytelling as a Pedagogical Approach for Meaningful Learning: Alternative Implementations of Technology in the Libyan EFL Context', show that digital storytelling can be a valuable instructional alternative to traditional teaching approaches in university EFL classrooms in Libya, evidencing their learners' favourable reaction to working collaboratively online. Abubaker and El-Badri's chapter is also a salutary reminder of what can happen in countries where infrastructure issues impact heavily on what teachers and students can do online. In 'Simple and Engaging Fiction for Adult Beginners', Pedro Malard Monteiro, Margaret Wilkinson and Martha Young-Scholten discuss an ongoing project, Simply Cracking Good Stories, aimed at producing and creating literature for learners with low level literacy skills. Their focus is on how writers are trained to write for such an audience, the guidance writers are given and the ways in which face-to-face and online training of writers differ. In her chapter, literary scholar Verena Laschinger reinvents the philological practice of annotating literary texts and visually exposes the obsolete notion of literature as the lone act of a genius author by engaging her students in Germany in collaborative, virtual annotation in digital classrooms. In the last empirical chapter, 'Writing the Future: Collaborative Creative Science-Fiction Writing in the Virtual EFL Classroom', Christian Ludwig and Elizabeth Shipley focus on issues of cooperation and creativity, presenting their classroom-based research on a collaborative online creative writing project at two German universities, in which the students produced science-fiction short stories and gained agency in online learning settings. Finally, the last chapter in the collection, Geoff Hall's 'Afterword: Closing Reflections on the Brave New World of Literature and Language Education Online', provides a thoughtful, reflective overview of the threads running through the various chapters.

A Look to the Future

We end with a consideration of the long-term implications of the changes that we witnessed in our lives and in education when digitization became the answer to the problems of maintaining contact in 2020. Moorhouse and Kohnke (2021), in a systematic review of the response to Covid-19 in the ELT world, suggest there were three main lessons learnt. These are valid for this collection as well. We have learned of the affordances of the move online, and in some areas of writing, publishing, teaching and learning about online literature, the global move towards virtual environments has been a motor for innovation. This is the result of the second lesson, which Moorhouse and Kohnke frame as 'the challenges, complexity and diversity of teaching online in ELT' (374). The established educational, research and publishing procedures, processes and objectives in teaching and learning were fundamentally challenged, and in some cases what had been 'previously unthinkable' (Puentedura 2012) publishing and teaching approaches, learning designs and forms of interaction became reality when human contact was possible exclusively online. And finally, the digital divide that Moorhouse and Kohnke (2021) talk about is also evident in various forms in the chapters here (see Hockly and Dudeney (2015) for a nuanced discussion of the digital divide and its manifestations).

We hope readers will find that this collection celebrates the vitality of response to the pandemic at the intersection of literature, language teaching and language teacher education, and that it will serve as a stepping stone for researching the phenomena we have witnessed. Focusing on researching continuities and changes in literary production, communicative interaction, task designs, online collaboration and feedback, the chapter authors provide insights into how creativity and crisis may lead to what would previously have been uncharted learning opportunities and innovations in human connections through literature. Importantly, we hope that the research presented in this volume will mark the first steps in the larger context of an ongoing technology-driven transformation of curricula and established teaching and research practices in the nexus of literature and foreign language learning.

References

Primary Literature

Eugenides, J. (2002), *Middlesex*, London: Bloomsbury.
Okri, B. (2020), 'We Need Art More Than Ever', *Financial Times*, 20 March. https://www.ft.com/content/efe229b4-6936-11ea-a3c9-1fe6fedcca75 (accessed 9 December 2021).

Secondary Literature

Bland, J., ed. (2018), *Using Literature in English Language Education: Challenging Reading for 8–18 Year Olds*, London: Bloomsbury.
Browner, S., S. Pulsford and R. Sears (2000), *Literature and the Internet: A Guide for Students, Teachers, and Scholars*, New York: Garland.
Dominguez Romero, E., J. Bobkina and S. Stefanova, eds (2018), *Teaching Literature and Language through Multimodal Texts*, Hershey, PA: IGI Global.
Gottschall, J. (2012), *The Storytelling Animal: How Stories Make Us Human*, Boston, MA: Houghton Mifflin Harcourt.
Hammond, A. (2016), *Literature in the Digital Age: An Introduction*, Cambridge: Cambridge University Press.
Hart, M. (1992), 'The History and Philosophy of Project Gutenberg'. https://www.gutenberg.org/about/background/history_and_philosophy.html (accessed 8 December 2021).
Hockly, N., and G. Dudeney (2015), 'Current and Future Digital Trends in ELT', *RELC Journal*, 49 (2): 164–78.
Jones, C., ed. (2019), *Literature, Spoken Language and Speaking Skills in Second Language Learning*, Cambridge: Cambridge University Press.
Kern, R. (2021), 'Twenty-Five Years of Digital Literacies in CALL', *Language Learning and Technology*, 25 (3): 132–50. https://www.lltjournal.org/item/3224.
Kirchhoff, P. (2019), 'Your Story in 280 Characters Max – Twitter Fiction für das kreative Schreiben nutzen', *Der Fremdsprachliche Unterricht Englisch*, 53 (160): 40–5.
Lima, C. (2013), 'Reading and Discussing Literature Online', in T. Pattison (ed.), *IATEFL 2012 Glasgow Conference Selections*, Canterbury: International Association of Teachers of English as a Foreign Language.
Moorhouse, B. L., and L. Kohnke (2021), 'Responses of the English-Language Teaching Community to the Covid-19 Pandemic', *RELC Journal*, 52 (3): 359–78.

Naji, J., G. Subramaniam and G. White (2019), *New Approaches to Literature for Language Learning*, Basingstoke: Palgrave Macmillan.

Puentedura, R. R. (2012), 'Transformation, Technology, and Education'. http://www.hippasus.com/resources/tte/ (accessed 9 December 2021).

Short, M., B. Busse and P. Plummer (2007), 'Investigating Student Reactions to a Web-Based Stylistics Course in Different National and Educational Settings', in G. Watson and S. Zyngier (eds), *Literature and Stylistics for Language Learners: Theory and Practice*, 106–25, Basingstoke: Palgrave Macmillan.

Tabbi, J., ed. (2020), *The Bloomsbury Handbook of Electronic Literature*, London: Bloomsbury.

Part 1

Literary Responses in Times of Crisis

1

Literary Narratives as Recordings of the Pandemic Present: The *New York Times Magazine*'s *Decameron Project*

Ingrid Gessner

Introduction

In March 2020, as the novel coronavirus spread across the world, governments issued travel bans and quarantine measures and people began to self-isolate, the editors of the *New York Times Magazine* asked a diverse group of contemporary authors to write new short stories inspired by the moment. The editors had gotten the idea for the anthology from Giovanni Boccaccio's *Decameron*, which was written as the plague, the Black Death, ravaged Florence in the fourteenth century. How are we making sense of the new pandemic reality? How will we remember it? As with early predictions on how we will remember the terrorist attacks of 9/11, we find ourselves without definite answers. On the one hand, there is the human need for detailed information, to have narratives that explain the incomprehensible, ranging from science-based narratives to those infused with conspiracy theories. On the other hand, we are faced with the current impossibility of closure; the lack of one coherent or authoritative version of the pandemic. This is where art steps in. Literature is called forth to contribute to the understanding of the shared experience of a historic and global crisis and to imagine a future. Or, as Rivka Galchen reminds us: 'Reading stories in difficult times is a way to understand those times, and also a way to persevere through them' (2020: xvi). In other words, the role literature plays in times of pandemics cannot be underestimated. Literature comes alive through the act of reading, and our choice to engage ourselves with a literary text includes a willingness to be changed by what we read. Consequently, when we read pandemic narratives in times of a pandemic, these fictions affect how we feel and how we make sense of the time we live in. The affective quality of pandemic narratives was most certainly on the minds of the editors of the *New York Times Magazine* when they asked for recordings of collective memories in the form of stories produced as literature on demand intended for digital dissemination and online reading. The latter is particularly relevant since the *New York Times* and the *New York Times Magazine*, its Sunday supplement, added 2.3 million digital-only subscriptions in 2020, more than in any previous year, possibly triggered by the pandemic, by the social unrest after the killing of George Floyd and by a contested presidential race (Tracy 2021). Because of their digital format the *Decameron Project* stories reached 7.5 million subscribers worldwide who could read the texts (whose layouts had been optimized for online consumption) on their digital devices. More people probably read the stories that are still available online after their initial publication due to widespread positive reporting, favourable reviews and discussion in scholarly circles (such as the symposium that triggered the publication of this chapter).

This chapter argues that the *New York Times Magazine*'s *Decameron Project*'s twenty-nine short stories are specifically produced figurative time capsules that defy (easy) closure or a commitment to a specific literary form. Together, they approach reality, memory and current history in more nuanced ways than biographical reconstructions in obituaries are able to. In fact, some of the earliest narratives of the global pandemic appeared in the form of obituaries in newspapers across the world. The 24 May 2020 front page of the *New York Times* presented names and biographical details of Covid-19 victims, calling attention to the death toll approaching one hundred thousand in the United States at that time. The list of names continued on three pages inside the newspaper's main news section. An interactive visualization of the victims' names, ages, hometowns and a short tag line about their lives are still accessible online (https://www.nyti mes.com/interactive/2020/05/24/us/us-coronavirus-deaths-100000.html).

The need to grieve, remember and find closure that might temporarily be satisfied with a list of confirmed 'real' names (such as in the *New York Times*) can equally be witnessed in the almost immediate wish to give a specific form to the pandemic experience as several memorial proposals as well as already completed monuments demonstrate. Amongst the completed monuments are the Blossom Memorial Garden in Queen Elizabeth Olympic Park, London, opened on 24 May 2021; the memorial *Resilienza, Comunità, Ripartenza* in Codogna, Italy, unveiled on 21 February 2021; and the *Monumento en recuerdo de las víctimas de la pandemia del Covid-19*, a circular piece of black steel with a flame, in Madrid, Spain, unveiled on 15 May 2020. Notable proposals for monuments include the planned 'World Memorial to the Pandemic', a large circular sculpture to be installed on water off the Uruguay coast (https://www.gomezplatero.com/en/proyecto/memorial-pandemic/); planting thirty-five thousand cypress trees in Milan's historic San Siro stadium to turn it into a public memorial to commemorate the Covid-19 victims, called 'san siro 2.0 – monumento per la vita' (http://www.angelorenna.com/), suggested by the Italian architect Angelo Renna; and finally the proposal by Miró Rivera Architects to construct a gigantic bowl-shaped structure in the middle of the Dead Sea, on the border between Israel and Jordan, as an inter-denominational floating burial site called 'Yarauvi' (https://www.mirorivera.com/yarauvi).

The memorials still in the planning stages are massive in size; probably to demonstrate the enormous influence the pandemic continues to have over our lives and deaths. However, unlike the monuments, the *Decameron Project* short stories do not commit themselves to a finite and unchangeable structure. In their entirety, they problematize the duality of time: the significant historicity of the present moment of crisis and the existential time that seems to have come to a standstill. The stories are radically open and defy closure by approaching the experience of the Covid-19 pandemic through motifs and plotlines clustered around issues of immobility and mobility as well as by employing settings that represent what Michel Foucault calls heterotopia or crisis heterotopia, 'sacred or forbidden places, reserved for individuals who are … in a state of crisis' (1986: 24). Furthermore, characters in the stories experience time as structured in a before and an after the beginning of the pandemic as well as in the form of Michel Foucault's concept of heterochronia, in which they are operating outside a social and political construction of time.

Boccaccio's *Decameron* and the *Decameron Project*

When the WHO declared the Covid-19 crisis a pandemic in March 2020, not only did people start rereading Katherine Ann Porter's famous novella *Pale Horse, Pale Rider* ([1939] 2011), which fictionalizes the 1918–19 flu pandemic, but quite a few turned to Giovanni Boccaccio's *Decameron* to look for guidance in the current crisis (Roper 2020: vii). Boccaccio began working on the project in 1349, after his father died of the plague, and completed the collection in 1353. The altogether one hundred stories, which Boccaccio called novellas, were largely versions of older and already familiar tales, which he sometimes restructured, combined and adapted to the reality of the fourteenth century. The frame narrative of the *Decameron* introduces ten young people who decide to quarantine themselves outside Florence during a plague outbreak in 1348. Most of the stories they tell each other in the literary work to pass the time are comedic, though some are tragic; they are about love and betrayal, life and death, but they do not explicitly focus on the plague. Towards the end of self-isolation 'we hear tales of those who behave with nearly unimaginable nobility in the face of a manifestly cruel and unjust world. Under emotional cover – it's only a story – the characters experience hope' (Galchen 2020: xvi). When the seven women and three men decide to return to Florence after fourteen days, they do not do this because the plague is over but because they have better understood the present and are able to see a (possibly hopeful) future. This realization is the essence of reading and engaging with literature, and it holds true for our present as well.

The new pandemic stories of the *New York Times Magazine*'s *Decameron Project* were published online on 7 July 2020, as part of an interactive website that included print art by Sophy Hollington and paintings by Shawna X, Aban, Kyutae Lee, María Medem, Monica Ramos, Alexander Harrison, Beya Rebaï, Linda Merad, Sophi Miyoko Gullbrants, Marly Gallardo, Zack Rosebrugh, Charlotte Edey, Jaedoo Lee, Flora Mottini, Derek Abella and Richard A. Chance (https://www.nytimes.com/interactive/2020/07/07/magazine/decameron-proj ect-short-story-collection.html). The print edition was published on 12 July 2020, in the magazine supplement of the Sunday issue of the *New York Times*. Featuring most of Hollington's relief print artworks but none of the paintings from the website or the magazine, the book version of the *Decameron Project* was published on 10 November 2020. The twenty-nine stories are heterogeneous regarding their length and the gender and ethnicity of their authors. They are between 654 ('The Walk' by Kamila Shamsie) and 3069 ('Line 19 Woodstock/Glisan' by Karen Russell) words long, authored by fourteen female writers, fourteen male writers and one non-binary writer; they represent a geographically and nationally diverse group: fifteen identify as American (including Haitian-American, Taiwanese-American, Chinese-American, Nigerian-American, Serbian-American, Ethiopian-American, African-American, Iranian-American, Moroccan-American and Austrian-American), one as Native American (Cheyenne and Arapaho), three as Canadian (including Arab-Canadian and Ghanaian-Canadian), two as South American (Chilean and Brazilian), seven as European (including English, Irish, Israeli-Polish, Italian, Franco-Moroccan and British-Pakistani) and one as Mozambican. However, writers of the Global North are overrepresented, while Africans, Asians or Pacific Islanders are conspicuously absent, except for Mozambican biologist and writer Mia Couto.

While primarily an English language endeavour, the multilingual aspect of the *Decameron Project* deserves attention. Although all stories were published in English, five of the twenty-nine were originally written in languages other than English, namely French (Leila Slimani), Spanish (Alejandro Zambra), Italian (Paolo Giordano), Portuguese (Mia Couto) and Hebrew (Etgar Keret).[1]

None of the stories focuses explicitly on the medical symptoms of a Covid-19 infection, and they do not have to since the pandemic is present in all of them in other ways. The stories' range of themes is similar to the original *Decameron*: love lost, sought and found, love between parents and children, between family members, lovers and strangers; stories about life and death, both violent and calm.

Among the stories, Margaret Atwood's takes a special position in that it directly references a novella from the *Decameron* transferred to a science-fiction setting. Entitled 'Impatient Griselda', it is a feminist rewriting of Boccaccio's tale of patient Griselda (Boccaccio 2009: X, 10; see also Däwes 2022). When the fictional listeners complain about the new ending, the octopus-shaped alien narrator refers to the cross-culturality of the moment: 'But storytelling does help us understand one another across our social and historical and evolutionary chasms' (Atwood 2020: 76). Indeed, storytelling can create empathy and lets us experience alternative situations. The *Decameron Project* stories offer imaginative renderings of both the present and an uncertain future, a crucial task that Aleksandar Hemon (2017) calls 'imagining the unimaginable'. However, in a moment of such radical instability, storytelling remains fragmentary and open, it points to the transitory nature of the moment with transient settings and a collectively shared sense of time and by aestheticizing practices of immobility and mobility.

Immobility and Mobility

The dichotomy between immobility and mobility is taken up in several *Decameron Project* stories. One of them is by Paolo Giordano, whose book *How Contagion Works* (2020a) was among the first non-fiction works about the coronavirus outbreak (Momigliano 2020). In his story, entitled 'The Perfect Travel Buddy' the college student Michele is stuck in time and space between Milan and Rome. While he physically arrives in Rome at the beginning of the story to self-isolate in a small apartment with his mother and stepfather, he continuously longs for his friends in Milan, whom he connects with virtually via video chat, listening to music and sharing a six-pack of beer on 'Houseparty Fridays' – as the autodiegetic narrator, Michele's stepfather, disapprovingly calls them (Giordano 2020b: 191). The disconnect between the older analog and younger digital generations becomes apparent in the stepfather's comment: 'I turned up the volume on the TV to cover Michele's laughter and the music blaring out of his laptop's speakers. The more he enjoyed himself, the lower my mood sank' (190). While Michele and his college friends use digital networks to their advantage and can be elsewhere (at least virtually), his stepfather perceives his situation as 'endless waiting' (191). There is a certain irony in the title of the story since Michele refers to himself as the 'perfect travel buddy' in a time where travel has come to a halt and movement outside a perimeter of '600 feet outside your own home' is forbidden (188). Readers will infer that Michele will eventually return to Milan, but the story ends before he arrives. The withholding or absence of physical arrival highlights a state of heterotopia and heterochronia, an altered experience of space and time, marked by immobility and standstill.

Similarly, Karen Russell's story 'Line 19 Woodstock/Glisan' ends before the bus arrives at its terminus. By not depicting the bus's arrival at the final station the story emphasizes the continuance of the journey and of the pandemic situation outside. If we read the bus as a container representing society, then the journey continues, as does the novel coronavirus. However, in the story the passengers communally overcome a moment of limbo, the lifting of time between minutes 8:48 and 8:49 pm (Russell 2020: 154), which can be read as the time of lockdown. While the imagined lockdown lies in the past, the time of crisis, the pandemic, has not yet passed.

At a time where movement is curtailed, the characters in many of the *Decameron Project* stories find ways to circumvent restrictions, in both more serious and playful ways. For example, in Kamila Shamsie's short story 'The Walk' Azra convinces Zohra to leave the house for a destination outside her usual park round: 'Everyone's doing it, even women on their own' (2020: 25). Their walk becomes a statement of women's emancipation: 'by accident, they found themselves on a road that was filled with walkers, several of whom they knew. Everyone waved, everyone was delighted to see one another and made a great show of keeping a distance, even when they weren't' (27). The final words of the story confirm the newly found freedom amid restriction: 'When this is all over, maybe we can sometimes walk here instead of endlessly round the track in the park, Zohra said. Maybe, Azra said' (27).

In Colm Tóibín's 'Tales from the L.A. River' the narrator convinces his boyfriend H. to order bicycles online to counter the monotony of their reading and movie-watching routines during the forced immobility of lockdown. When the narrator conjures up images of actual mobility (beyond the mobility merely consumed in fiction or films), he sounds like Beat poet Allen Ginsberg in 'A Supermarket in California' ([1956] 2012) and also plays with the name of the video communications platform Zoom that rose to the top of the market because of social distancing during the Covid-19 pandemic: 'I dreamed of us zooming through the suburban streets, passing the frightened bungalows, people cowering inside, zapping from channel to channel, hoping for redemption and washing their hands with prayerful zeal' (Tóibín 2020: 37). When the couple actually sets out on their bikes, they follow the mandated precautions and do so 'with helmets and masks on … flying down a hill with joy and glee and *controlled* abandon' (38, emphasis mine). The experience of restricted mobility alters the narrator's perception of space and time permanently. He perceives and acknowledges the L.A. River in a different way: it is, in fact, a legit river and not a weird, local curiosity. Celebrating the L.A. River in a story set in Los Angeles is also a political statement to combat what Norman M. Klein (1997) has aptly described as L.A.'s culture of forgetting and erasing its historical neighbourhoods and natural environment. The narrator states: 'I felt that I had found some element of the city that had been hidden from me. No car could come here. No images of this strange, sad spectacle would ever be sent out into the world. There would be no: "Come to L.A.! Ride your bike by a river!" No one in their right mind would be here' (38–9). But the narrator and his boyfriend are there, and they live and they laugh and they enjoy themselves, which recalls the Boccaccian message that says: we will get over this.

While the protagonists in Tóibín's story manage to revert their initial immobility into mobility with newly acquired bicycles, the opposite happens to the runner in Tommy Orange's story 'The Team'. The metaphor Orange uses for the pandemic experience is that of running a half marathon. We have heard the marathon simile of the 'long run' from politicians and health experts alike who kept referring to the large time window before we can expect the pandemic crisis to be over (Musu n.d.). For the narrator in the short story, the marathon was the 'last mass-gathering public-type thing' (Orange 2020: 54). He ran 'for 13 miles without stopping' to honour a family tradition of running (of the Cheyenne people but also of humans in general). Then the caesura, the standstill, from utter mobility to immobility: 'The world came to a screeching halt' (56). The Team, spelled with a capital T, shifts from meaning everything that was needed to complete the race, his running team, to the family as the new team. The new

Team is also 'isolation itself, what you did with it, against it. The new Team was *not running*, it was planning meals together and sharing news of the outside world' (56–7, emphasis mine).

> The new Team was the new future, which was yet to be determined, which seemed to be decided by individual communities and whether they believed in the number of lives lost and how it related to them … It was the Teamwork being done by the whole new world, all those not directly affected, to watch and wait, *to stay put*, it would be a marathon, all this isolation, but it was the only way the Team could make it, humans, the whole damn race. (57–8, emphasis mine)

The present pandemic experience, in Orange's story, is aestheticized as a marathon, usually a highly mobile and performance-oriented endeavour, yet in this case associated with 'not running' and with 'staying put'. Mobility and immobility are not paradoxical in the Teamwork that the marathon in the story requires, but each has its time. Ironically, one might add, the virus itself is a highly mobile and versatile agent that can only be immobilized in a communal effort of staying put.

Time as Caesura

Several stories follow an ordering of time into a before and an after, by designating a specific moment in time as a caesura, of what Aristotle would call 'the now' (*to nun*). Three stories mention a date to situate the narratives in time, and it is the same two consecutive dates in all three stories: 11 March and 12 March. On 11 March 2020, the WHO characterized Covid-19 as a pandemic. Although cases of the novel coronavirus had been reported since January, they began to jump at alarming rates in early March. On 11 March and the following days most countries of the Global North situated in the western hemisphere began issuing stay-at-home orders shutting down all non-essential businesses, travel and gatherings.

'Tales from the L.A. River' by Colm Tóibín begins:

> I kept a diary during the lockdown. I began by writing the date of my own personal shutdown – March 11, 2020 – and the place, Highland Park, Los Angeles. On the first day, I copied down a sign on a camper van I saw that morning: 'Smile. You Are Being Filmed.' After that first entry, I could think of nothing else. Nothing much happened after that. (2020: 31)

We have a starting date but not an end date. Tóibín's, like many of the stories, is radically open. In fact, 'nothing much happened' – there is no teleology, no purpose. The *Times* editors approached the authors in March 2020, when none of the authors could write a pandemic story from knowing how it will end. So, instead, quite a few stories start from what many perceive as the beginning of the pandemic. 'Clinical Notes' by Liz Moore begins:

> March 12, 2020
>
> *Fact*: The baby has a fever.
>
> *Evidence*: Two thermometers produce a succession of worrisome readings. 103.9. 104.2. 104.8. (2020: 43)

The baby's fever worries the parents. Their nocturnal struggle to decide what is the best way to react mirrors that of people around the world at the particular moment in time who are faced with the threat of a new pandemic, and the realization that the slightest increase in your body temperature could be more than just a temporary fever. The sudden awareness of the pandemic threat in early March 2020 was a globally shared experience narrativized in a myriad of fates, some of which we encounter in this and other *Decameron Project* stories. Of course, Covid-19 is not the world's first pandemic experience; there was the 1918 'Spanish' flu. But without an equivalent of today's communication systems and global media infrastructure and with most countries except for Spain censoring their media, the 1918 flu was a threat that was experienced locally and not shared globally – at least not at the time.

'Clinical Notes' is a parable promoting a scientific approach to dealing with the fever, that is, the pandemic threat, by collecting evidence and methodically assessing facts. However, no certainty can be attained because ' "there are a lot of unknowns here", the baby's mother says' (Moore 2020: 45); the parents' middle-of-the-night call to their doctor is redirected to an answering service. No guidance from science is available at this hour, neither about the baby's fever nor about where the pandemic is heading. Then the baby's condition seems to improve, judging from his outlook, behaviour and falling temperature. Momentarily assured by these signs and also by the eventual response from the doctor, the parents will wait until morning. The story ends with the mother touching one finger to the skin of the baby through the slats of the crib: 'Warm but not hot. Warm but not hot, she thinks – a chant, a prayer – though she cannot be certain' (50). Like the parents, readers of this story and people around the world will have to live with this uncertainty, which neither science nor religion can immediately resolve.

In Dinaw Mengestu's 'How We Used to Play' the first-person narrator drives from New York to Washington, DC, to help his 72-year-old uncle: 'It was March 12, 2020, and the virus was about to lay *siege* to the city. "We'll go to the grocery store," I said. "And stuff your freezer so you can grow old and fat until the virus disappears"' (2020: 138, emphasis mine). The story's title and the mentioning of the date divide time into a before and an after (cf. Aristotle 2018: *Physics* IV.11), which is further enhanced by likening the now to the beginning of a war or a siege. Once inside the taxi on the way to the store the two reminisce how they used to play, that is, how they used to imagine destinations: 'the Washington Monument, the museums along the Mall …, the Pacific Ocean, Disney World and Disneyland, Mount Rushmore and Yellowstone National Park, … Egypt and the Great Wall of China, followed by Big Ben and the Colosseum in Rome' (Mengestu 2020: 139). And although they could have easily continued to imagine journeys while waiting until – in the words of the story – 'the virus disappears' (138), the uncle refuses:

'I don't want to wait in a parking lot,' he said. 'I do that every day.'

'Then what do you want?'

He switched the meter off, and then the engine, but left the key in the ignition.

'I want to go back home,' he said. 'I want someone to tell me how to get out of here.' (142)

One might infer a death wish since the uncle has waited for passengers in parking lots his entire life. He wants 'to get out of here' – and readers might share this feeling, wishing to get out of this situation of crisis. The uncle wants 'to go back home' and we know from earlier in the story that home is his apartment, referred to as the last place he will ever live, where he will end his life.

Heterotopic Spaces

Foucault's theory of heterotopia relates to physical spaces that, while existing within society, are simultaneously separate from other spaces within society. Examples of heterotopic spaces include places of religious worship, prisons and gardens, each of which exists as a different type of heterotopia with unique social norms and ordering of time (Foucault 1986: 25). Airport lounges, border zones, bus or railroad stations are modern-day heterotopic spaces; as points of arrival and intended departure they are 'pointing to an elsewhere, they sustain, negotiate, mediate connections with the world outside and beyond a given dispensation' (Kunow 2011: 23; cf. Priewe 2011: 136). In the *Decameron Project*, several stories feature heterotopic settings, in which characters are suspended in time in space, such as the airport transit lounge in Laila Lalami's 'That Time at My Brother's Wedding', and an airplane in Alejandro Zambra's 'Screen Time'. In both stories, the heteronomic quality of the settings points to an elsewhere, another time and another place beyond the pandemic.

In Lalami's story a natural scientist from UC Berkeley is stuck in the transit area of Casablanca airport after attending her brother's wedding. Ms Bensaïd is waiting to be allowed to board a repatriation flight to the United States, the country of which she is a resident but not a citizen. Already the title of the story refers to the specificity and historicity of the present time as '*That* Time at My Brother's Wedding' (emphasis mine). Like in many of the other stories, the end of this story is left open. However, with the eventual arrival of the US consular officers, there is a glimpse of hope of escaping the transit area and – metaphorically – the pandemic crisis: 'I recognize the young man in the blue shirt. He was here two days ago. He's already walking in this direction; he must have noticed the blue passport in your hand. Go on. Perhaps I'll see you on the other side' (Lalami 2020: 230).

To the list of settings with a heteronomic quality one may add other non-permanent, in-between places, such as apartments or houses, which the stories' characters happen to find themselves in when the lockdown starts. Almost all of those places are located in the Global North, with few exceptions, such as Kamila Shamsie's 'The Walk' which is set in Karachi, Pakistan, or Julián Fuks's chronicle of pandemic life in Brazil in 'A Time of Death, the Death of Time.'

While physically stuck in time and space, many of the stories' figures go back to earlier times in their mind. They remember past places (through instances of analepsis) or envision future ones (through prolepsis). In 'The Cellar' by Dina Nayeri the Iranian-American academic couple whom the virus catches up with during their sabbatical abroad living in Paris recall their early courtship in the cellars of 1980s wartime Tehran. The story ends with the wife taking a 'stack of pillows, half a bottle of red, crackers and a book' running to the basement of their temporary Paris apartment in order to – as she says – 'wait out the daylight' (Nayeri 2020: 224) or actually to relive an earlier time where they hunker down and wait for things to become better.

Edwidge Danticat's 'One Thing' constantly deconstructs its actual situatedness in time and space through structural shifts. It begins: 'She is dreaming of caves and the rocks and minerals with which he's obsessed' (Danticat 2020: 283). Readers only gradually learn that Raymond and his wife Marie-Jeanne are not physically in the same space because Ray is ill and has recently been put on a ventilator in a hospital. The fact that Marie-Jeanne is banned from entering marks the hospital's heteronomic quality, as a place requiring the special circumstance of being ill or having to care for the diseased to enter and resolve the pandemic crisis.

Every night Marie-Jeanne 'speaks into the phone … placed next to his ear' (Danticat 2020: 284), which a nurse picks up in the morning to recharge. The nurse asks Marie-Jeanne what they talked about, which prompts an inner monologue that takes Marie-Jeanne back to the couple's New Year's Eve wedding in Brooklyn, only sixteen weeks earlier, and to the song 'Wild is the Wind' to which they danced. She recalls the places they were planning to see: Zambia, Peru as well as the cave mentioned in the story's first sentence. The cave bears Marie-Jeanne's name and is situated in the south of Haiti, the birthplace of both their parents. The story ends with her imagining standing in this cave and hearing what Ray 'whispered in her ear during their wedding dance. *One thing, MJ. This is our one thing*' (290, emphasis in original). Like the leaves in the song, they are clinging to the tree, to life and to hope that they are not carried away by the wild wind.

Practical Implications for Teaching the *Decameron Project*

Given the date of the publication of the *Decameron Project* short stories in early July 2020, the immediacy of the text production and the kind of reception this enables cannot be underestimated. In other words, the *Decameron Project* short stories represent a core object of investigation for literary and cultural studies and for literature in language learning and teaching to consider how the collective experience of emergency and crisis tends to prompt reflections and critique and how it inspires new conceptualizations and directions in the arts. One important task of language learning and teaching is to make sense of shifts as they happen. The *Decameron Project* short stories lend themselves to be analysed in the secondary school as well tertiary education classroom: from a critical analysis in the way outlined in this chapter, to problematizing the stories' materiality as digital publications, to researching their production and reception history, to an intermedial analysis of the rich illustrations that accompany the print and digital issues, to assigning creative writing projects.

An intermedial analysis of the illustrations that accompany the digital publication of the *Decameron Project* stories not only fosters students' visual literacy but also stimulates their learning processes and communicative competence (Rymarczyk 2005: 15). Monica Ramos's watercolour painting of a stylized runner, which prefaces Tommy Orange's story 'The Team', is just one of fifteen illustrations commissioned by the *New York Times Magazine* editors to grace the digital publication of the *Decameron Project*. All other illustrations – including Sophy Hollington's evocative black and white relief prints – equally lend themselves to a closer investigation.

In Ramos's painting, the blue pictogram-style figure of a runner takes up the entire canvas (Figure 1.1). In the background a snow-covered mountain range is dwarfed by a large sky that glows in multiple shades of red, orange, pink and purple. The fact that the figure wears a mask covering his nose and mouth establishes a connection to the pandemic reality. The runner's legs are larger and stronger than the upper body – emphasizing their importance and relevance. This is further enhanced by a succession of darker blue silhouettes on the figure's right arm and legs that illustrate the physical motoric of a person running. At the same time, the individual silhouette's apparent movement (reminiscent of Marcel Duchamps's *Nude Descending a Staircase, No. 2*) is contrasted by a bordered section on the bottom of the frame that represents eleven sitting figures. Students will infer that something has come to a standstill and read the illustration as a visual allegory of the Covid-19 pandemic. Like in Orange's story, the theme of mobility before the pandemic and immobility during the lockdown is visualized. In addition, twelve small suns arranged in a semicircle around the running figure symbolize the hours of the day, the passing of time, as well as the long duration of the run and the lockdown. During pandemic times and in the world of the illustration and Orange's story, they symbolize the passing of time as sitting and waiting (like the silhouettes at the bottom of the frame) but also as working together as a 'Team', represented by the coordinated movements of the silhouettes on the figures' limbs.

Drawing on Schoppe's teaching suggestion entitled 'Percept' (2014: 60) students verbalize what they perceive and share their first impressions of Ramos's watercolour painting in the classroom context. The following questions may frame the exercise: What can I see? What do I think? How do I feel? Another introductory activity requires students to come up with a title that they find suitable for the painting and explain their choices. To thoroughly analyse the painting, students stay on task by composing a profile, in which they list and explain elements and aspects depicted in the illustration. The teacher is available as a resource to answer questions and, if desired, reveal the actual title of the painting/story. For other illustrations from the *Decameron Project* website, in

Figure 1.1 Monica Ramos, illustration of 'The Team' by Tommy Orange. Courtesy of the artist.

which more than one central figure is represented, students may write dialogues among the objects and people depicted in the picture. Picking up the students' results by comparing initial and final thoughts allows for the integration of changing perspectives on visual art after an in-depth examination.

The class is now ready to engage in an online reading experience. As the *Decameron Project* website is enhanced to be displayed on mobile devices, it makes sense to allow students to read Orange's story 'The Team' on their mobile phones or, if available, tablets. Furthermore, with this particular story, an audiovisual experience is also possible since a link to a podcast that features the author, Orange, reading his own story is embedded in the website (see Chapter 3 for information on read-aloud talk of picturebooks). Students may read along while listening. The ensuing classroom discussion may centre around the story's metaphors of the marathon and running, as well as the significance that the narrator puts on the 'Team', which students might know from their own experience with professional as well as amateur sports activities in clubs. If not mentioned by the students, teachers may introduce the themes of time, movement/mobility and immobility that are central in both the story and the illustration. At the end, students may be asked to return to Ramos's illustration to assess whether they view it differently now, and if they discover new aspects. They might even be asked to create their own illustration of the story.

Concluding Remarks and Implications for Research

With regard to this corpus of twenty-nine short stories that I have previously referred to as figurative time capsules, they are indeed memorial compositions that bear witness to a pandemic crisis. Besides the aestheticization of a globally shared experience, which they bring to light in a myriad of fates, they are noteworthy for their dealing with the duality of time, that is, the specific historic moment *and* the existential time of what it means to live in and through a pandemic. Besides the heteronomic quality of time, space is especially important, as can be seen in most of the *Decameron Project* short stories because during pandemics secluded spaces, and the dichotomy of immobility versus mobility, play an important role. Many of the stories oscillate between mobility and immobility, the collective feeling of being stuck is creatively put into motion through walking (Kamila Shamsie), running (Tommy Orange), driving (Dinaw Mengestu and Karen Russell), biking (Colm Tóibín) and travelling (Paolo Giordano, Laila Lalami and Edwidge Danticat).

Although most of the stories are clearly set in the first months of 2020, and some specifically name a date in March (Colm Tóibín, Liz Moore, Dinaw Mengestu), referring to the historicity of the moment, they are also radically open since they refuse teleology and purpose. With an online publication date in early July 2020, and a print publication shortly thereafter, the *Decameron Project* writers wrote in and recorded what we now know was the beginning of a pandemic era. And because we are still living in it in 2021 (as I am writing this), the actual pandemic is sometimes easy to miss, too depressing or too hard to find words for. The *Decameron Project* stories have found a way, precisely through their openness that is so hard to bear. The challenge for language learning and teaching is to communicate, educate and become educated about the present condition. To this end, I suggest videotaping lessons on the *Decameron Project* at fixed intervals, such as once a year, and over an extended period of several years. The aim of such a long-term research project, which could be enhanced by interviews and group discussions before and after the lessons, is to investigate and thus better understand teachers' and students' reactions and learnings from the texts and images and how they help them to read their present. As Caitlin Roper writes in the preface to the hardcover version of the *Decameron Project*: 'It was a reminder that the best fiction can both transport you far from yourself but also, somehow, help you understand exactly where you are' (2020: ix).

Note

1 At the time of the publication of this volume, the *New York Times Magazine*'s *Decameron Project* has not been published in any language other than English. The originally non-English stories have not been published outside the *Decameron Project* either.

References

Primary Literature

Atwood, M. (2020), 'Impatient Griselda', in *New York Times* (ed.), *The Decameron Project: 29 New Stories from the Pandemic*, 67–76, New York: Scribner.

Boccaccio, G. (2009), *Decameron*, J. G. Nichols (ed.), New York: Everyman's Library.

Couto, M. (2020), 'An Obliging Robber', in *New York Times* (ed.), *The Decameron Project: 29 New Stories from the Pandemic*, 195–200, New York: Scribner.

Danticat, E. (2020), 'One Thing', in *New York Times* (ed.), *The Decameron Project: 29 New Stories from the Pandemic*, 281–90, New York: Scribner.

Fuks, J. (2020), 'A Time of Death, the Death of Time', in *New York Times* (ed.), *The Decameron Project: 29 New Stories from the Pandemic*, 231–7, New York: Scribner.

Ginsberg, A. ([1956] 2012), 'A Supermarket in California', in N. Baym and R. S. Levine (eds), *Norton Anthology of American Literature*, 8th edn, New York: W. W. Norton.

Giordano, P. (2020b), 'The Perfect Travel Buddy', in *New York Times* (ed.), *The Decameron Project: 29 New Stories from the Pandemic*, 183–94, New York: Scribner.

Keret, E. (2020), 'Outside', in *New York Times* (ed.), *The Decameron Project: 29 New Stories from the Pandemic*, 195–200, New York: Scribner.

Lalami, L. (2020), 'That Time at My Brother's Wedding', in *New York Times* (ed.), *The Decameron Project: 29 New Stories from the Pandemic*, 225–30, New York: Scribner.

Mengestu, D. (2020), 'How We Used to Play', in *New York Times* (ed.), *The Decameron Project: 29 New Stories from the Pandemic*, 135–42, New York: Scribner.

Moore, L. (2020), 'Clinical Notes', in *New York Times* (ed.), *The Decameron Project: 29 New Stories from the Pandemic*, 41–50, New York: Scribner.

Nayeri, D. (2020), 'The Cellar', in *New York Times* (ed.), *The Decameron Project: 29 New Stories from the Pandemic*, 213–24, New York: Scribner.

Orange, T. (2020), 'The Team', in *New York Times* (ed.), *The Decameron Project: 29 New Stories from the Pandemic*, 51–8, New York: Scribner.

Porter, K. A. ([1939] 2011), *Pale Horse, Pale Rider: The Selected Short Stories*, Modern Classics, London: Penguin.

Russell, K. (2020), 'Line 19 Woodstock/Glisan', in *New York Times* (ed.), *The Decameron Project: 29 New Stories from the Pandemic*, 143–57, New York: Scribner.

Shamsie, K. (2020), 'The Walk', in *New York Times* (ed.), *The Decameron Project: 29 New Stories from the Pandemic*, 23–7, New York: Scribner.

Slimani, L. (2020), 'The Rock', in *New York Times* (ed.), *The Decameron Project: 29 New Stories from the Pandemic*, 59–65, New York: Scribner.

Tóibín, C. (2020), 'Tales from the L.A. River', in *New York Times* (ed.), *The Decameron Project: 29 New Stories from the Pandemic*, 29–39, New York: Scribner.

Zambra, A. (2020), 'Screen Time', in *New York Times* (ed.), *The Decameron Project: 29 New Stories from the Pandemic*, 123–34, New York: Scribner.

Secondary Literature

Aristotle (2018), *Physics*, C. D. C Reeve (ed.), Indianapolis: Hackett.

Däwes, B. (2022), 'Molecular Mimicry, Realism, and the Collective Memory of Pandemics: Strategies of Narrative In/Stability in COVID-19 Fiction', *Diegesis* 11.1.

Foucault, M. (1986). 'Of Other Spaces', Jay Miskowiec (trans.), *Diacritics*, 16: 22–7. https://doi.org/10.2307/464648.

Galchen, R. (2020), 'Introduction', in *New York Times* (ed.), *The Decameron Project: 29 New Stories from the Pandemic*, xi–xvii, New York: Scribner.

Giordano, P. (2020a), *How Contagion Works: Science, Awareness, and Community in Times of Global Crises – the Essay That Helped Change the Covid-19 Debate*, New York: Bloomsbury.

Hemon, A. (2017), 'Stop Making Sense, or How to Write in the Age of Trump', *Village Voice*, 17 January. https://www.villagevoice.com/2017/01/17/stop-making-sense-or-how-to-write-in-the-age-of-trump/ (accessed 20 May 2022).

Klein, N. M. (1997), *The History of Forgetting: Los Angeles and the Erasure of Memory*, London: Verso.

Kunow, R. (2011), '"Unavoidably Side by Side": Mobility Studies – Concepts and Issues', in N. Franz and R. Kunow (eds), *Kulturelle Mobilitätsforschung: Themen, Theorien, Tendenzen*, Mobilisierte Kulturen 1, 17–32, Potsdam: Universitätsverlag Potsdam.

Momigliano, A. (2020), 'In Italy, Coronavirus Books Rush to Publication', *New York Times*, 9 April, sec. Books. https://www.nytimes.com/2020/04/09/books/italy-coro navirus-paolo-giordano-roberto-burioni.html (accessed 20 May 2022).

Musu, C. (2020), 'War Metaphors Used for COVID-19 Are Compelling but also Dangerous', *Conversation*. 8 April. http://theconversation.com/war-metaph ors-used-for-covid-19-are-compelling-but-also-dangerous-135406 (accessed 13 August 2021).

Priewe, M. (2011), 'The Commuting Island: Cultural (Im)mobility in the Flying Bus', in N. Franz and R. Kunow (eds), *Kulturelle Mobilitätsforschung: Themen, Theorien, Tendenzen*, Mobilisierte Kulturen 1, 135–47, Potsdam: Universitätsverlag Potsdam.

Roper, C. (2020), 'Preface', in *New Your Times* (ed.), *The Decameron Project: 29 New Stories from the Pandemic*, vii–ix, New York: Scribner.

Rymarczyk, J. (2005), '"To Nail One's Colours to the Mast!" Ein klares Ja zum bilingualen Kunstunterricht', *Der fremdsprachliche Unterricht Englisch*, 78: 14–21.

Schoppe, A. (2014), *Bildzugänge*, Stuttgart: Klett Kallmeyer.

Tracy, M. (2021), 'The New York Times Tops 7.5 Million Subscriptions as Ads Decline', *New York Times*, 4 February. https://www.nytimes.com/2021/02/04/business/media/ new-york-times-earnings.html (accessed 20 May 2022).

2

Pandemic Literature: What It Is, Why It Should Be Taught and How

Engelbert Thaler

Introduction

With the title 'Epidemics – Curse of the Past, Threat to the Future', an exhibition at the Hildesheim Roemer and Pelizaeus Museum (1 October 2021–1 May 2022) is dedicated to the dominant topos of the present (Sticht 2021). This exhibition on the medical and cultural history of epidemics takes visitors on a journey through time from Ancient Egypt to the present and highlights diseases such as the plague, tuberculosis, AIDS and Covid-19. It becomes clear that infectious diseases have always claimed more lives than wars or natural disasters. Recordings from the official opening of the exhibition show that viruses have existed since the beginning of humankind, that in spite of progress in medicine they still kill millions of people all over the globe and that we will have to live with them in the future, too (https://www.youtube.com/watch?v=VWOC JPQGcNw).

The simultaneously timeless and topical theme of epidemics is examined in this chapter but from a foreign language didactic perspective. Given the tremendous impact that pandemics have on our lives, foreign language teachers have the responsibility to address concomitantly arising private and public issues for individual and societal development and living per se through literary artefacts. The use of epidemic and pandemic literature in online (and face-to-face) teaching will be explored in a five-step approach, based on the classic wh-questions, that is, definition (What?), justification (Why?), venues (Where?), objectives (What for?) and methodology (How?).

Definition

The Covid-19 pandemic, first identified in 2019 and showing no sign of abating at the time of writing in 2021, is definitely not the first pandemic in human history (Vögele, Knöll and Noack 2016). One may distinguish between an epidemic, that is, an unexpected increase in the number of disease cases in a specific geographical area (e.g. yellow fever, smallpox, measles and polio in the United States); an endemic, a disease outbreak which is consistently present but limited to a particular region; and a pandemic, which affects a wider geographical area, infects a greater number of people than an epidemic and shows an exponential growth of the disease (Columbia Public Health 2021).

People have been afflicted by epidemics and pandemics for millennia. A pandemic (from Greek 'pan' for 'all' and 'demos' for 'people'), that is, a disease that spreads over a large area, has often decimated mankind, for example, the plague of Athens (with approximately 100,000 dead, around 430 BC), the Black Death (75–200 million dead in the fourteenth century), the Spanish flu from 1918 to 1920, HIV/AIDS, the 2009 flu pandemic (H1N1) and now Covid-19 (Vögele, Knöll and Noack 2016).

Since a pandemic has existential relevance, writers have always devoted themselves to this topos, seeking and discussing answers to pressing questions of life and death (for a comprehensive historic survey of literary treatments of plagues, see e.g. Emmrich and Geisenhanslüke 2020; also Georgi 2020 and Mylow 2020). Homer's *Iliad* begins with a plague that Apollo sent to the Greeks as punishment for capturing the daughter of Chryses, one of the god's priests. In Giovanni Boccaccio's *Decamerone* (1349–53), a plague epidemic in Florence forms the backdrop for the retreat of ten young women and men from the big city to a rural idyll to tell each other one hundred cheerful, sensual stories. (Notably, in March 2020, the *New York Times* initiated a *Decameron Project* for our times, commissioning a series of short stories on the pandemic and lockdown; see Gessner in Chapter 1 of this volume.) Nobel laureate Albert Camus's *La Peste* (1947), another canonical work of epidemic literature, experienced a new sales boom during the Covid-19 epidemic. In Gabriel García Márquez's magical realist bestseller *Love in the Time of Cholera* ([1985] 1988), two aged lovers realize that love may be infinite but increases when death is near, with the character of Femina Daza's doctor-husband having ironic parallels to the pop star status of contemporary TV virologists. In *Blindness*, José Saramago (1995) presents a world where crime and chaos reign, as an epidemic robs its victims of the essential sense of sight.

This multitude of relevant texts makes it clear that this genre is more than a mere pastime in difficult times. It offers escape and protection from inexplicable danger, criticism of social ills and human hubris, immunity and coping strategies against death as well as 'a historical archive from which one can read what tensions not only the plague but also epidemics such as cholera, diphtheria or polio inject into human conditions' (Emmrich and Geisenhanslüke 2020: n.p., own translation).

A number of writers have suggested reading lists of novels and stories that deal with pandemics (e.g. Carroll 2020; Davis 2020; see Kirchhoff (2019) for a discussion of issues of text selection). Table 2.1 provides a personal selection of works (all originally written in English) that deal with pandemics. As the reader will see, of the fifteen pieces, eight were written in the twenty-first century, which may be an indicator of the way in which we have turned our minds increasingly to these challenges.

Rationale

There are at least six arguments in favour of integrating fictional texts into foreign language teaching (Thaler 2014: 23; Tsang, Paran and Lau 2020), which hold true for pandemic literature.

(1) Language Learning

Dealing with fiction in the classroom promotes language proficiency, as literary texts are authentic examples of a wide range of styles and text types at all levels of difficulty. Thus communicative competences, that is, the basic skills of reading, writing, listening, speaking and mediating, as well as the linguistic domains of lexis, grammar, phonology and spelling (for Germany, cf. the national educational standards: KMK 2003; 2012), can be improved, for example, by

- listening to an audiobook version,
- viewing an adaptation of a literary text,
- discussing parallels between text and current situation (spoken interaction),
- posting an entry at the author's blog (written production),
- mediating key passages into L1,
- enlarging one's vocabulary with pandemic register,
- comparing original text and L1 translation with selected paragraphs (cross-lingual grammar analysis) or
- reading out some passages (pronunciation/intonation).

Table 2.1 Pandemic Fiction in English

Author. Year. *Title*	Blurb-like statements
Daniel Defoe. 1722. *A Journal of the Plague Year*	The author was just five when the plague swept through London in 1665, claiming nearly 100,000 lives. Calling on his own memories, the author of *Robinson Crusoe* later created this vivid chronicle of the devastating epidemic and its victims.
Mary Shelley. 1826. *The Last Man*	In this apocalyptic science-fiction novel, the author of *Frankenstein* depicts a future Earth in the late twenty-first century, desolated by a global pandemic. Shelley treats topics such as tragic isolation, the scope of scientific inquiry and the corrosion of Romantic ideals.
E. A. Poe. 1842. *The Masque of the Red Death*	In this short story by the granddaddy of horror literature, a disease known as the Red Death plagues a fictional country, causing its victims to die gruesomely. Death quickly comes to all mortals, and no artfulness can prevent the inevitability of Fate.
Katherine Anne Porter. [1939] 1990. *Pale Horse, Pale Rider*	Set around the Spanish flu pandemic in 1918, the eponymous title of this collection of three short novels focuses on a young woman falling in love with a soldier. Yet the pale rider, i.e. Death, takes away an entire era.
Richard Matheson. 1954. *I Am Legend*	In this sci-fi-horror-vampire-zombie novel, which has been adapted for the screen three times, the protagonist seems to be the only human survivor of a pandemic which has transformed the rest of mankind into blood-sucking vampires.
Michael Crichton. 1969. *The Andromeda Strain*	This techno-thriller novel is centred around a group of US scientists dealing with an epidemic, which has been caused by an extraterrestrial microorganism.
Stephen King. 1978. *The Stand*	The 'Master of the Macabre' here has created a post-apocalyptic novel, in which the virus is named 'Captain Trips', killing nearly the whole world population and making the remaining groups fight each other.
Stewart O'Nan. 1999. *A Prayer for the Dying*	In this slim, yet dreadful western-horror-post-Civil-War tale, the hero is the local sheriff, undertaker and priest, trying to manage an outpost consumed by a vicious epidemic.
Margaret Atwood. 2003. *Oryx and Crake*	A plague has wiped out much of humanity in this adventure romance by the great Canadian author. Told from the perspective of Snowman, the lone protagonist, a bioengineered apocalypse is gradually revealed.
Max Brooks. 2006. *World War Z: An Oral History of the Zombie War*	In this horror novel, a UN agent interviews survivors of a zombie plague, which began with rumours from China about another pandemic. The author deals with themes like government failure, survivalism and human uncertainty.

Table 2.1 Continued

Author. Year. *Title*	Blurb-like statements
Philip Roth. 2010. *Nemesis*	Political opacity, rampant fear and feelings of powerlessness prevail in this novel about a 1944 polio epidemic and its effects on a family-oriented Jewish community.
Emily St. John Mandel. 2014. *Station Eleven*	The Georgia flu spells the end of the world as we know it, but a Hollywood star, his would-be saviour and a theatre troupe roam the wasteland of the Great Lakes region, risking everything for the sake of art and humanity.
Louise Welsh. 2014–17. *Plague Times Trilogy*	The first book in this trilogy, called *A Lovely Way to Burn*, is really a lovely read – although the Sweats, a flu-like virus, is not so lovely.
Ling Ma. 2018. *Severance*	Contrary to the ordinary terror of apocalyptic novels, this amusing satire describes a plague which causes a debilitating attack of nostalgia. Shen fever, known as a 'disease of remembering', makes its victims endlessly repeat their old routines.
Mike Chen. 2020. *A Beginning at the End*	How do you start after the end of the world? This post-apocalyptic slice-of-life fantasy provides an answer after a disease known as MGS has eradicated over half of the population.
Lawrence Wright. 2020. *The End of October*	Coming creepily close to reality, this medical thriller by the Pulitzer Prize winner describes the global outbreak of a deadly pathogen. The protagonist, an epidemiologist working for the WHO, needs to find a cure for the mysterious virus.

(2) Intercultural Learning

Pandemic fiction contributes to the development of intercultural and transcultural competences. As a transcultural and worldwide phenomenon, a pandemic reminds us of the increasing global interconnectedness of nations. As early as 1948, Arnold Toynbee envisioned a 'single planetary society' in his famous lecture 'The Unification of the World' at the University of London, claiming that in spite of all barriers between nations the unification of the world cannot be stopped any more.

(3 and 4) Personal Enrichment and Motivation

Such an existential theme as a pandemic displays both topical and timeless relevance. It is the unfamiliar that makes these narratives so terrifying and appealing: 'mysterium tremendum et fascinosum' (Otto 1917). Science-fiction and pandemic literature are allowed to, indeed have to, break the rules of reality and venture into the domains of the (seemingly) unreal. They function as instruments to deal with current realities. They provide an outlet to visualize what could be. They allow the reflection on what is and the planning for what to do next. They force us to think about some existential questions, for example: how does fear affect us, that is, what are the causes, functions and pitfalls of fear? Who do we turn to for answers? Can we trust politicians who are only fixated on their popularity ratings? Are virologists really Jesus in a lab coat?

(5) Interpretational Openness

Of course, the novels or shorties mentioned above (cf. also Thaler 2016) open up interpretative freedom due to their complexity. Nearly every literary text lends itself to multiple interpretations, and this opinion gap between one's own interpretation and another's can be bridged by interaction (cf. reader-response theory e.g. Iser 1972).

(6) Social Prestige

Finally, fiction holds a high status in society. Reading 'Literature with a Capital L' (McRae 1994), for example, the titles by Defoe (1722), Shelley (1826), Poe (1842) or Atwood (2003), lends a certain social prestige to the reception process. Pupils, their parents and their teachers get the satisfying feeling that they are studying texts which are highly valued in society. Even if it is hard to draw the line between Capital L and small l literature, and to determine a generally accepted canon, aesthetically ambitious fiction is still valued by many readers. Yet other pandemic titles which rather belong to the small l category are often linguistically less complex and thus more accessible to teenagers.

Venues

Teaching literature does not have to be confined to the classroom but can also take place in (school/classroom) libraries, at home, in public places, on the internet, via MALL (mobile-assisted language learning) or distance learning (Böttger et al. 2021; Thaler 2014). In times of forced digitalization, homeschooling and distance learning with synchronous and asynchronous formats seem particularly relevant.

With the advent of the World Wide Web, internet reading has become an alternative to print-based literature classes. Access to a web browser guarantees the availability of round-the-clock literature sources, and as more and more websites offer full-text options, reading a whole pandemic novel is just a mouse click away. The permanent availability of internet literature also makes us aware that mobile reading is a modern-day option because Wi-Fi opens up immediate access to online texts.

Many electronic books can be stored on a light and portable device; are not vulnerable to natural damage; can be read in low light or total darkness; are often equipped with online dictionaries and audio or video that make comprehension and retention easier; use text-to-speech software; can be purchased online without having to visit a bookstore; have adjustable vision; and are often cheaper than paper books. One should, however, not ignore the advantages of paper books; for example, they are real and tangible treasures in your hands, do not strain the eyes on screen, do not require batteries and recharging, do not lack in quality checks and aesthetic design and are regarded as valuable cultural products and symbols of high-quality education (Edutech 2020; Leonhardt 2017).

Reading online seems suitable for reading for information (e.g. skimming or scanning shorter argumentative texts) rather than reading for fun (e.g. enjoying a novel), as scrolling down the pages, with your eyes fixed on a small screen for hours, makes it hard to get lost in the world of a novel – to be with it. Reading on a screen such as a Kindle or an iPad, however, may be more likely to enable this flow-feeling of 'be-with-it-ness' (Benson 2020). Although research on these facets of reading is scarce, some studies (e.g. Benson 2020) indicate that print texts are visually less demanding than digital ones and provide spatial and tactile cues to help readers process words on a page. Digital reading may impair comprehension and lead to superficial processing, possibly because of the shallowing hypothesis, that is, permanent exposure to fast-paced media trains the brain to process input less thoroughly. ' "Print reading is kind of like meditation – focusing our attention on something still," says Anne Mangen, a literacy professor at the University of Stavanger in Norway. "And it's a whole different kind of immersion than responding to digital stimuli" ' (cited in Benson 2020).

Objectives

Even though reading cannot be taught but must be caught, as Christine Nuttall states with the help of a virus simile and internal rhyme, teachers can contribute

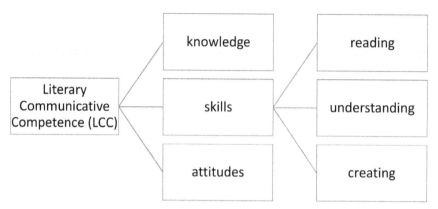

Figure 2.1 Model of literary communicative competence (LCC).

to spreading the reading virus. Literary communicative competence (LCC) can be postulated as the ultimate goal of this process (Thaler 2012: 258f.). Drawing on the two models of communicative language teaching (CLT) and intercultural communicative competence (ICC) (e.g. Michael Byram's five savoirs: Byram 1997), LCC also comprises knowledge, attitudes and various skills, that is, reading, understanding (analysing, interpreting) and creating. The three domains of knowledge, attitudes and skills as well as the three skills just mentioned must be seen against the backdrop of communication because they should not be dealt with as separate dimensions but foster literature-based communication and negotiation of meaning (Figure 2.1).

Concerning pandemic literature, the three pillars of LCC can be given as follows:

- Knowledge: The first pillar consists of literary theory (definitions, classifications, genres, aesthetics, rhetorical devices, textual criticism) and literary history (studying literary periods and persons: DWEMs (dead white English males) such as Defoe as well as Lit 21 or fiction of the twenty-first century and post-millennial authors such as Wright) plus background information on pandemics (Thaler 2019).
- Attitudes: This pillar comprises openness to pandemic literature, transcultural awareness of the phenomenon, enjoyment of reading as well as critical reflection on the political, social, economic, cultural and educational implications of current Covid-19 politics.
- Skills: The three sub-skills are reading, understanding and creating (Thaler 2014: 47–62).

Methodology

Due to the scope of this contribution and classroom relevance, this section will focus on skills, without ignoring the other two pillars completely. Of course, the techniques and approaches chosen will depend on the texts available, the type of school and the linguistic and cognitive abilities of the learners (Paran and Robinson 2016). A combination of asynchronous (for knowledge transfer) and synchronous (for interaction and reflection e.g. Zoom meetings) formats is recommended. In an upper secondary school course, the following online approach could be followed, which has already been experimented with at the university level (Stadler-Heer 2022).

After selecting a title, for instance, individually or in pairs, and supported by a list of books presented by the teacher, learners read the book, research background information, prepare a PowerPoint presentation with an audio commentary, present their product on a digital platform, upload it and finally receive feedback from their classmates and teacher. The latter can, of course, set additional tasks. In one of my university classes, we used the online platform Digicampus, and the following instructions for communication were given to my students:

- Use the FORUM (discussion/Q&A tool) for questions that are relevant to everyone.
- Go to BLUBBER (chat tool) for interaction between students.
- Use WIKI (collaborative writing tool) for cooperation (PPT, research paper).
- Write an EMAIL to me if the question is relevant only to you.

In addition to all these interactive online tools, background information on Covid-19 can be conveyed via non-fictional texts, with the greatest possible variety of different news sources to be considered here in order to counteract one-sided reporting. 'People are desperate for factual information to either assuage or verify their fears' (Doherty and Giordano 2020: n.p.). In this context, the following three non-fiction titles may be used (in excerpts):

- John Kelly, *The Great Mortality* (2006): This non-fiction book, which mixes fact with suspenseful storytelling, presents 'an intimate history of the Black Death, the most devastating plague of all time' (subtitle), which killed an estimated twenty-five million people.

- David Quammen, *Spillover: Animal Infections and the Next Human Pandemic* (2012): In this scarily prophetic non-fiction volume, the author scrutinizes pandemics that originate from animal infections, known as 'spillover' illnesses.
- Laura Spinney, *Pale Rider: The Spanish Flu of 1918 and How It Changed the World* (2017): Having heard comparisons between the deadly 1918 Spanish flu and the contemporary Covid-19 crisis, our learners will discover why these analogies seem eerily true – and may be given hope for the future.

To increase media range and motivational variety, the lessons should be enriched with intermediality, that is, the use of songs, music videos and films related to the topic. For example, 'No Time to Die' by Billie Eilish, the theme song of the eponymous James Bond film, is a suitable choice. Although it was produced before the Covid-19 outbreak, its title, orchestration, melody, singer's voice and lyrics evoke ominous associations with the current pandemic.

Quarantine and social-distancing restrictions have also influenced the production of music videos. Covid-19 times 'have seen an explosion in home-made, self-shot, DIY, hand-animated and Zoom-based music videos. Some of them have even been worth watching' (Savage 2020: n.p.). For example, American rock band Evanescence filmed the video for their comeback single, 'Wasted on You', in their homes, with each of the five members displaying feelings of loneliness and isolation. With their latest title 'Phenom', the Oakland-based band Thao and the Get Down set a standard for harnessing Zoom in a music video, showing people's drive to overcome social distancing in a nine-panel grid. Canadian alt-pop artist Jessy Lanza captured the melancholy mood of lonely repetition in her video for 'Over and Over' (2020), where a teenager permanently rides up and down a deserted escalator.

Of the numerous pandemic movies (see Goldsmith (2020) for a list), Steven Soderbergh's 2011 thriller *Contagion*, which depicts a deadly viral pandemic, shines out as it is solidly grounded in science and eerily anticipates current phenomena. One character provides an in-depth explanation of the concept of the R number, another spreads misinformation to destructive effect and governments administer an unprecedented vaccine. 'Viewed in retrospect, *Contagion* feels like a Covid play-by-play' (Heritage 2021: n.p.).

As far as the mode of reading is concerned, we can choose between six main approaches to reading novels or dramas (Thaler 2012), each of which has its benefits and drawbacks for pandemic titles as well.

1. Straight-through Approach: The whole novel (drama) is read at home by the students before classroom discussion starts. Knowing the whole makes understanding easier, enables topic-based explorations and leaves classroom time for discussion. However, it requires all students to have read the whole story; lazy readers may take the easy way out by skimming through web summaries, and this decreases suspense.

2. Segment Approach: In each lesson, one segment (or chapter, act) is discussed in class. This may be prepared at home or/and read at school. This approach covers the whole piece, keeps up suspense and does not expect too much reading per day. Yet it cuts up a text into easily digestible bits, enforces a uniform pace of reading and is time-consuming.

3. Sandwich Approach: Some chapters of the novel are read while others are skipped (and summarized, guessed or ignored). It saves time, skips less important passages and invites readers to catch up with the rest but makes understanding more difficult and may lead to a distorted impression.

4. Appetizer Approach: Only one excerpt from the whole book is read and discussed. This approach saves most time, focuses on important passages and allows for repeated reading and detailed analysis. However, it ignores the context, cannot lead to deep understanding and may frustrate learners who want the whole piece.

5. Topic Approach: Several books from the same literary genre, period, author or on a single issue are read in excerpts. This deepens the understanding of the topic (genre, period, author) but makes the appreciation of the whole novel impossible.

6. Patchwork Approach: Several books from various authors, genres and periods are read (in excerpts) and discussed. It is suited for a literary history en miniature unit, and as far as further benefits or drawbacks are concerned, it resembles the topic approach.

For an online unit on pandemic literature, we may use the Topic Approach and ask our students to choose one book each from a range of pandemic titles. Their individual choice could be facilitated if we combine this method with the Appetizer Approach and provide them with short excerpts from different titles at the beginning of the teaching sequence.

Next to reading and understanding fiction, students should also create their own products, which is one of the three sub-skills encompassed in LCC (see Figure 2.1 above). Independent creation need not be reduced to the now widely used creative writing, but we can also encourage our learners to produce something in various modes (Thaler 2014; 2009):

- Written creations: creative writing in all its numerous forms (acrostics on title, fan mail to author, review of book, writing an alternative ending etc.)
- Spoken creations: filling in indeterminacies and gaps, reading in various moods (e.g. sad or happy) or volumes (e.g. loud, whispering)
- Scenic creations: role playing, acting, miming, frozen tableau, hot seat etc.
- Visual creations: drawing pictures, designing collages, drawing a structure chart (including key phrases), making a pandemic fiction magazine etc.
- Acoustic creations: putting the text into sound, reading with suitable background music etc.
- Manual creations: designing objects from the text etc.
- Audiovisual creations: producing a YouTube clip, a short film etc.

All these activities allow learners to relate to a text on a creative level. Individually, in pairs or in small groups, they can present their personal perspectives on it.

Conclusion

To conclude, one could argue for a balanced form of literature teaching, which combines closed lessons and open learning and tries to strike a fair balance between six pairs of methods and procedures: teacher-fronted and learner-centred phases, working with a single title and intertextuality, text work and intermediality, intensive and extensive reading, close analysis and creative extension, deskbound approach and workshop approach.

The ultimate goal for our learners should be to understand and also enjoy literature, whether it is by reading DWEMs, LANGs (living authors, new genres), Lit-21 (postmillennial fiction) or pandemic literature. Infection researcher Tobias Welte recently stated: 'Infectious agents will always exist. The goal is not to overcome them, but to learn to live with them' (Sticht 2021) – and learning with them as well as from them can also be the goal of a teaching sequence on pandemic fiction.

Note

This is an updated and enlarged English version of Thaler (2021).

References

Primary Literature

Atwood, M. (2003), *Oryx and Crake*, Toronto: McClelland & Stewart.

Boccaccio (between 1349 and 1353), *Il Decamerone*, Project Gutenberg.

Brooks, M. (2006), *World War Z: An Oral History of the Zombie War*, New York: Three Rivers.

Byram, M. (1997), *Teaching and Assessing Intercultural Communicative Competence*, Clevedon: Multilingual Matters.

Camus, A. (1947), *La Peste*, Paris: Librairie Éditions Gallimard.

Chen, M. (2020), *A Beginning at the End*, Toronto: MIRA.

Crichton, M. (1969), *The Andromeda Strain*, New York: Knopf.

Defoe, D. (1722), *A Journal of the Plague Year*, Project Gutenberg.

Eilish, B. (2020), 'No Time to Die', Interscope Records.

Homer (*c.* 700/800 BC), *Iliad*, Project Gutenberg.

King, S. (1978), *The Stand*, New York: Doubleday.

Lanza, J. (2020), 'Over and Over', Hyperdub.

Ma, L. (2018), *Severance*, New York: Macmillan.

Mandel, E. St. John (2014), *Station Eleven*, New York: Knopf.

Márquez, G. G. ([1985] 1988), *Love in the Time of Cholera*, New York: Knopf.

Matheson, R. (1954), *I Am Legend*, New York: Gold Medal.

MGM (prod.) (2021), *No Time to Die*, Universal Pictures.

O'Nan, S. (1999), *Prayer for the Dying*, New York: Holt.

Poe, E. A. (1842), *The Masque of the Red Death*, Project Gutenberg.

Porter, K. A. ([1939] 1990), *Pale Horse, Pale Rider*, San Francisco: Houghton Mifflin Harcourt.

Roth, P. (2010), *Nemesis*, San Francisco: Houghton Mifflin Harcourt.

Saramago, J. (1995), *Blindness*, Lisbon: Caminho.

Shelley, M. (1826), *The Last Man*, Project Gutenberg.

Welsh, L. (2014–17), *Plague Times Trilogy*, London: John Murray.

Wright, L. (2020), *The End of October*, New York: Knopf.

Secondary Literature

Benson, K. (2020), 'Reading on Paper versus Screens: What's the Difference?' www.bra infacts.org/neuroscience-in-society/tech-and-the-brain/2020/reading-on-paper-ver sus-screens-whats-the-difference-072820 (accessed 16 August 2021).

Böttger, H., T. Hoffmann, D. Költzsch and S. Stadler-Heer (2021), 'Draußen lehren und lernen. Die Katholische Universität Eichstätt-Ingolstadt bereitet eine *Outdoor Faculty* vor. Wie das geht und was geplant ist', *Deutsche Universitätszeitung DUZ*, 30–3.

Carroll, T. (2020), 'Pandemics: An Essential Reading List'. www.vulture.com/article/best-pandemic-books.html (accessed 16 March 2021).

Columbia Public Health (2021), 'Epidemic, Endemic, Pandemic: What Are the Differences?' www.publichealth.columbia.edu/public-health-now/news/epidemic-endemic-pandemic-what-are-differences (accessed 16 August 2021).

Davis, S. (2020), 'The 16 Best Pandemic Books, Fiction and Nonfiction'. https://bookriot.com/best-pandemic-books/ (accessed 16 March 2021).

Doherty, J., and J. Giordano (2020), 'What We May Learn – and Need – from Pandemic Fiction,' *Philosophy, Ethics and Humanities in Medicine*, 15 (1). https://doi.org/10.1186/s13010-020-00089-0.

Edutech, Z. (2020), 'Pros and Cons of Online Reading and Book Reading'. https://medium.com/@ziyyaraedutech/pros-and-cons-of-online-reading-and-book-reading-8dae27c9eff5 (accessed 16 August 2021).

Emmrich, T., and A. Geisenhanslüke (2020), 'Literatur und Epidemie'. https://aktuelles.uni-frankfurt.de/forschung/literatur-und-epidemie (accessed 16 March 2021).

Georgi, S. (2020), 'Eine kurze Geschichte der Epidemien in der Literatur'. https://www.mdr.de/kultur/corona-epidemien-in-der-literatur-100.html (accessed 16 March 2021).

Goldsmith, A. (2020), 'How 10 Fictional Pandemics Compare to Ours'. www.townandcountrymag.com/leisure/arts-and-culture/g32419194/pandemic-movies/ (accessed 16 March 2021).

Heritage, S. (2021), 'What Does Covid Mean for the Future of Pandemic Movies?' www.theguardian.com/film/2021/feb/11/what-does-covid-mean-for-the-future-of-pandemic-movies (accessed 16 March 2021).

Iser, W. I. (1972), *Der implizite Leser: Kommunikationsformen des Romans von Bunyan bis Beckett*, Munich: Fink.

Kelly, J. (2006), *The Great Mortality*, New York: Harper.

Kirchhoff, P. (2019), 'Kanondiskussion und Textauswahl', in K. Stierstorfer and C. Lütge (eds), *Grundthemen der Literaturwissenschaft*, 219–30, Berlin: Walter de Gruyter.

KMK, ed. (2003), 'Bildungsstandards mittlerer Schulabschluss'. www.kmk.org/fileadmin/veroeffentlichungen_beschluesse/2003/2003_12_04-BS-erste-Fremdsprache.pdf (accessed 16 March 2021).

KMK, ed. (2012), 'Bildungsstandards allgemeine Hochschulreife'. www.kmk.org/fileadmin/veroeffentlichungen_beschluesse/2012/2012_10_18-Bildungsstandards-Fortgef-FS-Abi.pdf (accessed 16 March 2021).

Leonhardt, D. (2017), '18 Pros and Cons of E-Books'. https://thgmwriters.com/blog/18-pros-cons-ebooks/ (accessed 16 August 2021).

McRae, J. (1994), *Literature with a Small 'l'*, London: Macmillan Education.

Mylow, D. (2020), 'Literatur und Pandemie: Anregungen für den Literaturunterricht in Krisenzeiten'. https://www.erziehungskunst.de/nachrichten/pandemie/literatur-und-pandemie-anregungen-fuer-den-literaturunterricht-in-krisenzeiten/ (accessed 16 March 2021).

Otto, R. (1917), *Das Heilige*, Munich: Beck.

Paran, A., and P. Robinson (2016), *Literature: Into the Classroom*, Oxford: Oxford University Press.

Quammen, D. (2012), *Spillover: Animal Infections and the Next Human Pandemic*, New York: W. W. Norton.

Savage, M. (2020), '11 of the Best Music Videos from Lockdown'. www.bbc.com/news/entertainment-arts-53676767 (accessed 16 March 2021).

Spinney, L. (2017), *Pale Rider: The Spanish Flu of 1918 and How It Changed the World*, New York: Public Affairs.

Stadler-Heer, S. (2022, forthcoming), 'Teaching Current Crises: Designing Task-Based Online Lessons on US Structural Racism with the Help of Digital Tools', *F&E, Die Forschungszeitschrift der Pädagogischen Hochschule Vorarlberg*.

Sticht, C. (2021), 'Museum zeigt die Geschichte der Seuchen'. www.aerztezeitung.de/Panorama/Museum-zeigt-die-Geschichte-der-Seuchen-417484.html (accessed 16 March 2021).

Thaler, E. (2009), *Method Guide: Kreative Methoden für den Literaturunterricht*, Paderborn: Schöningh.

Thaler, E. (2012), *Englisch unterrichten*, Berlin: Cornelsen.

Thaler, E. (2014), *Teaching English Literature*, Paderborn: UTB.

Thaler, E. (2016), *Shorties: Flash Fiction in Language Teaching*, Tübingen: Narr.

Thaler, E., ed. (2019), *Lit 21: New Literary Genres in Language Teaching*, Tübingen: Narr.

Thaler, E. (2022), 'Pandemie-Literatur im Online-Fremdsprachenunterricht', in Simona Bartoli-Kucher (ed.), *Quo vadis, italiano? Letteratura, cinema, didattica e fumetti Literatur, Film, Didaktik und Comic*, Frankfurt/Main: Peter Lang, 61–74.

Toynbee, A. (1948), 'The Unification of the World and the Change in Historical Perspective', *Journal of the Historical Association*, 33. https://www.abebooks.co.uk/Unification-World-Change-Historical-Perspective-Toynbee/878619377/bd 1947 (accessed 16 March 2021).

Tsang, A., A. Paran and W. Lau (2020), 'The Language and Non-language Benefits of Literature in Foreign Language Education: An Exploratory Study of Learners' Views', *Language Teaching Research*. https://doi.org/10.1177/1362168820972345 (accessed 16 March 2021).

Vögele, J., S. Knöll and T. Noack, eds (2016), *Epidemien und Pandemien in historischer Perspektive*, Berlin: Springer.

Part 2

Researching and Teaching Literature for/to Young Learners

3

Identifying Quality in Asynchronous, Pre-recorded Picturebook Read-Alouds for Children Learning English as a Foreign Language

Gail Ellis and Sandie Mourão

Introduction

A picturebook is a form of children's literature where pictures, words and design are used to convey meaning (Bader 1976). It uses 'sequential imagery [to] carry much of the narrative responsibility' (Salisbury and Styles 2012: 7), and as such, the image is no longer seen as 'subordinate to the written word' (Salisbury and Styles 2019: 7); rather, meaning emerges from the interplay between these two codes. In a picturebook the illustrations overflow into the peritext (i.e. the covers, endpapers, title page, copyright and dedication pages etc.), resulting in a multilayered, aesthetic object that has been considered 'an experience for a child' (Bader 1976: 1). Not only has the relationship between the visual and verbal texts and the materiality of the picturebook been debated by picturebook scholarship since the 1980s but so have 'the pleasures [and] the learning processes evoked by picturebooks' (Kümmerling Meibauer 2018: 4).

Much has been written on the role of picturebooks in the development of the whole child in relation to their cognitive, linguistic, sociocultural and aesthetic development (cf. Nikolajeva 2014; Arizpe and Styles 2017; Kümmerling Meibauer 2018), including in the field of English language education (cf. Ghosn 2002; Bland 2013; Ellis and Brewster 2014; Mourão 2015), where picturebooks have been used as a rich and authentic source of meaningful input for over four decades (Mourão and Bland 2016). The fusion of trade publishing and age-appropriate ELT pedagogy offers a high quality, flexible and motivating approach to language teaching and learning and brings multimodal representation into the classroom (Ellis 2006; Bland 2013). In addition, picturebooks can be interpreted on many levels and thus satisfy children of different ages, at different points in their English language learning and from pre-primary through to secondary (Mourão 2013; Ellis and Brewster 2014; Mourão 2016).

A plethora of asynchronous picturebook read-alouds are available online. These are pre-recorded read-alouds for children to experience through online channels without real-time interaction and are produced by literacy charities, publishers, bookshops and picturebook creators, as well as by teachers, parents and carers. To our knowledge, very little research has been published around online read-alouds, and our chapter looks specifically at the issue of quality in these read-alouds with a particular focus on their affordances for EFL children in pre-primary and primary education.

Picturebook Read-Alouds and Quality Considerations

Empirical research has shown the benefits of reading aloud to children and providing access to children's literature for cognitive, language and literacy development (cf. Bus, van Ijzendoorn and Pellegrini 1995; van Kleeck, Stahl and Bauer 2003; Wells 2009). The research that investigates 'book reading quality' (Reese et al. 2003: 36) is associated with these benefits. Quality is often equated with the adult's behaviour and interactional style during a read-aloud and the support it affords for language and literacy development (Whitehurst and Lonigan 1998). Teale (2003: 129) asserts that it is 'the choice of how much, what, why, and how to read' which are relevant factors influencing the effect of reading aloud on children's learning and development. Nevertheless, Martinez and Roser claim that 'reading to children involves three components – the child, the adult, and the story' (1985: 168), and each is essential and has an influence over the other (Pellegrini and Galda 2003). This makes 'quality' a complex and multifaceted concept, for definitions will vary considerably depending on different educational and cultural contexts and the individualities of the adult and the child(ren) as well as their interests and needs.

Interactive Read-Alouds

Traditional read-alouds involve a reader focusing on the verbal text and reading *at* or *to* the children, which provides little or no opportunity for interaction and discussion around the visual-verbal narrative and is considered less effective (cf. Teale 2003). Interactive read-alouds (Greene Brabham and Lynch-Brown 2002), on the other hand, depend upon a teacher 'selecting books that meet students' interests as well as their social and developmental levels, modelling fluent reading, and encouraging students to contribute in active ways' (Wiseman 2011: 431–2). This means the reader reads *with* the children, and joint reflections and co-constructions of meaning take place through their interactions and collaboration. The reader respects children as equal partners in learning, although this will be influenced by the culture, practices and educational requirements of different countries.

Extratextual Talk and Behaviour

Typically, during face-to-face read-alouds, adults 'ask questions, paraphrase and explain story events, describe and label pictures [and] jointly construct understanding of the book' (Haden, Reese and Fivush 1996: 135–6). Referred to as 'extratextual talk', that is, talk that goes beyond reading the picturebook verbal text, this has also been identified as one of the aspects of the interactive read-aloud that is associated with children's language and literacy development (van Kleeck, Stahl and Bauer 2003) as well as their socio-affective and cognitive development (Greene Brabham and Lynch-Brown 2002; Wiseman 2011).

With a view to producing a standardized observational assessment of shared-reading quality for practitioners and researchers, the Systematic Assessment of Book Reading (SABR) examines adult 'extratextual behaviours' as it considers 'conversation *and* behaviours beyond the actual reading of the text' (Justice, Zucker and Sofka 2010: 5, our emphasis). Assessing two domains and seven constructs of extratextual behaviour, the SABR provides an opportunity to assess quality in relation to reading aloud for language and literacy development. The first domain is related to 'instructional support' and focuses on (1) vocabulary and oral language skills, (2) abstract thinking skills, (3) print-related and phonological awareness skills and (4) elaborative responses to the text. The second domain is more general and associated with the 'book reading context', focusing on adult behaviours that create a warm, supportive setting for shared reading, referring to the constructs of (5) book reading context, (6) reading delivery and (7) behaviour management. As a tool the SABR is unique in its objective to 'capture *what* the teacher is doing to teach students within the reading context' and '*how* the teacher organizes and delivers the shared-reading session' (4; original emphases). However we do not feel it covers all aspects of a reader's quality extratextual behaviour.

Scaffolding Functions

As noted, a successful interactive read-aloud respects and favours children's response. Sipe's (2008) five conceptual categories for adult talk during picturebook read-alouds testify to the variety of scaffolding functions undertaken by the teacher as they mediate children's interpretative responses during face-to-face read-alouds. This scaffolding contributes to developing children's literary understanding, through active meaning-making and exploration of the picturebook. The five categories are summarized in Table 3.1.

Several of Sipe's functions of adult talk can be mapped onto the SABR tool. The constructs of elaborative response align with Sipe's category of 'Clarifiers or Probers', and the book read-aloud context is apparent in the categories of 'Readers' and 'Managers and Encouragers'. However, the SABR tool includes no mention of making the most of the picturebook peritext, part of Sipe's 'Readers' category. Additionally, the collaborative role of Sipe's 'Fellow Wonderers', where the reader discovers *with* the children rather than *for* them, seems to have been ignored as well.

The Read-Aloud as Performance

Another concept that is relevant for understanding the quality of read-alouds is that of performance. Bauman's seminal work around oral storytelling refers to

Table 3.1 Sipe's Five Categories for Adult Talk

Category	Scaffolding functions
Readers	Reading the verbal text and guiding children around the book as object by pointing to and referring to its different parts (i.e. the peritextual features)
Managers and Encouragers	Managing discussion; bringing children's attention to details in illustrations through description or invited participation; giving praise; creating an atmosphere of respect and acceptance
Clarifiers or Probers	Supporting, extending, amplifying or contradicting; requesting more information; asking questions and making connections
Fellow Wonderers or Speculators	Questioning and wondering with the children
Extenders or Refiners	Amplifying children's contributions; grasping 'teachable moments'; summarizing; providing closure

Source: Sipe (2008: 200–203).

a 'performance event' (1986: 3), and we believe parallels can be made with the picturebook read-aloud. Performance is 'artistic action – the doing of folklore' and 'the situation, involving performer, art form, audience and setting' (Bauman 1984: 4). During a read-aloud, 'performance' refers to the doing of the read-aloud and 'the situation' denotes the three factors mentioned earlier – the reader, the picturebook and the children – together with the setting. Acknowledging also that interaction is key to the read-aloud, Ellis and Mourão (2021: 24) recommend that attention be paid to 'the potential interaction that might occur during a read-aloud event as each factor influences the other'. The reader will interpret the picturebook, and be influenced by its materiality (i.e. the way it is designed), its multimodality (i.e. the way the pictures and words interanimate) and its typographical features (i.e. weight, colour, size, slant, framing, formality and flourishes; cf. Serafini and Clausen 2012). The picturebook's materiality will influence the children as a group and as individuals, and they in turn will influence the reader and each other. During repeated read-alouds, this interaction will change, even if the same picturebook is being shared with the same group of children, for although a performance begins as a one-person show for the reader, it soon becomes collaborative as the children play an increasingly active part in the co-construction of meaning (Masoni 2019). The read-aloud is thus a dynamic performance event, and each performance is unique.

The Read-Aloud Skills

Considering the read-aloud as a performance event, enjoyment is derived in proportion to the skill of the performer – the reader (Bauman 1986: 3). As we have seen, this includes the use of extratextual behaviour to promote interaction, scaffold understanding and create rapport. However, a reader also requires the skills of reading aloud and performance (i.e. making effective use of their body, eyes and voice).

Reading Aloud

According to Garvie (1990) and Fox (2008) reading aloud is an acquired art. Both suggest there is no exact right way of reading aloud, other than to read aloud clearly, naturally and intelligibly and to be as interesting and as expressive as possible. Each reader should do this in the way they feel most comfortable, and each will have their own style. However, the reader should plan and rehearse to build their confidence in how to pronounce the words, in where to place correct emphasis and in being able to assimilate chunks of the verbal text by scanning ahead so they read coherently and smoothly. The punctuation should be used as a guide to know when to pause to convey mood and suspense, as well as to differentiate between dialogue and narrative, statement and question and so on (Garvie 1990). In addition, the typographical features of the verbal text, as referred to above, also have meaning potential (Serafini and Clausen 2012; Dowd Lambert 2015) and provide signposts to the reader so they can read with emotion and feeling and vary the intonation, tone and volume of their voice to bring the story alive and lift the words off the page.

Readers also need to be aware of pacing to maintain children's interest, motivation and perseverance to keep listening until the end. Reading *with* their audience requires that they look up from the page and make direct eye contact to connect, create rapport and engage them affectively so they 'feel part of the process' (Paran and Robinson 2016: 44). All of this combines with the way the reader interprets how the pictures and words interanimate so that children experience the 'drama of the turning of the page' (Bader 1976: 1) at the appropriate moment.

Performance Skills: Body, Eyes and Voice

According to Fox (2008), the body, eyes and voice all have an important part to play in reading aloud. So, a reader needs to be aware of how these performance skills can be used to convey emotion and meaning and how they contribute to children's construction and interpretation of the story as well as their heightened engagement. Use of the body involves the reader's gestures, facial expressions, actions, positioning and posture. Use of the eyes and gaze include showing and expressing meaning, feelings or emotions and making eye contact with the virtual audience. Finally, use of the voice and vocal variety involves using stress, intonation, tone, volume, pace and pause, as well as using different voices for different characters and sound effects. In addition, Fox warns against using a 'cutesy, sugary, patronizing voice' and suggests that readers should 'make a conscious decision *never* to talk down to children' (42; original emphasis).

Online Picturebook Read-Alouds

An 'on-screen picturebook experience' (Dunn 2013: 235) will never fully replace the excitement and intimacy of a face-to-face read-aloud event or the physical experience of holding a picturebook, but it offers a powerful digital alternative to using physical books. During the global pandemic the number of online picturebook read-alouds increased (Arizpe 2021), giving children continued opportunities to engage with quality literature during school closures and to support their social and emotional well-being (see also Chapter 4 by Summer in this volume for a discussion of some of the digital picturebooks that appeared during the first months of the pandemic).

The degree of social engagement that is possible when moving read-alouds online is dependent on whether the setting is synchronous or asynchronous. Stoetzel and Shedrow state that the key to meaningful instruction online is to rely less on structure (i.e. the organizational aspects of the read-aloud) and more on teachers' 'pedagogical knowledge to scaffold student engagement' (2021a: 749). Additionally, they recommend carefully considering the purpose and goals of the digital read-aloud experience and planning to intentionally develop language and literacy, even if relying on a recorded read-aloud. They describe the process a group of pre-service student teachers went through to create online picturebook read-alouds, highlighting the students' need for assistance to ensure that the dimensions of a quality, interactive read-aloud (i.e. explicitly fostering literacy growth) were an integrated part of the online read-aloud (Stoetzel and Shedrow 2021b). The checklist they created for the student teachers included:

- How will students see the text while you are reading?
- How are you modelling fluency and expression while reading?
- How many opportunities will you build into the reading for students to respond (by thinking, writing, or speaking)? (135)

We understand the term 'text' in this checklist as referring mainly to the verbal text rather than to the combination of pictures and words. It also appears to exclude the performance aspect of the read-aloud, but it is nevertheless a useful start for considering quality in relation to using a read-aloud with a clear focus on developing literacy. In an ELT context, where read-alouds provide access to continuous and coherent spoken discourse (Cameron 2001), as well as being an authentic resource to support meaningful listening practice, it is vital that the audience can see the reader and the picturebook to support understanding and engagement. Ellis and Gruenbaum (forthcoming) discuss the criteria for selecting asynchronous picturebook read-alouds by picturebook creators. A key selection criterion was the video production approach used (i.e. how they were filmed). Four approaches were identified, each offering different affordances for children at different stages in their English language learning. However, the 'interactive approach', which allows the audience to see both the reader and the picturebook at the same time, was, in their view, the most effective for e-learning, as the reader interacts with the virtual audience and encourages active participation in the meaning-making process.

To close this section on considerations around quality, we share recommendations provided by an expert librarian and storyteller, Alec Williams (see www.alecwilliams.co.uk/welcome.php), whose advice we sought. He explained that his main read-aloud tips for face-to-face encounters were to focus on 'reading for pleasure, so [my] tips are about "bringing the story alive", and about sheer enjoyment of the story experience' (personal communication, 22 June 2020). His additional advice for online picturebook read-alouds expanded on this slightly: 'My intention would be to recreate the best possible experience of a teacher or parent: clearly enjoying the story, reacting to words and pictures, putting drama into the telling … inviting participation, leaving time for children to comment … etc.' (personal communication, 22 June 2020). Particularly relevant here are the notions of the reader reacting to the picturebook and also inviting participation by the imagined virtual audience and leaving time for them to comment – all opportunities for extratextual talk. Sipe's (2008) five conceptual categories of adult talk presented in Table 3.1 are also evident in Williams's advice.

In this literature review we have identified aspects of quality in both face-to-face and online read-aloud contexts. These relate to the reader's skills of reading aloud, interacting and scaffolding meaning through using their body, eyes and voice and extratextual talk, as well as the approach used to film the read-aloud. We will now present a small-scale study which was undertaken with a view to answering the following question: What makes a quality asynchronous pre-recorded picturebook read-aloud for children of English as a foreign language?

Methodology

Context

During the flourishing of online picturebook read-alouds in the first months of the Covid-19 pandemic, we noticed that many readers focused only on reading the words aloud, which as we have shown above is considered to be a less effective practice. Between March and June 2020, we were also immersed in recording read-alouds for either our own young EFL students (in Portugal) or those of a colleague (in Poland) and had agreed to write a set of guidelines to support teachers in making their own recorded read-alouds for children learning English as a foreign language for the PEPELT project (see https://pepelt21.com/). This motivated us to work towards a better understanding of recorded picturebook read-alouds for this context.

Our epiphany came as we watched a recorded read-aloud of *Bunnies on the Bus* (Ardagh and Mantle 2020) by Alec Williams. We noticed the extratextual talk and behaviour Williams used and the opportunities this afforded for an imagined child participation. In addition, his judicious use of the picturebook peritext during this talk made his read-aloud extremely effective and demonstrated his attention to the picturebook as aesthetic object. Our hypothesis was that Williams's skill at using extratextual talk to read *with* his virtual audience rather than *to* them contributed to the success of his read-aloud. This prompted us to consider the role of this talk in online read-alouds for children learning English as another language.

At this stage, we also began to refer to the phenomenon as 'read-aloud talk' in order to situate it specifically within the read-aloud event itself and in our own context associated with English language education. We recognized its possible scaffolding functions, the additional exposure it provided to spoken English, as well as its collaborative nature in co-constructing meaning.

Data Collection

Taking a qualitative approach to understanding the phenomenon we had noticed, we planned two stages in our data collection, which began with an inductive baseline analysis in preparation for an inductive and comparative analysis of a small corpus of recorded read-alouds.

Stage 1: An Inductive Baseline Analysis

The first stage involved transcribing Williams's read-aloud of *Bunnies on the Bus* and undertaking a baseline inductive analysis (Patton 2014), for we already had a hypothesis about the role of the read-aloud talk and its relationship with the quality of the read-aloud. We were especially interested in the different functions the talk might serve. In this phase we identified segments in the transcription, coded them and then collated them into categories. This initial analysis enabled

Table 3.2 Alec Williams's Read-Aloud Talk

Category		Examples
1	Opening and closing the read-aloud event	[Introduction] It's Alec Williams here! Good to see you. I hope you're all ok …
		[Closing] So that's **Bunnies on the bus**, a new book by Philip Ardagh. Hope you liked it … Look after yourselves. And bye bye from me.
2.1	Commenting: referring to the picturebook creators, the peritext and using metalanguage	[Picturebook creators] So it's written by a man called Philip Ardagh … and the pictures are by Ben Mantel.
		[Metalanguage] Here is the <u>title page</u>, **Bunnies on the bus**.
2.2	Commenting: describing illustrations	There's a police car already and there's a train going across the bridge there, and over here you might just be able to see two little animals.
2.3	Commenting: modelling hypothesizing	I think they might be squirrels.
2.4	Commenting: making intertextual connections	They've got masks on so maybe they're burglars, like Burglar Bill.
2.5	Commenting: inviting participation	Now this is a sort of chorus. We could do it together couldn't we? Have a go! Ready? **Bunnies on the bus, bunnies on the bus. No wonder there's a fuss about the bunnies on the bus.**
3	Asking questions to engage the virtual listener	Do you think it's those bunnies?
4	Sound effects	Mehhh; Aheeee

Note: Bold typeface indicates picturebook verbal text; underlined text indicates peritextual metalanguage.

us to identify four main categories of read-aloud talk, which are listed in Table 3.2 with examples.

Three of Sipe's functions of adult talk are evident in these categories:

- 'Reader': Williams reads the verbal text and guides the viewers around the book by pointing to and referring to the peritextual features.
- 'Manager': Williams directs the viewers' attention to something in an illustration through description or invited participation.
- 'Fellow Wonderer or Speculator': Williams models hypothesizing and 'playfully contribute[s] to the creative flight of the [viewers'] imaginations'. (2008: 201)

The other two functions, 'Clarifiers or Probers' and 'Extenders or Refiners', were not evident, as Williams had no real children to interact with online.

Table 3.3 Contexts in Which the Picturebook Read-Alouds Took Place

Country	Children	Objectives for recorded read-alouds	Reader(s)
Portugal	25 Portuguese pre-primary children (5–6 years old); one weekly read-aloud session in English and 1 hour of English	i) To maintain an affective relationship with English during lockdown ii) To provide a familiar reassuring activity with someone the children already knew	Sandie Mourão
Poland	120 Polish primary children (6–9 years old) in mainstream education, with read-alouds in all English lessons, three times a week for 45 minutes	iii) To support children's socio-emotional well-being iv) To stimulate listening and comprehension skills in English *Additional objectives for Poland:* v) To provide wider exposure to English and access to different read-aloud styles and voices via people they did not know vi) To create a bank of read-alouds for children's own self-access use	Anneta Sadowska Gail Ellis Sandie Mourão

Stage 2: An Inductive and Comparative Analysis of the Target Corpus

This second stage of our analysis involved analysing a small corpus of recorded picturebook read-alouds which were made for two different groups of children learning English as a foreign language between March and June 2020, during the first three months of the Covid-19 lockdown. Table 3.3 summarizes the two contexts.

The selection of our corpus was made from a total of twenty-nine online picturebook read-alouds made by the teacher in Poland and the two authors. We selected four read-alouds of the same length: two read-alouds by readers who knew the children and spoke their language and two by readers who did not know the children and did not speak their language. An additional hunch was that the readers who spoke the children's language would be likely to include some use of this (Polish or Portuguese). Table 3.4 provides an overview of the selected read-aloud corpus.

The read-alouds were transcribed and the read-aloud talk was coded using the baseline categories constructed from Williams's read-aloud transcription

Table 3.4 Selected Recorded Picturebook Read-Alouds

Read-alouds	Picturebook	Synopsis	Audience	Reader	Length of recording
R–A1	*Peck, Peck, Peck* (Cousins 2013)	A baby woodpecker has just learnt how to peck and rejoices in pecking everything around him	Known primary children in Poland	Anneta Sadowska (speaks Polish)	05 min 48 sec
R–A2	*Wolf Won't Bite* (Gravett 2011)	Three pigs catch a wolf and show him off at the circus, only to discover that he is not as docile as they think	Known pre-primary children in Portugal	Sandie Mourão (speaks Portuguese)	05 min 4 sec
R–A3	*I'm Hungry* (Martín 2016)	A newly hatched dragon is very hungry and eats all the animals on her island until she is all alone	Unknown primary children in Poland	Gail Ellis	05min 55 sec
R–A4	*The Wall in the Middle of the Book* (Agee 2019)	A metaphorical book about a knight, a wall and an ogre which looks at how the invisible or unknown generates fear	Unknown primary children in Poland	Sandie Mourão	05 min 13 sec

as a guide. Qualitative data analysis is 'primarily inductive and comparative' (Merriam 2009: 175), and the comparative nature of this final phase enabled us to 'move back and forth between concrete bits of data [the baseline data and the corpus data] and abstract concepts, between inductive and deductive reasoning, between description and interpretation' (176). The analysis resulted in the construction of an extended and revised set of codes and categories.

Results and Discussion

Categories of Read-Aloud Talk

Six categories of read-aloud talk were identified during our analysis, which demonstrates that read-aloud talk can be used for different scaffolding purposes and contribute to creating a holistic picturebook read-aloud experience. However, these categories are not exclusive and sometimes overlap. As we moved back and forth between the baseline and corpus data, we moved away from separating 'commenting' from 'questions' and re-created our set of categories into slightly different subsets, which included the use of L1. In addition, the category 'sound effects' in the baseline categories (see Table 3.2) was removed as we felt it was more relevant to the skill of using voice and vocal variety. Table 3.5 presents the six categories with examples from the corpus.

In establishing the categories and selecting examples, it became increasingly clear that although read-aloud talk was indeed instrumental in its contribution to the quality of a read-aloud, this talk was part of the much bigger whole, an assemblage of read-aloud skills – read-aloud talk, reading aloud and performance (i.e. making effective use of the body, eyes and voice). In addition, the read-aloud, by virtue of being recorded, was transformed from a multimodal experience to a multimedial one which used technology to combine everything into a captivating experience for the children. Analysing read-aloud talk alone did not fully capture the richness of the combination of all modes – visual, verbal, aural and gestural – through which meaning was communicated in these pre-recorded read-aloud events.

The Read-Aloud as an Assemblage of Skills

With a view to exemplifying how the three skills outlined in the literature review combine to create a quality online picturebook read-aloud for children learning English as a foreign language, we analysed a sequence from read-aloud R–A1. The read-aloud was given using the 'interactive approach' (Ellis and Gruenbaum, forthcoming), so the virtual audience could see the reader and the picturebook. The two facing pages of the picturebook (i.e. each opening) were shown alongside the reader's upper torso and head. This meant that the reader's facial expressions, their posture and their hands were visible, the latter visible when pointing and giving meaningful gestures (Figure 3.1).

In this selected sequence, the double spread under analysis is Opening 6. The verbal text is on the verso against a yellow background, and the visual text is on the recto. The illustrations use Cousins's signature palette of bold primary colours, with thick black outlines, and are naive in their flat rendering style. They show a wallpapered wall with a framed picture of a ship and a coat rack, where a hat and jacket are hanging. On the floor, in a neat row underneath, are a small table with a flowerpot, some shoes and boots neatly lined up and an umbrella stand, where a tennis racket is placed. The baby woodpecker is balanced on the bumper guard of the tennis racket head and is pecking at the strings. Finally, there are two mats on the carpeted floor. The page has die-cut holes (i.e. small circular holes) on some

Table 3.5 Categories of Read-Aloud Talk

Categories	Examples
1. Opening and closing the read-aloud event	
1.1 Opening	R–A3 'Hello I'm Gail and I live in France and I'm going to read you a picturebook called *I'm Hungry!*'
1.2 Closing	R–A4 'I hope that you and Anneta have lots of fun talking about it. Bye, bye, stay well and keep safe.'
2. Managing the event	
2.1 Familiar routines	R–A2 'Shall we say hello to Morgan? Yes? [pause] One two three [pause] Hello Morgan!'
2.2 Inviting children to look at something	R–A2 'Let's just open the book and see what the little pigs have got at the end of the string.'
2.3 Inviting children to join in with repeated words, phrases or refrains either implicitly or explicitly	R–A4 'But wolf [pause and looks at audience] won't [pause and looks at audience] bite!' R–A3 **'Baby Dragon said sorry to her new friends …** who are all rather sad **Sorry! Sorry! Sorry!** [pause and looks at audience] **Sorry! Sorry! Sorry!'**
3. Referring to the picturebook as object	
3.1 Providing background information about the picturebook creators and the story	R–A1 'The book has been written by Lucy Cousins, whom you might remember as the author of the wonderful series *Maisy, Mysia* [trans: Maisy], the stories of Maisy.'
3.2 Talking around the picturebook peritext and using metalanguage	R–A3 'I'm going to show you the back cover.'
4. Asking questions	
4.1 Activating background knowledge	R–A3 'Look! Look at that egg. What do you think is in that egg?'
4.2 Encouraging prediction	R–A3 'And the text reads **On an island, far, far away, something is about to hatch** … What do you think it's going to be? **CRACK CRACK CRACK** Hmmmm?'
4.3 Prompting reflection to reflect on what the words say and the pictures show	R–A3 'Does he eat everybody on the island? Look here's a lovely pink elephant.'
5. Clarifying	
5.1 Translating a word or expression	R–A2 **'I can miss him every time.** Look can you see, miss, *não vai apanhar*' [trans: it won't catch them].
5.2 Repeating a word or expression	R–A1 **'I peck the hat. I peck the mat, the tennis racket** oh here tennis racket **and the jacket.** Hmmm, so let us have a look. A hat, a mat and a tennis racket and a jacket. Peck. Peck. Peck.'

Table 3.5 Continued

Categories	Examples
5.3 Expanding on the verbal text	R–A1 '**A tangerine, a green bean, an aubergine, a sardine, some margarine and seventeen jellybeans** one, two, three, four, five, six, seven, eight, nine, ten, eleven, twelve, thirteen, fourteen, fifteen, sixteen, seventeen jellybeans.'
6. Commenting	
6.1 Labelling or describing illustrations	R–A3 '**One by one, baby dragon ate everybody on the island** … look we can follow his tracks the cockatoo **chomp** a rabbit **chomp** and baby dragon's stomach is getting fuller and fuller […].'
6.2 Modelling being a good reader, i.e. thinking aloud, hypothesizing and wondering	R–A4 'Did you notice that when the main character was on this side of the book all of the words were also on that side of the book but then when he crossed over and he was saved, and of course then all the words went onto that side of the book.'

Note: Bold typeface indicates picturebook verbal text; book titles are in italics.

Figure 3.1 Anneta Sadowska reading aloud Opening 6 of *Peck, Peck, Peck* (Cousins 2013). Courtesy of Anneta Sadowska.

of the illustrated objects representing the woodpecker's pecking activity and near these holes are the words 'PECK' in handwritten lettering.

Table 3.6 provides an overview of twenty-four seconds of the pre-recorded read-aloud. The first column represents the picturebook verbal text, which will remain constant for all readers. Columns 1, 2 and 3 represent the read-aloud skills being used, and Column 4 identifies the categories of read-aloud talk being

Table 3.6 An Assemblage of Read-Aloud Skills: R–A1 [02m16s–02m40s]

The picturebook verbal text	1 Reading aloud	2 Read-aloud talk	3 Performance			4 Category of read-aloud talk
			3.1 Body/actions and gestures	3.2 Eyes/gaze	3.3 Voice	
I peck the hat. I peck the mat, the tennis racket	Uses the commas as a guide to pause after each item	–	Nodding head to the rhythm of the verbal text	Alternately looks at the audience and the verbal text on recto	Emphasizing the rhythm	–
		'Oh here's the' / pause/ 'tennis racket'	Points towards the visual text on verso	Looks at visual text on recto	Surprised tone	6. Commenting; 6.2 Thinking aloud
			Circles tennis racket with her finger		Emphasizing the rhythm and the rhyme	6. Commenting; 6.1 Labelling illustrations
and the jacket.	Uses the full stop, as a signal to use falling intonation on the second syllable of the word 'jacket' to mark the end of this page	–	Hovers over images and points to the jacket			–
		'Hummm, so let us have a look'	Hand to her chin and looks at visual text	Moves eyes across recto towards hat	Speaking quickly	2. Managing; 2.2 Inviting
		'a hat'	Points to the hat	Looks out at the audience	Emphasizing [hat]	6. Commenting; 6.1 Labelling illustrations
		'a mat'	Points to the mat	Looks at visual text on recto	Emphasizing [mat]	6. Commenting; 6.1 Labelling illustrations
		'and tennis racket, and the jacket.'	Points to the tennis racket and the jacket		Emphasizing the rhyming sounds	6. Commenting; 6.1 Labelling illustrations
		'Peck. Peck. Peck.'	Nodding head to the rhythm and turning the page.		Nonchalant manner	5. Clarifying; 5.2 Repeating

exemplified. The rows capture the multiplicity of what happens with each read-aloud skill and how these skills come together as an assemblage.

Notice, for example, how read-aloud talk (column 2) builds sequentially on, as well as expands upon, the reading aloud of the verbal text. The voice column (column 3.3) captures how the reader stresses the rhythm of the word 'tennis racket', which is further emphasized as she accompanies this with a nodding of her head (see column 3.1). Column 3.2 highlights how, at the same time, the reader alternates between looking at the picturebook pages and looking out at the audience to engage them in the read-aloud. The read-aloud talk comment in column 2, 'Oh here's the …', together with the pointing gesture (column 3.1), gives precedence to the importance of the imaginary virtual audience looking for and finding the objects in the illustrations. The remaining seconds in this sequence do exactly that, as the reader models looking for and finding objects in the illustrations, as well as emphasizing the rhyming sounds in the verbal text, which had just been read aloud. It is a rich extract, where the reader provides scaffolding through all three read-aloud skills to ensure their imagined audience is exposed to English meaningfully and is engaged and supported throughout the viewing.

This read-aloud was made by the children's teacher, who knew them and thus was aware of their individual needs, abilities and knowledge, and incorporated this awareness into her read-aloud. This brings us once again to consider the three components which make up a read-aloud – the child, the teacher/reader and the picturebook – which elsewhere we have described as the 'read-aloud triangle' to highlight how they influence each other (Ellis and Mourão 2021: 24). In a face-to-face context, the reader's understanding of picturebooks, their knowledge of the children, their pedagogical understanding and read-aloud skills will all influence how they read aloud and respond to the children. The children will also interact with the picturebook, the reader and each other, depending upon their age, their knowledge of English, the languages they speak, their knowledge of the world, their interests, their individual and collective personalities and so on. In a pre-recorded read-aloud, this real-time interaction and interpretation is restricted to the reader and the picturebook only, but the reader will be influenced by what they know of the imagined virtual audience and their imagined interaction with the picturebook. Figure 3.2 illustrates this, with the continuous two-way arrows symbolizing the real-time influences on the reader and the picturebook, and the dashed two-way arrows symbolizing an imagined participation, interaction and interpretation between the picturebook and the virtual audience, and the reader and the virtual audience.

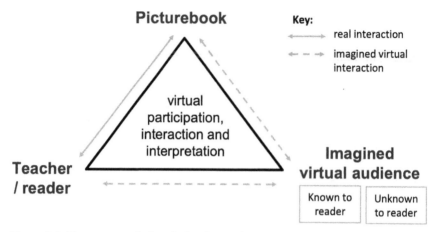

Figure 3.2 The pre-recorded read-aloud triangle.

Conclusion: Creating Quality Virtual Learning Conditions

Any read-aloud, whether recorded or live, involves a combination of the three read-aloud skills we have defined and discussed throughout this chapter. The use of read-aloud talk, in particular, will be influenced by the reader's knowledge of an imagined virtual audience and their likely response to the picturebook. However, this effective combination of skills becomes part of a greater, multilayered whole, evolving around the read-aloud as a performance event (see Figure 3.3).

The outer layer reminds us that any given read-aloud is a specific event that is bounded and which has a beginning and end. Understanding the read-aloud as an event enables us to suggest that these stages – the beginning and the end – need to be attended to, rather than the reader missing them out in order 'to get on with the story' (Roche 2015: 16), the middle. Read-aloud talk associated with opening and closing plays an important role in providing additional language exposure and demonstrating the social function of language, which is closely linked to creating rapport.

The second layer corresponds to the rapport and online presence nurtured between the reader and their imaginary virtual audience, which underpins the success of the read-aloud event. Most read-aloud talk categories contribute to recreating the 'shared social experience' (Ellis and Brewster 2014: 7) of the face-to-face read-aloud as they provoke response and contribute to building a relationship with the virtual audience (known or unknown) to keep them interested and engaged. This rapport is key to fostering engagement and motivation so that learning takes place.

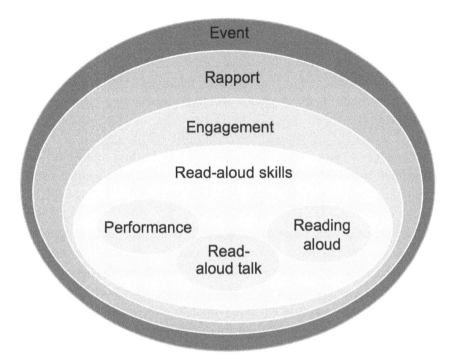

Figure 3.3 The read-aloud as a performance event.

In the third layer, the same areas of engagement and motivation that have been observed during face-to-face read-alouds can also be experienced by a virtual audience and are associated with the following:

- Affective engagement: The virtual audience connects with the reader's online presence and read-aloud style and experiences a sense of achievement, and thus motivation, at having understood the gist of an authentic picturebook read-aloud in the same way during face-to-face read-alouds.
- Aesthetic engagement: The virtual audience connects with the picturebook – its pictures, words and design, including its peritextual features – which allows them to appreciate the picturebook as an aesthetic object and recognize, and appreciate, how all these features contribute to conveying the narrative.
- Cognitive engagement: The virtual audience connects with the narrative, theme and concepts in which they can become personally involved, and develop inferencing, deduction and critical thinking skills by constructing meaning from clues via the illustrations and the reader's read-aloud skills

and predicting what is going to happen next. They are also developing the 'fifth skill of viewing' (Donaghy 2019).

- Multisensory engagement: The virtual audience connects with the reader through body, eyes and voice alongside the multimodal picturebook which contributes to the development of their visual literacy (Serafini and Moses 2014).

As can be seen, these areas of engagement link to the three read-aloud skills in the inner layer. All four layers contribute to creating a language-rich virtual environment by bringing the verbal and visual texts of the picturebook alive through the effective use of the read-aloud skills as we saw in Table 3.6. This provides children with a holistic virtual read-aloud experience as they are exposed to narrative as well as conversational discourse and engaged in affective, aesthetic, cognitive and multisensory learning. Although research has not been undertaken to confirm this, a virtual read-aloud experience affords children the opportunity to assimilate the target language and hopefully later transfer and use it in real-time, face-to-face interactions when they are ready and the opportunity arises.

Implications for Practice and Research

Training and reflection around the read-aloud skills we have identified would be useful in pre- and in-service teacher education and professional development, yet these skills are rarely given the relevant attention (cf. Stoetzel and Shedrow 2021b). In addition, teachers may need to reflect on their own theories and constructions of children and childhood, as well as the power dynamics in the adult-child relationship, to plan for an interactive approach to reading aloud.

For readers (pre- and in-service teachers, teacher educators, librarians, etc.), pre-recorded picturebook read-alouds might also provide opportunities to identify areas for self-improvement. For example, when revisiting our own read-alouds or observing read-alouds by others, we were able to notice missed opportunities for mediating through asking questions, encouraging prediction, better pausing and improved openings and closures. Such a practice would provide a valuable self-assessment and evaluation activity which can take place in the intimacy of individual or collective spaces.

Future research could also include the use of pre-recorded read-alouds in teacher education via classroom-based action-research, where practitioners identify improvements in their read-aloud practices and children's perceived learning and motivation. Additionally, a comparative study between children experiencing interactive read-alouds and traditional read-alouds might be relevant in relation to learning outcomes or engagement. Such a study could, for example, focus on comprehension and a transfer of acquired language to other situations, vocabulary acquisition and pronunciation, or even the development of literary understanding in a foreign language.

Finally, anecdotal evidence from our colleague in Poland indicates that primary children revisited the pre-recorded picturebook read-alouds independently. This suggests that these read-alouds can provide self-access to rich, authentic language exposure. Investigating the learning outcomes from these repeated exposures in relation to language acquisition and use in meaningful follow-up interactions would provide further avenues for research.

References

Primary Literature

Agee, J. (2019), *The Wall in the Middle of the Book*, London: Scallywag.
Ardagh, P., and B. Mantle (2020), *Bunnies on the Bus*, London: Walker.
Cousins, L. (2013), *Peck, Peck, Peck*, London: Walker.
Gravett, E. (2011), *Wolf Won't Bite*, London: Macmillan Children's Books.
Martín, J. (2016), *I'm Hungry*, London: Jonathan Cape.

Secondary Literature

Arizpe, E. (2021), 'The State of the Art in Picturebook Research from 2010–2020', *Language Arts*, 98 (5): 260–72.
Arizpe, E., and M. Styles (2017), *Children Reading Picturebooks. Interpreting Visual Texts*, 2nd edn, Abingdon: Routledge.
Bader, B. (1976), *American Picturebooks from* Noah's Ark *to* The Beast Within, New York: Macmillan.
Bauman, R. (1984), *Verbal Arts as Performance*, Long Grove, IL: Waveland.
Bauman, R. (1986), *Story, Performance and Event: Contextual Studies of Oral Narrative*, Cambridge: Cambridge University Press.
Bland, J. (2013), *Children's Literature and Learner Empowerment*, London: Bloomsbury.
Bus, A. G., M. H. van Ijzendoorn and A. D. Pellegrini (1995), 'Joint Book Reading Makes for Success in Learning to Read: A Meta-analysis on Intergenerational

Transmission of Literacy', *Review of Educational Research*, 65 (1): 1–21. doi:10.3102/00346543065001001.

Cameron, L. (2001), *Teaching Languages to Young Learners*, Cambridge: Cambridge University Press.

Donaghy, K. (2019), 'Advancing Learning: The Fifth Skill – "Viewing"'. https://www.one stopenglish.com/professional-development/advancing-learning-the-fifth-skill-view ing/557577.article (accessed 7 December 2021).

Dowd Lambert, M. (2015), *Reading Picture Books with Children*, Watertown, MA: Charlesbridge.

Dunn, O. (2013), *Introducing English to Children: Spoken language*, London: Collins.

Ellis, G. (2006), 'Teacher Competencies and a Story-Based Approach', in J. Enever and G. Schmid-Schönbein (eds), *Picture Books and Primary EFL Learners*, 93–108, Munich: Langenscheidt.

Ellis, G., and J. Brewster (2014), *Tell It Again! The Storytelling Handbook for Primary English Language Teachers*, London: British Council.

Ellis, G., and T. Gruenbaum (forthcoming), 'Reimagining Picturebook Pedagogy for Online Primary English Language Education', in D. Valente and D. Xerri (eds), *Innovative Practices in Early English Language Education*, London: Palgrave Macmillan.

Ellis, G., and S. Mourão (2021), 'Demystifying the Read-Aloud', *English Teaching Professional*, 136: 22–5.

Fox, M. (2008), *Reading Magic. Why Reading Aloud to Our Children Will Change Their Lives Forever*, New York: Harcourt.

Garvie, E. (1990), *Story as Vehicle*, Bristol: Multilingual Matters.

Ghosn, I.-K. (2002), 'Four Good Reasons to Use Literature in Primary School ELT', *ELT Journal*, 56 (2): 172–9.

Greene Brabham, E., and C. Lynch-Brown (2002), 'Effects of Teachers' Reading-Aloud Styles on Vocabulary Acquisition and Comprehension of Students in the Early Elementary Grades', *Journal of Educational Psychology*, 94 (3): 465–73.

Haden, C. A., E. Reese and R. Fivush (1996), 'Mothers' Extratextual Comments During Storybook Reading: Stylistic Differences over Time and across Texts', *Discourse Processes*, 21: 135–69.

Justice, T. A., T. A. Zucker and A. E. Sofka (2010), *Systematic Assessment of Book Reading: SABR Manual*, Columbus, OH: Preschool Language and Literacy Research Lab.

Kümmerling Meibauer, B., ed. (2018), *The Routledge Companion to Picturebooks*, Abingdon: Routledge.

Martinez, M., and N. Roser (1985), 'Read It Again: The Value of Repeated Readings during Storytime', *Reading Teacher*, 38 (8): 782–6.

Masoni, L. (2019), *Tale, Performance, and Culture in ELT Storytelling with Young Learners*, Newcastle Upon Tyne: Cambridge Scholars.

Merriam, S. B. (2009), *Qualitative Research: A Guide to Design and Implementation*, San Francisco: Jossey-Bass.

Mourão, S. (2013), 'Response to *The Lost Thing*: Notes from a Secondary Classroom', *Children's Literature in English Language Education Journal*, 1 (1): 81–106.

Mourão, S. (2015), 'The Potential of Picturebooks with Young Learners', in J. Bland (ed.), *Teaching English to Young Learners: Critical Issues in Language Teaching with 3–12 Year Olds*, 199–218, London: Bloomsbury Academic.

Mourão, S. (2016), 'Picturebooks in the Primary EFL Classroom: Authentic Literature for an Authentic Response', *Children's Literature in English Language Education Journal*, 4 (1): 25–43.

Mourão, S., and J. Bland (2016), 'Editorial: The Journey', *Children's Literature in English Language Education Journal*, 4 (2): ii–x.

Nikolajeva, M. (2014), *Reading for Learning: Cognitive Approaches to Children's Literature*, Amsterdam: John Benjamins.

Paran, A., and P. Robinson (2016), *Literature*, Oxford: Oxford University Press.

Patton, M. Q. (2014), *Qualitative Research and Evaluation Methods*, 4th edn, Thousand Oaks, CA: SAGE.

Pellegrini, A. D., and L. Galda (2003), 'Joint Reading as a Context: Explicating the Ways Context Is Created by Participants', in A. van Kleeck, S. A. Stahl and E. B. Bauer (eds), *On Reading Books to Children. Parents and Teachers*, 307–20, Mahwah, NJ: Laurence Erlbaum.

Reese, E., A. Cox, D. Harte and H. McAnally (2003), 'Diversity in Adults' Styles of Reading Books to Children', in A. van Kleeck, S. A. Stahl and E. B. Bauer (eds), *On Reading Books to Children: Parents and Teachers*, 35–54, Mahwah, NJ: Laurence Erlbaum.

Roche, M. (2015), *Developing Children's Critical Thinking through Picturebooks: A Guide for Primary and Early Years Students and Teachers*, Abingdon: Routledge.

Salisbury, M., and M. Styles (2012), *Children's Picturebooks: The Art of Visual Storytelling*, London: Lawrence King.

Salisbury, M., and M. Styles (2019), *Children's Picturebooks: The Art of Visual Storytelling*, 2nd edn, London: Lawrence King.

Serafini, F., and J. Clausen (2012), 'Typography as Semiotic Resource', *Journal of Visual Literacy*, 31 (2): 1–16.

Serafini, F., and L. Moses (2014), 'The Roles of Children's Literature in Primary Grades', *Reading Teacher*, 67 (6): 465–8.

Sipe, L. (2008), *Storytime: Young Children's Literary Understanding in the Classroom*, New York: Teachers College.

Stoetzel, S., and S. Shedrow (2021a), 'Making the Transition to Virtual Methods in the Literacy Classroom: Reframing Teacher Education Practices', *Excelsior: Leadership in Teaching and Learning*, 13 (2): 127–42.

Stoetzel, S., and S. Shedrow (2021b), 'Making the Move Online: Interactive Read-Alouds for the Virtual Classroom', *Reading Teacher*, 74 (6): 747–56.

Teale, W. (2003), 'Reading Aloud to Young Children as a Classroom Instructional Activity: Insights from Research and Practice', in A. van Kleeck, S. A. Stahl and E. B.

Bauer (eds), *On Reading Books to Children: Parents and Teachers*, 109–34, Mahwah, NJ: Laurence Erlbaum.

van Kleeck, A., S. A. Stahl and E. B. Bauer, eds (2003), *On Reading Books to Children: Parents and Teachers*, Mahwah, NJ: Lawrence Erlbaum.

Wells, G. (2009), *The Meaning Makers: Learning to Talk and Talking to Learn*, Bristol: Multilingual Matters.

Whitehurst, G. I., and C. I. Lonigan (1998), 'Child Development and Emergent Literacy', *Child Development*, 69 (3): 848–72.

Wiseman, A. (2011), 'Interactive Read Alouds: Teachers and Students Constructing Knowledge and Literacy Together', *Early Childhood Education Journal*, 38: 431–8.

4

Digital Picturebooks in Times of Crisis: From Picturebooks about Covid-19 to Developing Critical Environmental Literacies

Theresa Summer

Introduction

Thinking back to the beginning of the global pandemic in early 2020 will evoke a mixture of different feelings among people. Whereas some may have felt completely isolated and experienced personal loss, others might have enjoyed spending a lot of time with their loved ones and felt joy while rediscovering the natural world at their doorstep. Accordingly, the lockdown in our global village shifted some people's ideology from a human and anthropocentric worldview to an ecocentric one (Verma and Prakash 2020).

Another important element in the response to the pandemic is the emergence of various digital texts published online to inform people about Covid-19. These include digital picturebooks, many of which explain what the virus is and how it is affecting society. Taking this as a starting point, this contribution explores these digital picturebooks and their features, which then, focusing on one example, leads to a discussion of how to further an ecocentric worldview in foreign language education with the aim of developing critical environmental literacies (Deetjen and Ludwig 2021). As such, the aim of this contribution is twofold: it seeks to identify the features and potential of digital picturebooks published during times of crisis in order to highlight how to make the most of these picturebooks in foreign language education while at the same time focusing on environmental learning.

Picturebooks, defined by Bader as 'text, illustrations, total design; an item of manufacture and a commercial product; a social, cultural, historical document; and, foremost, an experience for a child' (1976: 1), comprise multimodal texts that become alive with the readers' interaction. As Mourão notes, picturebooks are thus 'an excellent springboard for expanding students' understanding of a topic as well as motivating and supporting them to look beyond their own worlds and positively experience others' (2015: 203). In English classrooms for young learners, picturebooks have for many years been considered an important component of storytelling (Bland 2013; Ellis and Brewster 2014). They provide a meaningful context, allow the teacher to present new target language and offer opportunities for authentic and intercultural communication (Shin and Crandall 2014). What is more, in our increasingly digitalized world today, digital picturebooks and apps have 'become a major force' among child readers (Yokota and Teale 2014: 577).

An important development that started with the first major lockdown is that several picturebooks were published online free of charge. These include a whole range of digital picturebooks such as *Coronavirus and Covid: A Book for Children about the Pandemic* (Jenner et al. 2021), which explains Covid-19, what it is, how you can catch it, why people worry, what the vaccine does and what children can do to help (see the section 'Digital Picturebooks in Times of Crisis' for a fuller discussion of these picturebooks). Whereas books such as this one explain Covid-19 to children or try to help them cope with their worries, an example that stands out thematically is *What Happened When We All Stopped* (Rivett-Carnac and Rivett-Carnac 2020). The story initially raises the reader's awareness of current environmental challenges: 'For the trees had almost gone and the bees had almost gone', speaking of 'one wild chance for *rebirth*' and suggesting that 'this moment can lead us back home' (17, 20, 27; emphasis in original). It addresses environmental issues and thus falls into the category of explicit eco-picturebooks, that is, picturebooks that explicitly focus on various environmental problems and whose narratives directly foster an ecocritical reading and invite the reader to participate in pro-environmental behaviour. Although no clear-cut distinction can be made in all cases, as I argue elsewhere (Summer, forthcoming), explicit picturebooks contrast with implicit eco-picturebooks, which also include an environmental narrative, but do not contain factual ecocritical information or invite the reader to get actively involved in promoting a sustainable environment. Considering the story's explicit environmental content, the fact that it relates times of crisis to environmental concerns, its easy accessibility online and its high quality, this contribution explores three key issues: (1) the importance of developing critical environmental literacies in times of crisis, (2) digital picturebooks published during these times of crisis and (3) the practical dimension of working with digital picturebooks in English language education. An analysis of digital picturebooks published during the pandemic leads to a discussion of what we can do with such picturebooks in practice in terms of competence development. The final section of this chapter discusses research implications.

Developing Critical Environmental Literacies in Times of Crisis

Sustainability and environmental issues have been on the education agenda for several years. The outline of the seventeen Sustainable Development Goals (SDGs) (United Nations n.d.) provides a starting point for engaging with topics such as 'good health and well-being' (SDG 3) and 'responsible consumption and production' (SDG 12). This global programme calls upon educators worldwide to raise learners' awareness of current global issues and encourage them to become active citizens. In English language education, addressing the SDGs is important for our society, can increase learners' awareness of sustainability issues and further language-based competencies (Bastkowski 2019).

The concept of critical environmental literacies aligns with this understanding of foreign language education and subsumes knowledge, skills, attitudes, awareness and active participation (Deetjen and Ludwig 2021). In terms of knowledge, this includes knowledge about local and global environmental challenges and their historical, political and cultural contexts, as well as knowledge about how different types of media communicate information about environmental issues. Skills include topic-related language skills that help learners communicate about environmental issues. Attitudes refer to moral concerns as learners develop a sense of planetary responsibility for dealing with environmental crises. Awareness describes students' ability to identify themselves as responsible citizens by participating in environmental discourses. Finally, active participation refers to learners' participation in (media) discourses and taking action towards overcoming environmental problems (Deetjen and Ludwig 2021). Seeing the development of critical environmental literacies as a key goal of education and understanding the five elements subsumed within these literacies can provide educators with a valuable starting point for integrating environmental learning into their teaching.

Combined with a consideration of the development of digital competence (Vuorikari et al. 2016), I propose seeing the development of digital and global competence as a key goal of foreign language education, subsuming six competence domains: content literacy, engagement, (re-)design, responsible use, problem-solving and critical-reflexive thinking (Summer 2021: 195). Crucially, digital adaptations and creations of picturebooks with environmental themes, which I call eco-picturebooks (Summer, forthcoming), can foster digital and global competence, for instance, if teachers encourage and support a critical response to digital formats. This includes writing an online commentary or a book review or recreating (or remixing) a text from a different perspective. The following section identifies key features of this format and suggests a categorization deemed useful for research and practical teaching before looking at practical implications and one digital picturebook example in detail.

Digital Picturebooks: Categorization and Pedagogical Implications

Digital media play a key role in the lives of young learners today and often bring students in contact with the English language. That is why it is crucial to develop young learners' media literacy, encompassing the effective use, critical evaluation and creation of media (Kolb 2021). The Covid-19 pandemic resulted in a noticeable increase of digital picturebooks made available online in a variety of formats. These formats feature a range of different written, visual, spatial, tactile, gestural, audio and oral modes – subsumed under the concept of multimodality (Kalantzis and Cope 2012). In acknowledging that today's classrooms need to take into account the great variety of multimodal communications and thus foster the development of multimodal literacy, the question arises what role digital picturebooks can play in foreign language education. To address this question, we need to systematically categorize and describe digital picturebooks. Based on previous attempts to categorize digital transformations of picturebooks (e.g. the fourfold categorization by Yokota and Teale 2014), I suggest a fivefold categorization that seems to work for most formats and can enable a systematic analysis and research of digital picturebooks available today while also facilitating their practical use in or for foreign language education.

The first type, basic digital picturebooks, also called 'scanned picturebooks' (Yokota and Teale 2014: 578), refers to online versions of print picturebooks or basic digital formats without significant supplementary or interactive features. I avoid the term 'scanned picturebooks', however, because this may suggest that these picturebooks are available in print, which is not always the case. The term 'basic' suggests this category offers only limited additional digital and interactive features. These books are often either available as PDF documents or they can be accessed in other formats online. This can have important implications for teaching practice because teachers who want to use digital picturebooks in classes in which all learners are equipped with a tablet (called *Tabletklassen* or 'tablet-classes' in German), for instance, will need to make sure that every student has registered and can thus easily access the digital picturebook. In a young learners' classroom, where not all learners may have an email address (or may not remember it), this creates an unwanted and unneeded obstacle to access.

The second category, interactive digital picturebooks, includes additional digital affordances that go beyond written and visual modes. These can be an added reading audio in which the child can choose a "Read to me" mode; added sound and music; or added hotspots in which illustrations are programmed to respond to a click with sound and animation (Yokota and Teale 2014).

The third category is picturebook apps, also called story apps (Brunsmeier and Kolb 2017), which comprise applications that contain visual images, animations and/or sounds that can be controlled by a touchpad or a digital device. Serafini, Kachorsky and Aguilera (2016) identify three features of such apps: (1) tableau features (visual features such as the opening screen, view of two pages, possibly voice-over narration), (2) transitional features (how readers transition from one screen/tableau to another, often accompanied by sound effects) and (3) interactional features (ways in which readers interact with elements of the app such as hotspots that can be swiped, additional content and connections to social media sites or games). Although various challenges arise from this format for educational practice – for instance, game-like features might break the reading flow or interactional features might be of poor quality – these apps can provide additional resources and encourage learners to look up new words (Serafini, Kachorsky and Aguilera 2016). Due to the complexity regarding content and language involved in discussing environmental issues (such as climate change, for instance), these possibilities could be particularly beneficial for foreign language learning.

The fourth type, audiovisual picturebook creations, are film adaptations or transformations (often of print or basic digital picturebooks). Such digital adaptations are often strictly based on the text and storyline provided in the (original) picturebooks, or they offer new interpretations of a text with some substantial changes made to the story. Especially animations and the integration of sounds and music can add further layers of meaning to such audiovisual creations. As Yokota and Teale point out, this format 'puts the director in charge visually and auditorily' (2014: 579). In creative phases of an English lesson, learners can equally take on the role of a director and (re-)create a story.

The fifth category, picturebook read-aloud videos, typically includes a storyteller reading out the print picturebook to their viewers, offering a digital asynchronous alternative to storytelling in the classroom. With the emergence of homeschooling, online picturebook read-alouds have become more prominent as picturebook creators uploaded read-alouds of their books to enable teachers and learners to use literary texts outside the classroom (Hasegawa 2021). In an analysis of read-alouds, Ellis and Gruenbaum (2021) identify four video production approaches: (1) the interactive approach (the reader is shown holding the book showing close-ups of different pages, interacting with the audience), (2) the alternating approach (the reader holds the picturebook and the audience sees close-ups from selected pages), (3) the performance approach (the reader acts out the story to convey meaning) and (4) the bird's eye approach (filmed at an overhead shot camera angle in which the audience sees the pictures, the words and the reader's hands, with limited eye contact). Ellis and Gruenbaum (2021) point out that these approaches have different pedagogic benefits and constraints. Due to their wide and free availability online, however, their biggest potential for foreign language education seems to be that they allow teachers and learners anywhere in the world with internet access and a digital device to encounter picturebooks. (See also Ellis and Mourão, Chapter 3 of this volume, for a discussion of online read-alouds and ways of identifying quality in such read-alouds.)

Given the great variety of digital picturebooks described above, it is challenging to draw general conclusions concerning their use, benefits and potential pitfalls. Focusing on print picturebooks, Ellis and Brewster (2014) list five main objectives of language teaching for a consideration of selection criteria: linguistic, psychological, cognitive, social and cultural objectives. In selecting appropriate picturebooks, the level, literary devices, content/subject matter, illustrations/layout, educational potential, motivation, values, global issues and language/content play a crucial role. In addition, the digital element of digital picturebooks brings with it several more issues worthy of a critical analysis. Various researchers have discussed the affordances and challenges of digital tools (e.g. Whyte and Cutrim Schmid 2018; Kolb 2021). On the one hand, digital picturebooks can offer a range of affordances such as promoting reading skills through rich input, providing enhanced interaction, supporting autonomous learning and fostering independent reading and reading motivation. On the other hand, digital elements within literary texts can present numerous challenges such as a predominance of drills that leave little room for creative output, superficial interactivity, cognitive overload and disorientation (for instance, by distracting the reader from the content of the story through playful elements).

Essentially, as is the case with print picturebooks, the quality of digital picturebooks or apps can determine their educational affordances as well as their practical implementation. Yokota and Teale (2014) identify three general criteria of digital picturebooks: high literary standards of the story, skilfully crafted language and skilful illustrations that illuminate or extend the text. As such, if a digital picturebook is linguistically, visually and cognitively accessible to young learners and if the content is relevant to learners' lives, it holds pedagogic potential. Moreover, if digital elements provide added value instead of distracting readers from the story, digital picturebooks can be a useful and inspiring medium. Teachers thereby play a key role in (pre-)selecting appropriate picturebooks for young learners particularly in times of pandemic crisis. One essential point is that teachers need to know their learners – listed as the first principle ('know your learners') in TESOL's list of six principles for exemplary English teaching (Shin, Savić and Machida 2021). If teachers gain relevant information about their group of learners, they can determine correct practices and choose suitable resources.

Digital Picturebooks in Times of Crisis

The times of crisis focused on in this contribution refer to two crises: the global Covid-19 pandemic and the global environmental crisis. Anthropogenic activities such as the burning of fossil fuels throughout the past decades have resulted in several environmental problems such as pollution and climate change (also referred to as the climate crisis or catastrophe). As a response to the global pandemic, however, the lockdown acts resulted in less vehicular movement and consequently in an improvement of air quality and fall in CO_2 emissions; some inhabitants of big cities experienced clear skies for the first time in their lives. The use of fossil fuels also fell due to the lesser demand of power industries and, therefore, the ecosystem recovered to some extent (Verma and Prakash 2020). As the media reported these positive developments in different parts of the world, some people became more aware of environmental problems and of the importance of minimizing the use of the planet's resources. However, despite the close connection between the global pandemic and (other) environmental threats, digital picturebooks published during the start of the pandemic did not frequently respond to this interplay. Against this background, it is worth pointing out and discussing those picturebooks that did rise to the challenge. This section presents some of the more interesting picturebooks published during the pandemic and then discusses the features that make them worthy of exploration.

Various digital picturebooks published during the outbreak of the Covid-19 pandemic responded to people's need to inform their children about the virus and talk to them about how it has affected our daily lives. These digital picturebooks have a number of features in common, which are of interest for discussing potential affordances for foreign language education. Here I present some books considered suitable for young learners from primary up to early secondary school that deal with the pandemic and its impact on society. (Readers might be interested in finding other books; a particularly helpful website for finding digital coronavirus picturebooks in the New York City School Library System is https://nycdoe.libguides.com/covid-19ebooks/free).

The picturebooks in this list come from a variety of countries and approach the topic in a variety of ways. The picturebook *Everybody Worries* (Burgerman 2020; free log-in required) from England is a supportive 32-page basic digital picturebook with short and simple verbal texts with rhyming couplets, telling children that it is okay to worry about Covid-19. The positive tone combined with the colourful illustrations offers reassurance stating, for instance, 'It's okay to worry when things don't stay the same' (19), thus aiming to support children's mental health. *The Inside Book* (Griffiths 2020) from South Africa, which is available in various languages and explains to children why they are stuck inside, comes in two formats: as a basic digital picturebook and as an audiovisual picturebook creation. The latter takes the form of a partly animated video in which the writer Matthew Griffiths and his friend Naledi Majola, both of whom introduce themselves briefly in the beginning of the video, read aloud the picturebook in turns. Some of the images of the picturebook are animated in the video, thus adding more life to the story, which may further support comprehension; and the alternating male and female voices might make the audiovisual listening and viewing experience relatable and appealing for children. The short humorous comic *The Princess in Black and the Case of the Coronavirus* (Hale, Hale and Pham 2020) is a basic digital picturebook available as an 8-page PDF booklet and offers three tips for fighting the virus: (1) wash your hands, (2) stay at home and (3) make some space. *My Hero Is You: How Kids Can Fight COVID-19* (IASC 2020) is another basic digital picturebook aimed at helping families worldwide to cope with the pandemic, thus available in 125 different languages. The story presents Sara and her mother, who is a scientist and tells her about Covid-19. The website of the IASC (Inter-Agency Standing Committee on Mental Health and Psychosocial Support in Emergency Settings), which published this book, reports on a great variety of further digital adaptations, including a video of a hand puppet play as well as various other video animations in different languages. Several more basic digital picturebooks were published in response to the pandemic: the previously mentioned *Coronavirus and Covid* (Jenner et al. 2021), which is an informative picturebook about the coronavirus from England and is available as a free audio edition; *Even Superheroes Stay Home* (McGaw 2020) from the United States, which aims to inspire children to be helpful superheroes by staying at home; and the famous witch Winnie and her cat Wilbur feature in *Winnie and Wilbur Stay at Home* (Thomas and Paul 2020), which illustrates their stay-at-home adventure trying an online exercise class and creating rainbows.

All in all, these digital picturebooks offer an opportunity for young language learners to explore relevant lexical items while also discussing the impact of the pandemic on our daily lives and mental health. What is more, due to their cultural diversity, they offer various opportunities for multilingual approaches and an inclusive cultural involvement (Coelho 2012). As concerns their digital and interactive components, however, these remain somewhat limited (except for the audiovisual picturebook creations) as most of the Covid-19 picturebooks are basic digital picturebooks and do not offer further interactive components such as hotspots, which could make the reading experience more engaging for learners.

Despite these shortcomings, the digital picturebooks explored above exhibit four key features that are worthy of exploration for educational contexts: they are (1) relevant, (2) free of charge, (3) goal-oriented and (4) action-oriented. A discussion of these features will provide an insight into their potential for foreign language education.

First, these digital picturebooks are thematically relevant. As a response to the pandemic, many of these picturebooks explicitly address the Covid-19 pandemic and what we can do to stop spreading the virus (e.g. Hale, Hale and Pham 2020; Jenner et al. 2021), and some offer reassurance for children feeling worried about the virus – thus potentially supporting their mental health to a certain degree (e.g. Burgerman 2020). Other books relate the pandemic to environmental issues that have been brought to our attention in response to the pandemic (Rivett-Carnac and Rivett-Carnac 2020), as the following section will illustrate, although this category seems to be an exception. Such thematically relevant content is highly learner-centred, adapts to learners' needs by building on their current knowledge and experiences and also meets their affective needs (Bremner 2021), and this learner-centredness can motivate learners to engage with literary texts.

Second, the picturebooks published online about Covid-19 are frequently free of charge and easily accessible; even renowned illustrators such as Axel Scheffler (Jenner et al. 2021) made their work available free of charge. This is highly relevant for education because a problem associated with the use of literary texts in the classroom is that setting up a school library or even a smaller collection of texts requires financial support. As governments are investing huge sums in the digitalization of education in some parts of the world, digital technology such as laptops and tablets can result in an easier accessibility to literary texts. In Germany, for instance, the initiative of the *DigitalPakt Schule* is providing at least 5.5 billion euros for German schools, which amounts to an average of 500 euros per student (n.n. 2020: 5) – money that can be spent on digital technology. If teachers and learners have a digital device such as a tablet or laptop at hand (an obvious prerequisite for working with digital picturebooks), literary texts can more easily find their way into a classroom as this involves no additional costs. This, however, requires two basic things: literary texts need to be available online and, more importantly, educators need to know where to find them and how to work with them in the classroom. If teachers know which digital picturebooks might be suitable for their class and if learners also know how to navigate online to find books they may enjoy reading in free voluntary reading scenarios (Krashen 2011), for instance, free and easy accessibility can be a major advantage. As such, the free availability of digital picturebooks can potentially contribute to a wider usage of literary texts in the classroom. The third feature, goal-orientedness, refers to the fact that digital picturebooks published in times of crisis usually have a clear goal related to challenges evolving from this global crisis. As my comments on the books above show, they often inform readers about the pandemic and what each individual can do to help, and some also aim to mentally support and comfort their readers. They therefore provide teachers with an opportunity to discuss student-centred themes and encourage learners to communicate about feelings and life during pandemic times in English.

Finally, the digital picturebooks published in times of crisis are frequently action-oriented. They aim to contribute to changes and initiate action while informing children about the virus. In *The Princess in Black and the Case of the Coronavirus* (Hale, Hale and Pham 2020), for instance, readers get three tips for fighting the coronavirus: washing hands, staying at home and making space. As the content as well as the linguistic and visual depiction of such actions in picturebooks differ, learners could compare digital picturebooks in the foreign language classroom to identify how writers and illustrators aimed to inform and mentally support children. In lessons designed for younger learners at secondary schools, teachers could explore the concept of solidarity, global cooperation and active citizenship with learners by discussing how each individual's action can potentially contribute to change in a global pandemic. This relates to the concept of global participation within the context of environmental learning (Deetjen and Ludwig 2021).

Against this background, the example I discuss in the next section, *What Happened When We All Stopped* (Rivett-Carnac and Rivett-Carnac 2020), stands out thematically among the texts presented above as it relates pandemic times to environmental and sustainability issues. This story thus offers the chance to further not only communicative competencies but also critical environmental literacies.

Digital Picturebook Example:
What Happened When We All Stopped

What Happened When We All Stopped is a digital picturebook written and illustrated during the first Covid-19 lockdown by two siblings from South West England, Tom (the writer) and Bee Rivett-Carnac (the illustrator) (Rivett-Carnac and Rivett-Carnac 2020). The story takes the reader on a journey illustrating how the first lockdown can lead us to a greener and more sustainable future. As people 'looked up from their day to day tasks … and their day to day masks' during the Covid-19 lockdown and observed the Earth realizing that 'the trees had almost gone and the bees had almost gone', nature speaks to them 'like thunder' (8, 17, 32). People then begin to realize that they need to get active so that the Earth can be renewed. This story, as Jane Goodall expressed in an interview, aims to help us 'overcome the disconnect between our clever brains and our loving, compassionate hearts' and find a way of living in harmony with nature (Cowan 2020).

The story was (at the time of writing this contribution) available in two main formats: as a basic digital picturebook and as an audiovisual creation. The former was a 32-page picturebook, which was initially available as a free PDF document online. However, this is no longer available, and instead it has been published in print under the title *When We All Stopped* (Rivett-Carnac and Rivett-Carnac 2022). The written text resembles a poem. In line with Bland's (2013) outline of linguistic features of well-craftedness, this is a well-crafted text due to its lexical density and stylistic cohesion. This becomes evident at the beginning of the story, which starts as follows:

> It starts as a whisper
> A word on the air
> It can't quite be heard
> But you know that it's there.

(Rivett-Carnac and Rivett-Carnac 2020: 3)

The textual mode merges creatively with the visual modes of the illustrations in the picturebook. The latter, mostly drawings in natural shades of brown, green and blue, depict the simplicity and beauty of nature, showing a young girl with long hair and a long dress, almost resembling a tree, and leaves, plants, a forest and an owl that seems to help the human characters reconnect with nature – all of which are creatively integrated into the natural surroundings, providing various triggers for communicative interaction. The girl, who can be seen in the excerpt of the digital picturebook (27–8), is reaching out to an owl holding a plant; a green elf-like character is also reaching out its arms to take the plant, suggesting a reconciliation of humans with nature. Drawers labelled 'seeds', 'leaves' and 'flowers' are shown, as well as a book on the shelf with the title 'The Future We Choose'. This message, which is almost hidden due to the small size of the illustration of the book and its title on this double spread, is intertwined into the textual and visual modes and is an example of how the visual counterparts help to make the writers' intention more understandable. In telling readers that we can choose our future, the author and illustrator suggest that each individual can contribute to a more sustainable future on this planet. This aligns with the concept of critical environmental literacies that, as outlined above, includes participation as one important component.

The audiovisual creation is an animated (TED-Ed) video available on YouTube narrated by the British scientist and conservationist Jane Goodall and has received over 761,000 clicks (as of 29 November 2021, https://www.youtube.com/watch?v=gX0HOy8Pi54). The video includes additional animated images and thus adds further layers of meaning to the story. This is a prime example of the way in which various modes, including oral, written, visual, gestural, tactile and spatial, are coming together – described with the term *synaesthesia*, 'a process of shifting backwards and forwards between different modes of meaning' (Kalantzis and Cope 2012: 195). Contemporary communication thus takes place not only verbally but also through multiple modes. The audiovisual creation of *What Happened When We All Stopped* offers additional support for comprehension by portraying messages not only through a written or spoken sentence but also with accompanying moving images and sound.

The thought-provoking background music, mostly piano and string instruments, and nature sounds, such as birds singing, help listeners imagine nature and take on Mother Earth's perspective, which might involve a sense of fright and disbelief in response to the destructive actions of humans on this planet. By communicating the same environmental message through different modes, the video not only provides the learners with support for comprehension but also encourages them to emotionally relate to the serious situation people are facing on planet Earth with the rapid decrease of biodiversity and the effects of climate change. An engagement with the video can thus offer additional opportunities for comprehension and content engagement.

According to Klippel, picturebooks should not only be seen as 'vehicles of information' (2006: 83) but should also 'help the children understand the story or grasp the information shown' (85). Audiovisual creations of picturebooks offer additional support for students' comprehension due to the multiple modes and, in the context of environmental learning, the aesthetic dimension and an emotionally engaging, interesting, visually appealing and creative story can potentially motivate reluctant readers to engage with an English text. The following section addresses more specifically how to integrate this artefact into practice.

Implications for Practice

As the pandemic has digitalized foreign language education across many countries in the world, this could also result in an increase in the use of digital literary texts. This, however, requires guidelines for text selection, lists with suitable texts made available to teachers and a conceptual framework. Almost two decades ago, Klippel (2006) called for more collaboration between parents, publishers, authors, libraries and children so that picturebooks in primary education can achieve a greater acceptance. The situation today requires an additional consideration of digital formats and suggestions for the fulfilment of particular learning goals.

The goals for working with a digital picturebook can be subdivided into two main categories: general educational goals (e.g. environmental learning) and language-based goals (e.g. communicative competence). The former can include the development of critical environmental literacies and digital competence or DigCompGlobal (Summer 2021); the latter can involve various skills and language elements. The basic task sequence in Table 4.1 provides an overview of the ways in which teachers can combine the two categories of learning goals while focusing on the environment and sustainability as the main content themes. The concept and some of the tasks are partly based on Ellis and Gruenbaum's picturebook e-lessons developed in early 2020 for children to complete at home (https://pepelt21.com/overview/). The lessons place a key emphasis on personal response and self-evaluation, which is also central in the context of environmental learning. In addition to the widely known pre-, while- and post-reading phases, participation plays a central role (in the PWP+P sequence). This idea derives from the concept of critical environmental literacies aimed at encouraging learners to participate in ecological projects to 'become active in their areas of interest' (Deetjen and Ludwig 2021: 17). Through the suggested task sequence (Table 4.1), learners can gain new insights into environmental concerns by entering new storyworlds and becoming active global citizens. Compared to work with print picturebooks, this sequence focuses on audiovisual comprehension and multiple literacy and the fourth participation phase invites learners to take part in a digital environmental discourse such as the (re-)creation of pro-environmental texts.

Table 4.1 A Task Sequence for Working with Digital Eco-picturebooks

Phase	Tasks
1. Pre-viewing/ reading	Analysis of • title/cover/screenshot
2. While viewing/ reading	Listen and watch • e.g. ticking things shown in the video, marking words/ pictures from the story, identifying different modes
3. Post-viewing/ reading	Personal response • From my perspective, the story is about … • What I learnt … • I would like to find out more about … • Questions on my mind … • What I liked about the story …
4. Participation	• Developing a social media campaign • Initiating a sustainability project at school/the local area • Creating a clip, poster, journal, trailer

Table 4.2 Task Examples for *What Happened When We All Stopped*

Phase	Tasks
1. Pre-viewing	*Task 1a*: Thinking back: How were people across the world affected by the (first) coronavirus lockdown? Write a few sentences.
	Things you can write about: People had to ... People spent time ... Maybe some people felt ... (e.g. always, often, sometimes/ happy, scared, sad, bored, alone/they missed ...); what they did (watched films, played games, phoned friends, chatted with etc.)
	Task 1b: Now talk to your partner and compare your impressions from Task 1a.
	Questions you can ask: What did you write? What did people do? How did the people feel? → IN-CLASS: You can share your impressions with the class.
	Task 2: Imagine: A story was written during the coronavirus lockdown. The three sentences are text samples from the story. What could the story be about?
	[Think – Pair – Share]
	• 'This moment can lead us back home.' • 'For the trees had almost gone and the bees had almost gone.' • 'One wild chance for rebirth.'
2. While viewing/ reading	*Task 3a*: Watch the animated video of the story and tick what you see often.
	Nature: • beaches • rivers • leaves • trees Animals: • dinosaurs • owls • unicorns • elephants
	Task 3b: What kind of music (or special sound effects) can you hear? How does it relate to the story?
	Task 4: Read the story.
	a) Focus on the text: Who is 'It'? What do the words 'whisper' and 'thunder' symbolize in the story? Write down your ideas. b) Focus on the text and the pictures: What illustrated ideas can you find?
3. Post-viewing	*Task 5*: Discuss the questions with your partner and take notes.
	• What did you learn? • What would you like to find out more about? • What did you like about the story? Do you prefer the digital book or video?
	Task 6: Find out more about the global goal 'Life on Land' by doing online research and relate it to the story.
	Task 7: Listen to the words (online/teacher). Match those that rhyme.
	air – hail – tasks – earth – sorrow – best/test – rebirth – prevail – tomorrow – there – masks

(continued)

Table 4.2 Continued

Phase	Tasks
4. Participation	*Task 8*: How can you give Earth a chance for rebirth? Choose a task:
	• Write a list of things that you could/want to do. You can check your carbon footprint online (carbon footprint calculator) to get some ideas.
	• Give a mini presentation on what you would like to change in your school/local area.

To illustrate more specifically how the task sequence can be put into practice, Table 4.2 presents a collection of tasks for the PWP+P sequence when working with *What Happened When We All Stopped*. It is a list of task ideas that can be rearranged, substituted and used very flexibly in the classroom depending on the learning and teaching contexts. A trigger warning might be necessary for learners depending on which potentially traumatizing experiences they went through during the pandemic. By focusing on people's experiences in the pandemic rather than learners' personal experiences in the pre-task, learners can reflect on others' experiences from an outsider's perspective and in a more objective way, which could be supported through the provision of pictures (e.g. children painting rainbows on walls etc.). For the while-reading/viewing phase and in well-equipped schools, an option would also be to split up a class and invite one group to read the basic digital picturebook while the other group focuses on the audiovisual creation. In that way, the two artefacts could be compared in pair work and learners could be given an opportunity to talk about important differences.

Implications for Research

The goal of this contribution is to provide the reader with a fuller understanding of digital picturebooks focusing on those formats published during the beginning of the global Covid-19 pandemic. After discussing the importance of developing critical environmental literacies in times of crisis through digital picturebooks, for which I presented a categorization and an outline of their key features, my aim was to relate theoretical considerations to practical implications by focusing on one example text. Implications for research relate to two main areas: future innovations in the creation of digital picturebooks and future empirical classroom research.

First, the development of further digital eco-picturebooks could offer various learning opportunities in foreign language education. Picturebook apps with interactive features that assist the reading process, encourage learners to stay focused on the storyline and support their language proficiency development through individualized feedback would be an important desideratum. As previous studies showed that story apps often include drills and form-focused activities rather than meaning-focused and creative tasks (e.g. Elsner 2014), designers and creators of such apps should pay special attention to the methodological approach of apps. Including supportive language learning functions in which important vocabulary or content is explained, for example, would be valuable especially for younger learners. Furthermore, this could include multilingual components in which learners can choose between different languages and compare various languages that they might be familiar with. As Yokota and Teale (2014) highlight, another important aspect is personalization. By personalizing a 'Read to me' function or embedding the child's name into a text, for instance, children could get motivated to engage with a text (Yokota and Teale 2014). A prerequisite for all of this is a collaboration between writers of high-quality texts, illustrators, designers, researchers and teachers, which could contribute to the development and the more frequent use of high-quality digital picturebooks, and picturebook apps in particular, which offer additional interactive learning opportunities. The picturebooks about the coronavirus and Covid-19 described in this contribution have shown that these are mostly basic digital picturebooks; in the future technological innovations that can be easily applied to literary texts and which make use of the affordances of digitalization would be a desideratum.

Second, empirical research projects should investigate the potential of digital picturebooks for developing critical environmental literacies. It would be interesting to find out if print picturebooks differ from digital picturebooks in the extent to which they can, for instance, foster learners' attitudes in terms of developing a sense for planetary responsibility. Although there has been some research within this field focusing on the use of print picturebooks in early elementary education (e.g. Muthukrishnan 2019), I have not come across any research of this kind either in the context of foreign language education or with a focus on digital picturebooks. Especially the variety of modes such as animated images, music and sounds in audiovisual picturebook creations analysed in the example above (see the section 'Digital Picturebook Example') seems to offer additional learning opportunities compared to print picturebooks. Identifying the specific learning potential of digital media in that respect or the extent to which this may distract learners from developing communicative competence or engaging with the content of a story would be desirable. It would be interesting to identify the extent to which print and digital picturebooks can foster critical environmental literacies as well as basic communicative competencies. If, in this context, digital picturebooks are made available for free – one of the features of digital picturebooks published in times of crisis in this contribution – this could provide essential learning opportunities for English learners across the world. What is more, investing money not only in digital devices but also in content such as digital picturebooks and apps would be essential for the development of various literacies.

In addition to the two fields of research outlined above, investigations of whether and how digital (eco-)picturebooks are used in classrooms would also be of interest. In this way, teacher education could be developed bottom-up by identifying important benefits and limits of digital picturebooks in practice. The text in focus throughout this contribution, *What Happened When We All Stopped* (Rivett-Carnac and Rivett-Carnac 2020), is one compelling example that shows how digital formats and multiple modes can potentially contribute to learners' development of critical environmental literacies. In the future, we can hope not only that global crises will result in high-quality and easily accessible digital picturebooks but also that there will be support for their creation and goal-oriented use in everyday educational practice in whatever 'normal' we find ourselves after the pandemic.

References

Primary Literature

Burgerman, J. (2020), *Everybody Worries: A Picture Book for Children Who Are Worried about Coronavirus*, Oxford: Oxford University Press. https://www.oxfordowl.co.uk/api/interactives/29765.html.

Griffiths, M. (2020), *The Inside Book*. https://mattcgriffiths.com/.

Hale, S., D. Hale and L. Pham (2020), *The Princess in Black and the Case of the Coronavirus*, Somerville, MA: Candlewick. https://www.princessinblack.com/download/pib-coronavirus.pdf

IASC (2020), 'My Hero Is You: How Kids Can Fight COVID-19!' https://interagencystandingcommittee.org/iasc-reference-group-mental-health-and-psychosocial-support-emergency-settings/my-hero-you-storybook-children-covid-19.

Jenner, E., K. Wilson, N. Roberts and A. Scheffler (2021), *Coronavirus and Covid: A Book for Children about the Pandemic*, London: Nosy Crow. https://nosycrowcoronavirus.s3-eu-west-1.amazonaws.com/Coronavirus_PDF_UpdateV3.pdf.

McGaw, J. (2020), 'Even Superheroes Stay Home'. https://www.jamiemcgaw.com/#/even-superheroes-stay-home/.

Rivett-Carnac, T., and B. Rivett-Carnac (2020), 'What Happened When We All Stopped'. https://whathappenedwhenweallstopped.com/.

Rivett-Carnac, T., and B. Rivett-Carnac (2022), *When We All Stopped*, Rolling Meadows, IL: Cottage Door.

Thomas, V., and K. Paul (2020), *Winnie and Wilbur Stay at Home*, Oxford: Oxford University Press. https://www.oxfordowl.co.uk/for-home/find-a-book/library-page/.

Secondary Literature

Bader, B. (1976), *American Picturebooks from* Noah's Ark *to* The Beast Within, London: Macmillan.

Bastkowski, M. (2019), 'Global Goals im Englischunterricht: Wie die Global Goals entstanden und was sie für den Englischunterricht bedeuten', *Englisch 5–10*, 47 (3): 28–31.

Bland, J. (2013), *Children's Literature and Learner Empowerment: Children and Teenagers in English Language Education*, London: Bloomsbury.

Bremner, N. (2021), 'Learner-Centredness', *ELT Journal*, 75 (2): 213–15. https://doi.org/10.1093/elt/ccab002.

Brunsmeier, S., and A. Kolb (2017), 'Picturebooks Go Digital – the Potential of Story Apps for the Primary EFL Classroom', *Children's Literature in English Language Education*, 5 (1): 1–20.

Coelho, E. (2012), *Language and Learning in Multilingual Classrooms*, Bristol: Multilingual Matters. https://doi.org/10.21832/9781847697219.

Cowan, K. (19 June 2020), 'What Happened When We All Stopped', A Beautiful Animated Poem Narrated by Jane Goodall, Creative Boom. https://www.creativeboom.com/inspiration/what-happened-when-we-all-stopped-a-beautiful-animated-poem-narrated-by-jane-goodall/.

Deetjen, C., and C. Ludwig (2021), 'Introduction: Developing Students' Critical Environmental Literacies in the EFL Classroom', in C. Ludwig and C. Deetjen (eds), *The World Beyond: Developing Critical Environmental Literacies in EFL*, 9–24, Heidelberg: Winter.

n.n. 'DigitalPakt 360^0: Eine Schritt-für-Schritt-Anleitung für den DigitalPakt Schule. Informationen für Schulträger' (2020). https://www.wirmachendigitalisierungeinfach.de/bildung/digitalpakt/.

Ellis, G., and J. Brewster (2014), 'Tell It Again! The New Storytelling Handbook for Primary Teachers'. http://www.teachingenglish.org.uk/sites/teacheng/files/D467_Storytelling_handbook_FINAL_web.pdf (accessed 7 December 2021).

Ellis, G., and T. Gruenbaum (2021), 'Using Picturebook Video Read-Alouds in Primary ELT', Slides from a British Council Webinar. https://www.teachingenglish.org.uk/sites/teacheng/files/V2BC_Slides_TG_EG_July_2021.pdf;

presentation: https://www.youtube.com/watch?v=jl23FTWl8Fg (accessed 7 December 2021).

Elsner, D. (2014), 'Multilingual Virtual Talking Books (MuViT) – a Project to Foster Multilingualism, Language Awareness, and Media Competency', in D. Abendroth Timmer and E.-M. Hennig (eds), *Plurilingualism and Multiliteracies: International Research on Identity Construction in Language Education*, 175–90, Frankfurt/ Main: Peter Lang.

Hasegawa, A. (2021), 'Recommended Resource: Picturebooks in European Primary English Language Teaching (PEPELT) Mini e-Lessons', *Children's Literature in English Language Education*, 9 (1): 82–6.

Kalantzis, M., and B. Cope (2012), *Literacies*, Cambridge: Cambridge University Press.

Klippel, F. (2006), 'Literacy through Picture Books', in J. Enever and G. Schmid-Schönbein (eds), *Picture Books and Young Learners of English*, 81–90, Berlin: Langenscheidt.

Kolb, A. (2021), 'Digital Teaching and Learning in the Primary EFL Classroom', in C. Lütge and T. Merse (eds), *Digital Teaching and Learning: Perspectives for English Language Education*, 125–40, Tübingen: Narr.

Krashen, S. (2011), *Free Voluntary Reading*, Santa Barbara, CA: Libraries Unlimited.

Ludwig, C., and C. Deetjen, eds (2021), *The World Beyond: Developing Critical Environmental Literacies in EFL*, Heidelberg: Winter.

Mourão, S. (2015), 'The Potential of Picturebooks with Young Learners', in J. Bland (ed.), *Teaching English to Young Learners: Critical Issues in Language Teaching with 3–12 Year Olds*, 199–217, London: Bloomsbury.

Muthukrishnan, R. (2019), 'Using Picture Books to Enhance Ecoliteracy of First-Grade Students', *International Journal of Early Childhood Environmental Education*, 6 (2): 19–41. https://naturalstart.org/using-picture-books-enhance-ecoliter acy-first-grade-students.

PEPELT (Picturebooks in European Primary English Language Teaching) YouTube channel (since 25 September 2018), https://www.youtube.com/channel/UCcPH EWqeXGUDVOLnB4JBooA/featured.

Serafini, F., D. Kachorsky and E. Aguilera (2016), 'Picture Books in the Digital Age', *Reading Teacher*, 69 (5): 509–12. https://doi.org/10.1002/trtr.1452.

Shin, J. K., and J. Crandall (2014), *Teaching Young Learners English: From Theory to Practice*, Boston, MA: National Geographic Learning.

Shin, J. K., V. Savić and T. Machida (2021), *The 6 Principles for Exemplary Teaching of English Learners: Young Learners in a Multilingual World*, Alexandria, VA: TESOL International Association.

Summer, T. (2021), 'Digital Competence in a Global World', in C. Lütge and T. Merse (eds), *Digital Teaching and Learning: Perspectives for English Language Education*, 185–206, Tübingen: Narr.

Summer, T. (forthcoming, 2022), 'Eco-Picturebooks for Older Learners: Features, Selection Criteria, and Practical Suggestions', in G. Alter and T. Merse (eds), *Re-thinking Picturebooks for Intermediate and Advanced Learners*, Tübingen: Narr.

United Nations (n.d.), *Sustainable Development Goals*. https://sustainabledevelopment.un.org/sdgs.

Verma, A. K., and S. Prakash (2020), 'Impact of COVID-19 on Environment and Society', *Journal of Global Biosciences*, 9 (5): 7352–63. doi: www.mutagens.co.in/jgb/vol.09/05/090506.pdf.

Vuorikari, R., Y. Punie, S. Carretero Gomez and G. Van den Brande (2016), *DigComp 2.0: The Digital Competence Framework for Citizens. Update Phase 1: The Conceptual Reference Model*, Luxembourg Publication Office of the European Union. EUR 27948 EN. doi: 10.2791/11517.

Whyte, S., and E. Cutrim Schmid (2018), 'Classroom Technology for Young Learners', in S. Garton and F. Copland (eds), *The Routledge Handbook of Teaching English to Young Learners*, 338–55, London: Routledge.

Yokota, J., and W. H. Teale (2014), 'Picture Books and the Digital World', *Reading Teacher*, 67 (8): 577–85.

Part 3

Researching and Teaching Literature in Online Teacher Education

5

Exploiting the Educational Potential of Literature in English Language Teaching: Continuity and Change in Digital Literature Teaching

Christine Gardemann

Introduction

Digitalization in education is by no means a new phenomenon, though the recent Covid-19 pandemic has given new impetus to the question of how to sensibly and meaningfully implement digital tools in the EFL classroom. While the pull of the pandemic has boosted the use of digital tools in Germany, it has also shown that multiple problems exist when it comes to taking lessons to the digital space. The frequency and quality of digital tool use were thus likely determined by several factors, including available resources, data protection laws, learners' technical equipment at home, teachers' digital competencies and experiences, and many more. Before the pandemic, the ICILS study (2018) found that more than 60% of German teachers of all subjects were using digital media at least weekly when teaching; 23% of them even daily (Eickelmann, Bos and Labusch 2019). Younger teachers were more likely to use digital media more frequently than their older colleagues (Drossel et al. 2019). Most teachers (about 44%), however, mainly used digital media as a supplement or substitution for teacher input and roughly a third of German teachers, a number low in international comparison, believed that digital media can be used to improve academic performance (Eickelmann, Bos and Labusch 2019). Teachers, in other words, were using digital media mostly to work with it themselves.

This insight into the practical use of digital media in German classrooms is interesting because those in favour of implementing more digital tools often highlight how these tools can be used to engage learners. However, Schopf, to choose but one critical voice from educational research, claims that it is impossible to imagine anything 'more frontal' than learning while sitting in front of a screen (2020: 406), echoing Gruschka's earlier observation as to the excessive *Didaktisierung* of content, that is, an oversimplification or trivialization of subject matter that he describes as 'teacher-proofed-student-food' (2011: 29). Although Schildhauer (2020) is in favour of the implementation of digital tools in everyday teaching, he nevertheless criticizes an implicit notion often found in the reception of Puentedura's (2006) widely quoted model of transforming education through digitalization. Schildhauer (2020) argues that the suggestion that there might be a proportional relationship between an increase in the use of digital tools in the classroom and better learning outcomes is untenable and obscures the particular strength of analogue forms of teaching and, in particular, possible hybrid forms. All in all, there should be no doubt that digital tools can enrich learning experiences both at home and in the classroom, but like all tools, they should be evaluated critically and chosen carefully. It is clear, though, that they have already become a crucial prerequisite for participation in society (KMK 2017).

Lee, Ceretto and Lee (2010) were able to show that teachers are open and interested in using digital media in their classrooms if they perceive them as a tool to promote motivation and communication and facilitate work. Too often when discussing digitalization, though, there is a strong focus on the *change* it might bring to educational practice, often combined with an underlying accusation of teachers' current practice being outdated, curiously mirroring the notion that teachers' understanding and teaching of literature is so as well. The focus on change is most prominently exemplified in the abovementioned model by Puentedura (2006), which describes the highest level of transformation as a 'redefinition' of education. Instead of demanding such radical change (or even implying that the implementation of digital media must lead to it), I would like to suggest that it might be worthwhile to add a perspective of *continuity of practice* to the focus on change. In this chapter, I argue this by using the example of English literature teaching. To this end, I will first summarize selected studies from empirical research on the current use of literature in German EFL classrooms and connect it with a perspective from the point of view of professionalism research. Drawing on the results of a study at the nexus of literature teaching and teacher professionalism (Gardemann 2021), I will present three types of teachers that I identified by analysing semi-narrative interviews using the Documentary Method (Nohl 2007; see section on current classroom practices). This chapter aims to outline possible ways in which teachers can move towards an increased use of digital tools in literature teaching. To this end, teachers' current practice when it comes to teaching literature in an analogue EFL setting at German secondary schools will be used as a starting point. I will then suggest different approaches to integrate digital tools into literature teaching that emphasize a focus on continuity of the teacher types' existing practice.

Theoretical Background: Potentials of Literature in the EFL Classroom

There is a strong consensus across the EFL research community that literary texts can and should be conceptualized as being more than just comprehensible input (Krashen 1993) for fostering students' reading, writing, speaking, listening and mediating skills. The exact definition of the potential added value (Klieme and Hartig 2007: 22), however, has long since been the topic of controversial debate as it is located in an area that eludes the measuring and testing logic of the Common European Frame of Reference for Languages (Council of Europe 2001) and the German Educational Standards (KMK 2004). From a didactic point of view, it is mainly the interpretative openness of literary texts that should be seen as their central characteristic. Since the texts and their *Leerstellen* (semantic gaps that readers need to fill; cf. Iser 1994) can serve as impulses for readers to find and negotiate meaning, they can be used to assist students in developing their own readings, selecting texts for their own reading needs and getting to know new and different perspectives. These perspectives can raise awareness of certain issues, stimulate self-reflection and world reflection and provide an opportunity for (inter)cultural learning. When teachers make use of methods that reflect the texts' interpretative openness, students are invited to involve themselves as active readers. The fictional space of literature can open up opportunities for imagination and creativity but also serve as a safe space for students to draft and express understandings, opinions and ideas without real-life consequences and, if necessary, do so indirectly through a character's point of view. A teacher who takes students' readings seriously can motivate them to learn the foreign language and in a more general sense. That motivation can be inspired through topics and themes explored in literature, which allow students to discover parallels or disparities with their own selves and lives.

To fully exploit these potentials, learners' voices need to be heard and taken seriously. While teachers will bring knowledge and experience related to literary texts to the classroom and remain experts on their subject and their teaching, learners should neither be pushed nor dragged towards a certain reading of a text. Klippel (2000) assumes that EFL lessons are significantly shaped by the teachers, based mostly on their advanced level of English competence. This is backed by one of the findings of the German DESI study on English lessons in year 9 that has shown English teachers to have twice as much talk time as all of their learners combined (Klieme 2006). EFL teachers then have a special mediating role to play when it comes to bringing literature and learners together (Delanoy 2002). Examined in the light of didactical approaches such as reception theory (for the German context, see Bredella and Burwitz-Melzer 2004), the meaning of a literary text is only created by the reader and not inherent in the text itself. According to Iser (1994), literary texts are incomplete in that they never fully explain, describe or include all the information that would be needed to paint a complete picture of a character or situation. Involved readers fill these gaps in the text by employing both their creative imagination as well as their knowledge of the world. Consequently, readers must be understood as an integrative part of the literary communication process instead of being reduced to addressees of a text or even receivers of an author's intentions. Teachers' focus of attention should thus be on the specific readers in their classrooms. Learners bring knowledge, experiences and attitudes to a reading of a text and cannot but read and understand it in a very individual way. Their readings can and should become visible, either during or after the actual reading process. Ideally, different individual readings of different learners and the teacher can then not only be exchanged but negotiated with each other. In such discussions, elements of readings can be added, edited, adapted or discarded (Bredella 2002) while also being coordinated with the text's internal perspective to make sure subjective readings are not detached from what the text offers.

Such openness of understandings and discussions, such ambivalence and polyphony, however, can create challenges for learners. In EFL classrooms, their ability to express themselves is limited by the foreign language competence they have at any given time. This reduction of self-expression alone can lead to uncertainty, frustration and self-doubt (Arnold 2011). The more we press for acknowledgement of interpretative openness, the more we risk pushing learners to a place where they do not feel enriched by the multitude of perspectives but rather unsatisfied with the seemingly inconclusive result. It is important, then, that the development of tolerance for ambiguity is understood as a crucial learning goal whenever engaging with literature in the EFL classroom. Several empirical studies conducted in the field of EFL literature teaching and related disciplines have highlighted that while the texts might be open to interpretation, teachers' and pre-service teachers' approaches to teaching literature are often not (see Caspari 2003; Schädlich 2008). It would be premature, however, to make far-reaching assumptions about school practice because of the still small number of empirical works in this area, and it is worth adding the perspective of teacher professionalism research before delving deeper into how literature is currently being taught.

The complexity of everyday teaching means that individual teachers will choose different approaches, based on their general understanding of teaching EFL and more specific understandings of teaching literature. It is important to note that while the observation of classroom practice allows insight into *which* methods are chosen by teachers when using literature, it does not enable researchers to deduce *why* these methods were chosen. Teachers who make use of learner-activating methods, for example, from the pool of cooperative learning or drama pedagogics, could thus *still* hold the belief that literary texts have definite, objective meaning and try to suggestively lead learners to a predefined understanding of a text. On the other hand, Delanoy (2002) suggests that teacher-dominated lessons (e.g. measured by talk time) could *still* lead learners to truly engage with a text and develop individual readings. One should also keep in mind that teachers are influenced by instructional trends that might lead to the use of certain procedures (Caspari 2003) but do not reflect the teachers' actual attitude towards literature or literature teaching. Last but not least, decisions on teaching methods are also made based on time limitations, curricular demands or availability of resources and can sometimes even contradict a teacher's underlying pedagogical and methodical convictions (Dann 2000). Finally, engaging with literature is just one part of EFL lessons that needs to be related to grammar teaching, vocabulary, (inter-)cultural learning, assessment and so on (Delanoy 2002: 37).

Studies of teachers of various school subjects have shown that professionally experienced teachers tend to have internalized and routinized patterns of actions in their everyday teaching practice. Such patterns have been shown to be rather inaccessible to change or can only be changed with difficulty (e.g. by positive eye-opening experiences or negatively marked professional crises). For example, Asbrand and Martens (2013) in a study of maths teachers have shown that, generally, many teachers are oriented towards preservation and reproduction of actions; likewise, Bennewitz (2005) has shown that teachers of maths, German, music and history are conservative when it comes to the implementation of reforms. In a cumulative review of studies on the effectiveness of in-service training offers, Lipowsky (2010) summarizes that teachers seem to be particularly resistant to what they perceive as top-down interventions by school-related institutions. In the same way, while staged interventions by academic researchers lead to teachers implementing a conceptually faithful realization of the learning environments developed by the researchers, this does not usually result in lasting change (Lipowsky 2010). To achieve this, the principles guiding teachers' actions, that is, their implicit orientations, attitudes, beliefs and convictions, would have to be addressed. Of those, we still know rather little when it comes to teaching literature in the EFL classroom.

In an early study by Benz (1990), 226 sixth-form pupils from different grammar schools in Hesse (Year 13) and 114 students of English at Gießen University reported on their recollections of literary texts used in their English (as a foreign language) and German (as a first language) lessons at school in a questionnaire study. Pupils and students alike remembered a limited repertoire of methods that mostly focused on text analysis. Participants also stated that in their opinion, English teachers were even more insistent on guiding learners to a seemingly correct understanding of a literary text than German teachers. Since Benz only worked with quantitative data, reasons for this perspective cannot be deduced from the study. Taking into consideration the greater difficulty learners might experience when reading a text in a foreign language rather than their native language, the learners' assessment of the teachers' approaches might be correct and incorrect at the same time. The difference in learners' perceptions might be based on the expectations teachers explicitly or implicitly convey in a classroom setting. An English teacher might already consider the content-based deciphering of a text in a foreign language a success, whereas the same level of reading competence would be deemed insufficient by a German teacher teaching native speakers of German. Kelchner's (1994) interview study, however, points in a different direction: sixteen of the eighteen interviewed EFL teachers are classified by Kelchner as having a positivist view of literature, that is, holding the conviction that a literary text has one identifiable meaning.[1]

More recently, Schädlich (2004, 2008) found that pre-service teachers of French as a foreign language bring an outdated concept of literature to the university and seemingly do not abandon it despite attending seminars focusing on modern understandings of literature and related teaching approaches. In the same way, Caspari (2004) deduces from a series of interviews with experienced foreign language teachers that knowledge acquired at the university seems to have had little influence on both the convictions and actions of teachers, at least based on their recollections of factors that had an impact on their understanding of teaching and learning.

It would be unwise, however, to present a mostly negative view of teachers' current practice. Rather than assessing their actions by the theoretical models of literature's potential and normative perspectives on what constitutes good literature teaching, one must acknowledge that all knowledge, whether explicitly acquired at the university and during in-service training or more implicitly acquired through teaching, will invariably be adapted and recontextualized by teachers in their everyday practice. Teachers perform a 'translation service' (*Übersetzungsleistung*; Asbrand and Martens 2013: 115) when they merge subject-specific knowledge, pedagogical knowledge and educational policies. In recent years, such recontextualization processes have been observed in teachers' work on curriculum and educational policy reforms (Tesch (2010) for French; Asbrand and Martens (2013) for maths). These studies show that theoretical knowledge cannot be implemented into practice without undergoing changes due to both the number of factors influencing teachers' decisions during everyday practice and their complexity.

Current Classroom Practice: Teachers as Authors' Agents, Pragmatists and Mediators

In my project LITES 1 (Gardemann 2021), I was able to show that the way a certain teacher teaches literature in the EFL classroom does not so much depend on that teacher's understanding of literature or view of their learners. Instead, as part of EFL teaching practice, literature teaching is fundamentally tied to the teachers' general understanding of their professional self as teachers. The study, therefore, confirms earlier results by Caspari (2003), who found that knowledge of literature and literature didactics does not seem to have direct effects on French (as a foreign language) teachers' actions in the classroom. The fundamental attitudes that Caspari assumes influence teachers not only in their teaching of literature but rather in their overall approach to teaching can best be understood by reconstructing precisely how a certain attitude to literature (or, more generally speaking, subject matter), pedagogical convictions and conceptualizations of the teacher's and the learner's roles in the classroom are interwoven in teachers' professional self-conceptions.

I conducted semi-narrative interviews for the qualitative part of my study to reconstruct teachers' frames of orientation. Interviewees were systematically chosen to be maximally contrasting cases, drawing on the results of a representative quantitative study including 368 secondary school English teachers in Hamburg.[2]

It should be noted that all data was collected before the pandemic and thus does not include particular reference to digital teaching. The results do, however, supply us with a comprehensive picture of how literature is currently being used in classrooms in Hamburg, which was specifically chosen for the reason that teachers here have greater flexibility than in all other German federal states, due to local curricula making relatively few specifications. The way they teach is, therefore, more up to individual teachers' decisions than in the rest of Germany. The details of the larger study and justifications of choices both of methodology and methods are extensively explained in Gardemann (2021), where I also explain my overall mixed methods design, the use of quantitative data to carefully select the teachers for the qualitative study and the steps undertaken to identify the teacher types using the documentary method (Nohl 2007). The theoretical framework connected to the documentary method, which draws on insights from *Wissenssoziologie*, views people as belonging to different experiential spaces, each of which is characterized by its own inherent logic that shapes the thinking and behaviour of its members. This inherent logic is conceptually close to the concept of *Habitus* developed by Bourdieu (1970). It encompasses constitutions of meaning and action as well as the structure of practice and is defined, in the terminology of the documentary method, as a 'framework of orientation'. This term is used to describe the entirety of the implicit, atheoretical knowledge that has a guiding influence on a teacher's specific practice. The frames of orientation for all teachers were reconstructed from the semi-narrative interviews in the strictly structured three-step analysis and interpretation procedure prescribed by the method (for more on the method, cf. Nohl 2007). Three different types of teachers were thus reconstructed based on teachers' frameworks of orientation regarding their professional identity, conceptualization of students and teaching style as well as understanding of literature. The types are referred to below not only by their descriptive type name but also by the teacher pseudonyms representing them in the LITES 1 project. The pseudonyms were carefully created by modifying and extending a suggestion made by Loviglio (2012), considering Grinyer's (2002) thoughts on names carrying connotations related to social class, age, ethnicity and so on.

Type 1 – the Authors' Agent: Birgit Wichmann is a reader and lover of literature. Her relationship to a literary text is first and foremost shaped by her personal appreciation for the text. Only when she approves of a text in her role as a private reader does she consider bringing that text into the classroom. On one occasion, this even makes her manipulate a group of learners to vote for a favourite novel of hers that she presents as being one of two alternatives for reading in class. With the text, she brings her own understanding of it to the classroom. She also shows great appreciation for the texts' authors. In her eyes, they are artists as well as artisans: they cleverly make use of stylistic and rhetorical devices to create certain effects, they employ narrative perspectives to allow readers to understand different characters' points of view and they guide the reader through the fictional universe they have created. In Birgit Wichmann's understanding, it is the reader's task to follow the path outlined by the author. In this sense, she conceptualizes her role as a teacher as the Authors' Agent: in the same way that an author leads a reader through a literary text, Birgit Wichmann leads the learners through it, directing their attention to certain stylistic devices or choices and explaining their effects. It becomes clear then that her role is that of an instructor. She believes that learners need guidance, and rather than allowing them the space to develop their own readings, she tries to lead them to an appreciation of the great artistry of authors.

Type 2 – the Pragmatist: While Birgit Wichmann bases her classroom practice mostly on her expertise, Nicole Dewitz's starting point for teaching literature is externally set goals (e.g. the curriculum, standardized testing). She chooses literary texts by screening them according to whether or not they will allow her to teach certain skills and competencies needed for assessments and exams. Still, she is critical of the educational system she works in and laments the workload, limited resources and time constraints she experiences daily. As a private reader, she enjoys literature as a holistic form of art. To her, it does not seem appropriate to dissect a text or to read it cut up into pieces, thus destroying its overall effect. At school, however, the analysis of literary texts seems to be to her what is demanded by the educational standards and the curriculum. These two different perspectives on literature appear to be irreconcilable to Nicole Dewitz. Her attempt at asking learners to read a full novel as a whole at home must be classified as doomed for failure: she refers to the learners' backgrounds as being problematic and acknowledges that they do not enjoy reading in general. She also combines this seemingly freer reading of a text with the task of keeping a reading diary that she then collected and graded, thus subordinating reading pleasure to the institution's testing logic. The frustration that follows this and other brief experiments could lead to a fundamental change in action or to resigned pragmatism. Since Nicole Dewitz feels burdened by her workload already, the only logical conclusion for her is to act like a (Resigned) Pragmatist. This goes beyond the immediate context of choosing texts or methods for her lessons and extends to an attitude that conceptualizes learners as being responsible for their own learning success: in Nicole Dewitz's view, learners in Year 10 can either work with literature according to the curricula's demands or they cannot. In the latter case, they will simply fail exams or not be allowed to move on to Sixth Form education. To put it bluntly, it is what it is.

Pragmatism, however, can also take on the form of the Doubtful Pragmatist. Tobias Jessen also plans and teaches according to expectations set in curricula and standardized testing. In the same way as Nicole Dewitz, his main focus is on the final exams; his task as a teacher is to prepare learners for these exams. Contrary to Nicole Dewitz, though, he refuses to take on the role of gatekeeper. Instead, above all, he conceptualizes himself as being responsible for his learners' success (which at times, causes him considerable self-doubt as to his abilities as a teacher). Since he is not a trained teacher of English but has taken on that additional role as a native speaker, he is not part of the English department at his school. As such, he is not included in decision-making processes that involve choosing the novels supposed to be read in certain years. In his teaching practice, he undergoes three steps: first, his main goal is to have as many learners as possible pass the final exams. Second, he knows that literature will not be part of this year's final exam. Third, when he feels that his learners mostly struggle with the novel given and take little away from it, both on a content as well as on a personal level, he decides to abandon the novel. Instead, he gives his learners additional time to prepare and practice for the final exams. Whether that is the right thing to do, when the curriculum explicitly requires him to have the learners engage with literature, is something he still wonders about weeks after having made that decision.

Type 3 – the Mediator: Bianca Hemschrodt does not seem to think her private reading preferences are of any interest to her work as an EFL teacher of literature at the school. Throughout her years of having been a teacher, she has realized that most literary texts that might interest learners on a content level will be too difficult to read. In the same way, texts on an appropriate level of difficulty might be too boring for them. She also acknowledges the great and manifold differences between individual learners, considering both interests and English competence. Since supply and demand are thus never a good fit, she conceptualizes her task as a teacher to be in a mediating position and to make things fit. This leads to her taking a very active, sometimes proactive approach to teaching. Making things fit includes choosing texts that will be easy to read and enriching the teaching unit with additional materials, among other strategies. While this causes her to spend extra time preparing her lessons, it also helps her avoid frustration in the long run. Other teachers might spend time on finding texts that can be used as they are and struggle with the fact that learners' interests differ both from what the text offers and from what other learners are interested in. Bianca Hemschrodt never assumes that one day she will find the perfect fit but accepts her role as a Mediator as being her main task.

Despite the differences between the types when it comes to how they perceive themselves as teachers, their learners and their teaching, all teacher types have in common that they ultimately conceptualize the learners in a receiving role of their EFL learning. It is worth noting that the teachers' reasons for positioning the learners in this role differ greatly. Nicole Dewitz subordinates the learners' interests and voices to the requirements of the school system and, in particular, the perceived need to complete the curriculum, for example, working through the entire coursebook or placing a main focus on the standardized testing routines. It almost seems as though the learners and their individual experiences or struggles might get in the way of reaching this self-imposed goal. Bianca Hemschrodt, in her role as Mediator, seems to find a better balance between externally set educational goals and the learners' interests, but she also takes on an instructive role. Birgit Wichmann considers learners to need guidance which she feels she can provide, both as an expert on literature and as an educator. In the same way, Tobias Jessen perceives a need for guidance for his learners, though mainly due to their lack of foreign language competence, which leads to him rather giving up on the idea of engaging his learners with literature in favour of more measurable, short-term goals in the form of upcoming final exams.

If one now contrasts the theory-based conviction as to the need for an active role of readers in the literary reading process with the empirical finding that learners are ascribed a primarily receiving role in lessons by their teachers, this begs the question of whether the educational potential of literature can be fully exploited by any of these teacher types. In the interviews, momentary snapshots appear that point to existing alternative approaches to either literature teaching or the learner's role in the classroom. Birgit Wichmann, for instance, is ready to accept that one of her classes refuses to engage with a certain topic taken from a novel that she was convinced would be relevant for the learners and be met with great interest. Tobias Jessen, while doubting both his learners' competence as well as his teaching skills, recounts a lesson during which the learners took on an active and highly involved role in trying to write and perform role plays. Nevertheless, these short narratives remain exceptions.

One has to wonder, then, what kind of experiential crises (positive or negative) could still trigger a fundamental change in teachers' frames of orientation when underlying professional convictions and beliefs seem to be stable both in theory and empirical study (Gardemann 2021). The recent pandemic that forced teachers and learners to adapt to alternative settings could represent such a crisis. The challenge for teachers in the future will then be to take literature online. As I have argued above, it makes sense to not only press for fundamental *change* here but rather draw on teachers' existing practice outlined above, and as such, on a *continuity of practice*, to allow for a smoother transition into the digital space. Drawing on the teacher types reconstructed in the LITES 1 project, such a focus on 'continuity first, change second' will be presented for each type in the following.

Going Digital: A Tailor-Made Focus on Continuity and Change

To be able to identify the type of focus on continuity that I believe is most likely to convince the teacher type in question to use digital tools (or more/ other digital tools than they already do), it is necessary to focus on each type's professional needs and worries that I deduce from my analysis of the types. The suggestion of specific digital tools and tasks for each type that follows is based on both my theoretical knowledge and practical experience of using digital tools in teaching. The Author's Agent is an instruction-focused type of teacher. They need to feel in control of what is happening in the classroom because they conceptualize their learners as needing guidance on all levels (language and content). They use literary texts to bring a worthwhile topic to the classroom, to illustrate the use of rhetoric devices to achieve certain effects and, ideally, wish to convey their love of literature to the learners. Because of their perceived higher expertise in choosing adequate topics, understanding the art and craft that is writing and what makes certain pieces of literature worth reading, they worry that the learners lack knowledge, skills and insight to be allowed more metaphorical space in the classroom. The Author's Agent will thus feel most inclined to try out digital tools if we highlight those tools that are an addition or enhancement (as per Puentedura's model, 2006) to their existing practice. They could make use of teaching approaches such as the flipped classroom by using existing video material or podcasts available online to provide their learners with the high-quality input they feel is necessary and might be more open to allowing learners to research and discuss additional information more freely then. To allow the learners to take on a more active role when dealing with a literary text, collaborative writing tools and/or collaborative concept mapping tools such as Padlet can be used to have learners collectively mark passages, leave comments and questions that can then be saved and sent to the teacher for additional commenting, feedback or corrections before such information is then shared with the entire group. It can be assumed that the Author's Agent might feel particularly uneasy about breakout sessions in video conferences, during which learners will be in separate rooms without the teacher. If that is a worry, it is worthwhile discussing suitable tasks (both in terms of cooperative learning skills as well as subject matter and time restraints) in the context of such settings before expecting this teacher type to move on to more complex and time-consuming tasks.

Both subtypes of Pragmatists are worried that changes to the routine might be problematic. To briefly recap, the Doubtful Pragmatist Tobias Jessen fears that his deviation from the curriculum might get him or his learners in trouble; the Resigned Pragmatist Nicole Dewitz explains how any deviation from the fixed order of topics in the coursebook will result in having to catch up on missed content and, ultimately, additional work and stress for the teacher. Both kinds of Pragmatists want to make sure that what they do is 'safe' in the context of the system. The switch from analogue to digital coursebooks might then be a suitable focus on continuity that this type of teacher will need. This way, they can make sure that all required topics and skills can be covered to then, ideally, feel more comfortable to explore other offers from publishers such as vocabulary learning apps, quiz features and additional material that would not fit the restraints of a printed book. Especially the Resigned Pragmatist will profit from games, quiz apps and fill-in-the-gap activities online, which offer learners the opportunity to have their entered results checked by software rather than the teacher being required to collect and mark written work. Many analogue methods that this type of teacher will likely use in the classroom can easily be transformed into a digital form: a blog can take the place of the reading log and be enriched with pictures, sounds or even video clips as well as allow other learners (or the teacher) to comment and thus engage with the content. Role plays can be practiced and recorded to then be played to the class, adding classic film elements such as music, title pages or credits; not to mention filters that most learners are familiar with from their social media use. Saving the role play to be stored and watched again can also enhance learners' feeling of their work being appreciated rather than a brief, one-time performance in class. If several role plays are created and recorded, they can later be watched in chronological order to illustrate and analyse a character's development through a novel and allow for that to be done in a much easier and more reliable way than having learners go over the written dialogues in their exercise books. Drawing on learners' experiences with social media, Instagram stories can be created for characters to introduce the idea of writing portraits or characterizations later. Instead of writing dialogues between characters to better understand their positions, WhatsApp messages or Snapchats can be imagined that characters would send to each other. Freeze frames can be reimagined as pictures a group of characters would upload to their social media profile.

The Mediator is likely to be the most open of the three types when it comes to trying new methods, seeing as they already do not expect to be able to use texts and tasks as they are in existing coursebooks or teaching materials. If this type of teacher struggles to find adequate digital tools, they might also find the switch to digital coursebooks most sensible at first. The additional material available will allow the Mediator to pick and choose as necessary, then branch out into other options. GoogleMaps, StreetView and similar services can allow learners to zoom into any existing city a novel or short story might be set in. New street maps can be created by learners for places in fictional towns. A character's movement through a city can be sketched out on the map; places and sights mentioned in the story can then be researched by learners easily. Instead of looking for material to enrich the reading experience themselves, teachers could send learners on online quests for information, background knowledge and related themes.

Conclusion and Implications for Research

All digital tools and tasks suggested in the previous section are closely tied to each teacher type's existing practice. They do not require teachers to radically change the way they teach but rather substitute digital options for analogue tasks they already ask pupils to work on, thereby enhancing and enriching lessons while also allowing for a continuity of practice. The tools and materials mentioned already exist and as such, their implementation requires relatively little time. Last but not least, many of the ideas given put work in the hands of the pupils, allowing them to take on a more active role in the reading process. Thus, the substituted tools and tasks have one goal in common: freeing up time and mind space for teachers to reflect on existing practice, evaluate digital tools and feel more comfortable in providing learners more space in lessons. Rather than waiting for teachers to experience negative experiential crises when being challenged with implementing digital tools they have not chosen themselves, there should be a focus on enabling teachers to experience positive eye-opening moments when going digital. Case studies with teachers willing to be interviewed before and after such implementations of digital tools could lead to interesting insights into their attitudes, beliefs and experiences, whereas classroom observation studies could focus on the way pupils accept or reject their new role as more active co-contributors to literature lessons.

One of the main results of the quantitative study in LITES 1 was the continued importance of EFL coursebooks, which seem to take on the role of a hidden curriculum, often becoming a decisive factor as to which texts are being dealt with and which tasks learners will work on (Gardemann 2021). The existing coursebooks, however, too often still focus on grammatical progression over communicative language teaching and learning. If teacher educators and policymakers are interested in facilitating teachers' switches to digital tools, they need to be provided with high-quality material that will enable them to do so without feeling that digitalization is superimposed on their classrooms and practice. In-service training, as well as day-long, research-based workshops at schools, could allow experienced teachers to try out new tools themselves, possibly working on ideas cooperatively as to how to implement those sensibly in their classrooms. Most importantly, routine follow-up evaluation and discussion are needed after having introduced digital tools rather than considering such seminars or workshops to be one-time events. Researchers might want to look into such teacher-chosen and teacher-driven changes at schools and should consider not only evaluating the results but also attempting to understand the processes that lead to sustainable change.

However, providing material for in-service teachers will not be enough. If teacher educators take seriously that pre-service teachers arrive at university with an already quite stable set of convictions and beliefs about how teaching and learning work (for their motivations, knowledge and attitudes: Gröschner and Schmitt (2008) and König and Rothland (2013)), this will now inevitably include their attitudes towards the use of digital tools. Successful teacher training must consider students' existing convictions more, explicitly making them the starting point of seminars. Since there is still little empirical research on the individual development of students' convictions during their university studies, following some pre-service teachers throughout their entire training (at university and school), analysing how they make sense of their theoretical knowledge, integrating it into their previously held convictions – or adapting and/or revoking those convictions – would be a very valuable addition to professionalism research that still mostly focuses on measuring subject matter knowledge and competencies deemed necessary for future teachers at the time of graduation.

Both the interpretative openness of literary texts as well as the willingness to take risks in the EFL classroom (e.g. by trying out new methods and tools) relate to the concept of tolerance of ambiguity. Dealing with such ambiguity and uncertainty should be a core competence especially for today's prospective teachers, which we urgently need to further promote within the framework of university teacher education. Given the interpretative openness of texts, the field of literature didactics offers itself as an exemplary field of work to make pre-service teachers understand the need to be open to learners' readings of texts and to come to terms with the fact that there is no such thing as a 'correct' solution when it comes to discussing literature. Empirically researching the way pre-service teachers react to pupils' readings of specific literary texts (presented in the form of lesson, group discussion or interview transcripts) might be worth looking into: do they immediately classify pupils' understandings of texts as correct/incorrect, or are they willing to engage with them? Such input, taken from actual lessons, could facilitate pre-service teachers' mediation of literary and pedagogical theory and the ever-present wish for practical application of such knowledge.

Considering the described insights of professionalism research, the implementation of digital tools in the EFL classroom not just as an occasional treat or to spice up lessons but as a natural part of teachers' existing repertoire of teaching methods can only succeed if teachers are taken along in the transformation process. In the context of the pandemic, many teachers' hands were forced. The sudden school closures left little time to thoughtfully initiate appropriate processes, both individually and collectively at the school level, so that the quality of digital tool implementation in many places will have been determined by the degree of digitalization (knowledge, equipment, resources) that was already present before the pandemic. The few empirical results that are available so far on the learning status of pupils who have since returned to in-person teaching in Germany, as well as anecdotal observations by various educational researchers, indicate that the implementation of distance learning was indeed problematic in many cases – and not only in Germany. From their systematic evaluation of 109 international studies, Hammerstein et al. (2021) conclude that most distance learning measures applied by teachers during the initial school closures were not beneficial to pupils' learning success. Furthermore, a first empirical survey on the state of reading literacy in primary schools in Hamburg concluded that while children from socially less privileged families were often particularly disadvantaged by the situation, there was also a smaller number of children with high proficiency levels than before the pandemic, which researchers tentatively attribute to the increased media consumption during the school closures (Deutsches Schulportal 2021).

Looking forward into the time past the acute situation, the question that arises is not just how to implement specific digital tools in a meaningful way but also how to accompany teachers in this ongoing process. Doing so, scholars should focus research on learner-orientation in a double sense – focusing both on learners in the EFL classroom as well as teachers in teacher education (see the chapters in Parts 2 and 3 of this volume for research on best practice examples in teacher education developed during the first and second waves of the pandemic) and extra-occupational training.

Notes

1   Unfortunately, Kelchner does not supply the reader with more information on the way the interviews were conducted or his method of analysis. From today's point of view, both methodology and methods of Benz's and Kelchner's studies must be evaluated rather critically.
2   This study had a participation rate of 27.7% of all English secondary school teachers, comfortably exceeding the previously calculated minimum sample size for representativity and representing 88% of all grammar schools and 85% of all comprehensive schools in Hamburg (Gardemann 2021).

References

Arnold, J. (2011), 'Attention to Affect in Language Learning', *International Journal of English Studies*, 22 (1): 11–22.

Asbrand, B., and M. Martens (2013), 'Kompetenzorientierter Unterricht. Eckpunkte des didaktischen Konzepts', *Schulmagazin, 5–10*, 81 (5): 7–10.

Bennewitz, H. (2005), *Handlungskrise Schulreform. Deutungsmuster von Lehrenden zur Einführung der Förderstufe in Sachsen-Anhalt*, Wiesbaden: Springer VS.

Benz, N. (1990), *Der Schüler als Leser im Fremdsprachenunterricht*, Tübingen: Narr.

Bourdieu, P. (1970), *Zur Soziologie der symbolischen Formen*, Frankfurt am Main: Suhrkamp.

Bredella, L. (2002), *Literarisches und interkulturelles Verstehen*, Tübingen: Narr.

Bredella, L., and E. Burwitz-Melzer (2004), *Rezeptionsästhetische Literaturdidaktik mit Beispielen aus dem Fremdsprachenunterricht Englisch*, Tübingen: Narr.

Caspari, D. (2003), *Fremdsprachenlehrerinnen und Fremdsprachenlehrer. Studien zu ihrem beruflichen Selbstverständnis*, Tübingen: Narr.

Caspari, D. (2004), 'Über berufliches Selbstverständnis nachdenken – Entwicklung, Durchführung und Evaluation eines Bausteins für Lehrerfortbildungsveranstaltungen im Bereich Fremdsprachen', *Zeitschrift für Fremdsprachenforschung*, 15 (1): 55–78.

Council of Europe (2001), 'Common European Framework of Reference for Languages: Learning, Teaching, Assessment'. https://rm.coe.int/1680459f97 (accessed 20 September 2021).

Dann, H. D. (2000), 'Lehrerkognitionen und Handlungsentscheidungen', in Martin K. Schweer (ed.), *Lehrer-Schüler-Interaktion. Pädagogisch-psychologische Aspekte des Lehrens und Lernens in der Schule*, 79–108, Opladen: Leske + Budrich.

Delanoy, W. (2002), *Fremdsprachlicher Literaturunterricht. Theorie und Praxis als Dialog*, Tübingen: Narr.

Deutsches Schulportal (2021), 'Lernstandserhebung in Hamburg. Bundesweit einmalige Daten zeigen Lernverluste durch Corona'. https://deutsches-schulportal.de/ schule-im-umfeld/bundesweit-einmalige-daten-zeigen-lernverluste-durch-corona (accessed 20 September 2021).

Drossel, K., B. Eickelmann, H. Schaumburg and A. Labusch (2019), 'Nutzung digitaler Medien und Prädiktoren aus der Perspektive der Lehrerinnen und Lehrer im internationalen Vergleich', in B. Eickelmann, W. Bos, J. Gerick, F. Goldhammer, H. Schaumburg, K. Schwippert, M. Senkbeil and J. Vahrenhold (eds), *ICILS 2018 #Deutschland. Computer- und informationsbezogene Kompetenzen von Schülerinnen und Schülern im zweiten internationalen Vergleich und Kompetenzen im Bereich Computational Thinking*, 205–40, Münster: Waxmann.

Eickelmann, B., W. Bos and A. Labusch (2019), 'Die Studie ICILS 2018 im Überblick – Zentrale Ergebnisse und mögliche Entwicklungsperspektiven', in B. Eickelmann, W. Bos, J. Gerick, F. Goldhammer, H. Schaumburg, K. Schwippert, M. Senkbeil and J. Vahrenhold (eds), *ICILS 2018 #Deutschland. Computer- und informationsbezogene Kompetenzen von Schülerinnen und Schülern im zweiten internationalen Vergleich und Kompetenzen im Bereich Computational Thinking*, 7–32, Münster: Waxmann.

Gardemann, C. (2021), *Literarische Texte im Englischunterricht der Sekundarstufe I. Eine Mixed Methods-Studie mit Hamburger Englischlehrer*innen*, Berlin: Metzler.

Grinyer, A. (2002), 'The Anonymity of Research Participants: Assumptions, Ethics and Practicalities', *Social Research Update*, 36: 1–4.

Gröschner, A., and C. Schmitt (2008), ' "Fit für das Studium?" - Studien- und Berufswahlmotive, Belastungserfahrungen und Kompetenzerwartungen am Beginn der Lehramtsausbildung. Empirische Befunde der wissenschaftlichen Begleitforschung zum Praxissemester an der Universität Jena', *Lehrerbildung auf dem Prüfstand*, 1/2: 605–24.

Gruschka, A. (2011), *Verstehen lehren. Ein Plädoyer für guten Unterricht*, Ditzingen: Reclam.

Hammerstein, S., C. König, T. Dreisörner and A. Frey (2021), 'Effects of COVID19 Related School Closures on Student Achievement – a Systematic Review'. https://psyarxiv.com/mcnvk (accessed 20 September 2021).

Iser, W. (1994), *Der Akt des Lesens. Theorie ästhetischer Wirkung*, Munich: Wilhelm Fink Verlag.

Kelchner, H.-R. (1994), *Lyrik und Hermeneutik im fremdsprachlichen Literaturunterricht: Studien zu Einstellungen und Rezeptionsfähigkeit von Lernern*, Frankfurt: Peter Lang.

Klieme, E. (2006), *Zusammenfassung zentraler Ergebnisse der DESI-Studie. Deutsches Institut für Internationale Pädagogische Forschung*, Frankfurt: Main.

Klieme, E., and J. Hartig (2007), 'Kompetenzkonzepte in den Sozialwissenschaften und im erziehungswissenschaftlichen Diskurs', in M. Prenzel, I. Gogolin and H.-H. Krüger (eds), *Kompetenzdiagnostik*, 11–32, Wiesbaden: VS Verlag für Sozialwissenschaften.

Klippel, F. (2000), *Englisch in der Grundschule. Handbuch für einen kindgemäßen Fremdsprachenunterricht*, Berlin: Cornelsen Scriptor.

KMK – Sekretariat der ständigen Konferenz der Kultusminister der Länder der Bundesrepublik Deutschland (2004), *Bildungsstandards für die erste Fremdsprache (Englisch/Französisch) für den mittleren Schulabschluss*, Beschluss vom 15.10.2004, Munich: Luchterhand.

KMK – Sekretariat der ständigen Konferenz der Kultusminister der Länder der Bundesrepublik Deutschland (2017), *Bildung in der digitalen Welt. Strategie der Kultusministerkonferenz*, Beschluss vom 08.12.2016 in der Fassung vom 07.12.2017, Berlin: KMK Eigendruck.

König, J., and M. Rothland (2013), 'Pädagogisches Wissen und berufsspezifische Motivation am Anfang der Lehrerausbildung. Zum Verhältnis von kognitiven und nicht-kognitiven Eingangsmerkmalen von Lehramtsstudierenden', *Zeitschrift für Pädagogik*, 59 (1): 43–65.

Krashen, S. (1993), *The Power of Reading: Insights from Research*, Englewood, CO: Libraries United.

Lee, J., F. A. Ceretto and J. Lee (2010), 'Theory of Planned Behavior and Teachers' Decisions Regarding Use of Educational Technology', *Educational Technology and Society*, 13 (1): 152–64.

Lipowsky, F. (2010), 'Lernen im Beruf. Empirische Befunde zur Wirksamkeit von Lehrerfortbildung', in F. H. Müller (ed.), *Lehrerinnen und Lehrer lernen. Konzepte und Befunde zur Lehrerfortbildung*, 51–70, Münster: Waxmann.

Loviglio, D. (2012), 'Picking Pseudonyms for Your Research Participants'. https://blog.mozilla.org//ux/2012/05/picking-pseudonyms-for-your-research-participants (accessed 20 September 2021).

Nohl, A.-M. (2007), *Interview und Dokumentarische Methode. Anleitungen für die Forschungspraxis*, Wiesbaden: Springer VS.

Puentedura, R. (2006), 'Transformation, Technology and Education'. http://www.hippasus.com/resources/tte/puentedura_tte.pdf (accessed 20 September 2021).

Schädlich, B. (2004), ' "… an der Quelle Durst zu leiden": Überlegungen zum Verhältnis von Literaturdidaktik und Hochschullehre am Beispiel der romanistischen Literaturwissenschaft', in L. Bredella, W. Delanoy and C. Surkamp (eds), *Literaturdidaktik im Dialog*, 289–312, Tübingen: Narr.

Schädlich, B. (2008), 'Reliterarisierung des schulischen Französischunterrichts – was kann die Lehrerausbildung beitragen?', *Fremdsprachen Lehren und Lernen*, 37: 298–311.

Schildhauer, P. (2020), 'Rezension zu Burwitz-Melzer, Eva/Riemer, Claudia/Schmelter, Lars (2019) (eds.): Das Lehren und Lernen von Fremd- und Zweitsprachen im digitalen Wandel. Arbeitspapiere der 39. Frühjahrskonferenz zur Erforschung des Fremdsprachenunterrichts', *Journal für Medienlinguistik*, 3 (1): 1–6.

Schopf, H. (2020), 'Ist da jemand? Skeptische Anmerkungen zu (neuen) Höhlen und Maulwurfsbauten im Zusammenhang mit Didaktik und "digitaler" Bildung. Eine Provokation', in R. Bauer, J. Hafer, S. Hofhues, M. Schiefner-Rohs, A. Thillosen, B. Volk and K. Wannemacher (eds), *Vom E-Learning zur Digitalisierung. Mythen, Realitäten, Perspektiven*, 401–15, Münster: Waxmann.

Tesch, B. (2010), *Kompetenzorientierte Lernaufgaben im Fremdsprachenunterricht. Konzeptionelle Grundlagen und eine rekonstruktive Fallstudie zur Unterrichtspraxis (Französisch)*, Frankfurt/Main: Peter Lang.

6

Conducting Story-Based Activities in Times of Social Distancing

Annett Kaminski

Introduction

One of the central themes in publications for pre-primary and primary EFL specialists is holistic learning. There is consensus that very young second language learners aged between three and ten years need to be provided with a language learning environment which incorporates the L2 in purposeful activities that engage them physically, emotionally, socially and artistically as well (Brewster, Ellis and Girard 2002; Moon 2005; Dunn 2014; Mourão and Ellis 2020; Read 2020). Young learners need to experience the L2 in a context that allows them to construct meaning from it – decoding L2 samples in an environment that is familiar to them (Cameron 2004). Although a holistic approach to learning has also been recommended for older language learners, for example, as part of humanistic approaches to language learning (Arnold and Murphey 2013), it seems to be paramount for the success of early L2 programmes. The fact that learners at pre-secondary level are still developing abstract thought and therefore require a contextualized learning environment (Piaget and Inhelder 1969) necessitates the incorporation of language learning in the wider context of children's growing understanding of their environment (Cameron 2001). Thus, in primary language programmes holistic learning equates to meaningful learning by experiencing 'English not as a subject to be learned, but as a means of communication, where the focus is on meaning not the form of the language' (Moon 2005: 2). The aim is to design classroom activities that support 'development in all areas – through English' (Mourão and Ellis 2020: 11), including personal, physical, creative, literacy and numeracy development.

Children's literature, comprising of rhymes, poetry, stories and drama, has repeatedly been found to lend itself to holistic learning (Cameron 2001; Brewster, Ellis and Girard 2002; Pinter 2006; Read 2007; Bland 2013; Ghosn 2013). Stories are a rich resource inviting children to step into an 'imaginary world, created by language, that they can enter and enjoy' (Cameron 2001: 159). They encourage young learners to think about characters and plot (Ghosn 2013) as well as about missing pieces in the verbal or visual storyline (Bland 2013), guide their growing understanding through peritextual features (Mourão 2013) and can initiate a creative response from young listeners (García Bermejo and Fleta Guillén 2013).

Principles for good practice in early language learning as listed in educational policies include holistic language learning, a visual approach, multisensory learning and the use of stories (Edelenbos, Johnstone and Kubanek 2006). The recent awareness of multi-literacy has only confirmed and strengthened the argument for holistic approaches in early language learning, and thus it has been suggested that activities around picturebooks, for example, can cater for the development of nature, visual, emotional, cultural and learning literacies (Ellis 2018).

If teacher education aims at preparing pre-service teachers for the demands of real classrooms, it follows that the management and facilitation of holistic learning has to play a major role in seminars at university. Student teachers need to develop a good understanding of how to organize and conduct activities in the primary language learning classroom that allow for a holistic learning experience. Likewise, if good practice in Teaching English to Young Learners (TEYL) entails the use of stories, then student teachers need to be able to develop expertise in making effective use of this resource, especially since this 'requires a great deal of sensitivity and a wide range of varied skills by the teacher' (Read 2006: 11). This involves not only a sound knowledge of different types of stories and the ability to select appropriate texts but also the ability to analyse linguistic as well as peritextual features that can support children's understanding of the story during shared story time or story-based activities (Mourão and Ellis 2020; Kaminski 2020).

Before the pandemic, face-to-face seminars for future primary teachers at our university campus in Landau addressed this by simulating a classroom environment, in which student teachers could carry out preparation activities, core activities and cross-curricular follow-up activities such as artwork, singing, cooking, dance and physical exercise as part of their TEYL seminar. This seminar forms a compulsory part of student teachers' primary EFL programme in the MEd phase of their studies. With the restrictions on face-to-face tuition during the pandemic and the introduction of emergency remote teaching, the question arose as to how student teachers could be prepared for the demands of real-life classroom situations in virtual seminars. In this chapter, I show how seminar content was adapted over the course of two terms, analyse affordances and restraints of the digital delivery mode on the basis of student evaluations and discuss implications for teacher education.

Research on Digital Teaching

The unprecedented halt to traditional face-to-face teaching that was experienced in primary, secondary and tertiary education across the globe resulting from the Covid-19 pandemic in early 2020 has triggered a surge in interest in online tuition, and in the course of the pandemic reports that share insights into different remote teaching formats have been published widely on different internet platforms and open access journals. However, prior to the Covid-19 crisis, a substantial body of research on digital learning had already been developing for about three decades. In the following, I discuss research undertaken both before and during the pandemic. I am particularly interested in, firstly, the question of what constitutes online education; secondly, what experiences have been reported with student response to digital resources in tertiary education; and thirdly, the use of digital tools in primary L2 education.

Online Education and Emergency Remote Teaching

Within educational technology research, online education is perceived as an umbrella term that refers to a range of 'highly variable design solutions' (Hodges et al. 2020: 1) called distance learning, blended learning or mobile learning among others, with effective online programmes being a product of 'careful instructional design and planning' (2). Several variables need to be considered, such as pacing, student-instructor ratio, pedagogy, role of online assessment, online communication synchrony and source of feedback (Means, Bakia and Murphy 2014). These variables each provides several options; for instance, within 'online communication synchrony', a programme might either be asynchronous only, synchronous only or both to some extent. It is noteworthy that these options are interdependent: the decision for or against a certain design option in one variable impacts directly on the decision of which other design options can be used. Decisions around class size, for example, influence pedagogy as well as feedback. With growing class size, opportunities for practice and high-quality teacher feedback decrease (Hodges et al. 2020).

Bernard et al. (2009) found that asynchronous distance learning that included different types of interaction such as student-content, student-student and student-teacher resulted in higher achievement levels, suggesting that the use of different interaction types is a decisive factor for learning outcomes. The underlying understanding is that learning is not 'merely a matter of information transmission' but both 'a social and a cognitive process', and therefore the focus is on providing social support alongside instructional content (Hodges et al. 2020: 2).

In a similar way, Palloff and Pratt (2011: 7–8) argue that 'establishing presence is the first order of business in an online class' in order to 'create a sense of connection with learners who are otherwise separated by time and space' (2011: 7–8). This includes communicating who we are and forming a social bond with the people within the virtual classroom. Palloff and Pratt suggest that establishing presence needs more effort in an online environment compared to a face-to-face teaching environment. For this, synchronous tools that allow participants and instructor to communicate in real time should also be considered. The learning community formed in this way serves as a social support framework and ensures that the learners' need to belong is met, learner isolation is reduced, learning outcome is improved and 'a shared goal for learning' is established (8).

While the integration of a social support system receives some recognition in online education now, it was not necessarily part of traditional distance learning programmes in the past when 'distance education was conceptualised mainly as interaction of the learner with learning resources' (Paran, Furneaux and Sumner 2004: 338). This view changed due to a changing understanding of learning and to affordances of modern technology, and online courses have been expected to be interactive since the mid-1990s (Paran, Furneaux and Sumner 2004). At the time, Moore (1993), for example, argued that modern means of communications, such as teleconferences, could increase the level of student-instructor dialogue and also allow for peer support. This, it was suggested, would reduce the so-called transactional distance, which had been defined as the space created by the physical separation of instructors from their learners (Moore 1972) – a space that carries the risk of misunderstanding. And yet a few decades later, online teaching at tertiary level was still usually associated with distance degree programmes that would mostly rely on asynchronous online tools (Yamagata-Lynch 2014).

For undergraduate and postgraduate students working on campus, face-to-face teaching was the standard before the Covid-19 pandemic, although there was increasing interest in online learning on the grounds that this would make university education more accessible, would allow more flexibility and would be more cost-efficient (Dziuban et al. 2006; Graham, Woodfield and Harrison 2013). Amidst all the enthusiasm for online learning, it was already pointed out at the time that the quality of course design was crucial for successful implementation, especially the effective use of online tools that would also foster interaction (Dziuban et al. 2006).

With all of the above in mind, teachers making use of digital technology for their formerly traditional face-to-face classes need to be aware that not only does it entail 'technical proficiency, e-safety and information literacy' (Selwyn 2020: 2) but there also needs to be an understanding of the 'social, emotional and affective aspects of technology-based education' (4). Due to the Covid-19 pandemic and the subsequent requirement to teach online, there are specific challenges that teachers face, for example, the fact that learners' different home environments and unequal working conditions become more pronounced when all of them are physically at home while attending class. This leads to additional requirements for more flexibility to access material, more generous timing, more need for improvisation, and greater empathy with students who feel isolated and depressed during lockdown (Selwyn 2020).

The fact that because of the pandemic online teaching had to be implemented without a careful planning process and often also without the necessary human, financial and technical resources has caused some concern. Hodges et al. (2020) argue that the lack of proper design means that it will be impossible to benefit from all the affordances that online education has to offer and that, therefore, online education will continue to be considered as the 'weak option'. New terms have been suggested for these online programmes, such as 'emergency remote teaching' (Hodges et al. 2020) or 'temporary distance education' (Selwyn 2020). At the same time, one must also acknowledge that the motivation for improving online education has indeed sometimes been triggered by times of crisis (Palloff and Pratt 2011).

Student Response to Digital Technology

As part of tertiary education, digital tools have been used in two very different learning contexts: firstly, as a support system for residential students attending mostly face-to-face classes and, secondly, as a means of content provision for students on distance degree programmes. While the former represent the majority of the student population, the latter only represent a fraction of it.

With regard to the use of digital resources in distance university education, students have been found to articulate clear preferences for certain digital tools as well as reluctance to use others, which seems to be based on their previous experience and in part also on a heightened awareness of time-efficient learning practice. In an early study, Paran, Furneaux and Sumner (2004) examined computer-mediated communication as part of a UK-based postgraduate distance TEFL programme and found that, contrary to their expectations, students reported time constraints as a reason for their limited use of computer-mediated student-student interaction, rather than a lack of internet or computer access. Teacher-student interaction in the form of email communication, on the other hand, was seen as helpful, specifically for the purpose of receiving more feedback (Paran, Furneaux and Sumner 2004).

In a study with participants of an online graduate-level course that consisted of 50% synchronous whole-class meetings and 50% asynchronous discussions, Yamagata-Lynch (2014) found that students were apprehensive about the synchronous elements in the course and reluctant to invest time for weekly meetings, expressing concern that technical issues with conferencing tools might disrupt learning. However, students later stated that they had experienced a 'sense of stability' and 'a stronger connection with other students while engaged in spontaneous conversations during synchronous meetings', and that the blending of synchronous with asynchronous elements had helped them to stay on task (203). It is noteworthy that at the same time as affording more structure to a course, synchronous elements also reduce the amount of flexibility for the student. The provision of flexibility, however, has always been at the heart of distance learning (Naidu 2017) in order to make education accessible to a diverse group of participants.

With regard to undergraduate programmes, research with students suggests that rather than 'transforming' university education, digital technologies are still very rarely used for the actual purpose of learning. Henderson, Selwyn and Aston, in a study that asked students to identify and justify 'particularly helpful' or 'useful' digital technologies, found that the three most frequent reasons cited were 'organising and managing the logistics of studying', 'flexibility of place and location' as well as 'time-saving' (2015: 5). 'Reviewing, replaying and revisiting' material, such as recordings of lectures, only ranked in fourth place. Moreover, although this resource was seen as a useful form of back-up, students also noted that they did not necessarily make use of it. Only 11.7% of 4,594 respondents reported using technology for 'deeper' learning in the sense of processing information in a different way, such as by watching videos from sources outside the university.

These findings suggest that mainstream tertiary education in many countries was by no means prepared for a shift from traditional face-to-face teaching to online tuition when the pandemic struck. There was not sufficient experience with asynchronous online tools, and even less with synchronous ones, for campus-wide learning. Once all teaching and learning had to be moved online in the spring of 2020, this consequently caused considerable upheaval for mainstream university education in countries across the globe. De Oliveira Dias, de Oliveira Albergarias Lopes and Teles (2020), in a paper that discusses the use of Zoom classes that were introduced mid-April in Brazil, only one month after the start of lockdown, illustrate the challenges that university teachers were confronted with when they moved an MBA course online. On the basis of self-observation data and semi-structured interviews with students, the authors argue that it is impossible to reproduce the same learning environment online and point out that students can more easily withdraw from classroom activities (de Oliveira Dias, de Oliveira Albergarias Lopes and Teles 2020). They report problems with unstable internet connections, security issues and background noise when participants did not turn their microphone off, yet also a lack of interaction when students switched their camera off. They highlight that exercises that involved physical interaction between participants had to be replaced by simulations and that 'the absence of face-to-face contact in virtual negotiations' meant that students missed 'the subtleties and important visual cues' of non-verbal language (212).

It seems that even when synchronous digital tools are applied, additional effort is necessary to decrease the transactional distance imposed by the physical separation of teacher and student in online education. To make full use of all the advantages of synchronous course elements, such as real-time interaction and a closer connection between participants, the technical equipment has to work reliably for everyone involved, all participants need to be encouraged to switch on their camera and security within the virtual classroom has to be ensured so that participants are comfortable with being heard and seen. Furthermore, the absence of a shared physical space restricts the range of activities that can be carried out in a meaningful way.

Digital Technology in Primary L2 Education

When designing online courses in primary language teacher education, another relevant issue is the question of how digital tools are already used for second language learning, specifically at primary level, and how emergency remote teaching can contribute to developing student teachers' digital competence.

Publications on the use of digital technologies in second language education show that there have been many efforts to integrate modern technology in different educational settings, such as formal online courses providing learners with material and regular synchronous speaking classes, computer-based online environments, so-called virtual worlds and also Massive Open Online Courses (MOOCs; see Hockly (2015) for an overview). In order to improve listening, speaking, reading and writing skills teachers have experimented with the use of tablet PCs and smartphones, interactive white boards, electronic dictionaries, ePortfolios, blogs, chats and automatic speech recognition among others (Golonka et al. 2014).

With regard to primary level L2, which is the level that the student teachers in this study will be working at, there have been projects on the use of videoconferencing with modern foreign language (MFL) learners. Phillips (2010) reports on her introduction of twice-weekly videoconferencing sessions between her L2 French learners in the UK and a French school in order to create meaningful communicative situations. She found that motivation increased across different ability groups and higher confidence levels for speaking the foreign language were detected. Videoconferencing has also been tried as a resource to counterbalance shortage of specialist MFL staff, for instance, in the UK where secondary school teachers were asked to teach French to primary school children (Pritchard, Hunt and Barnes 2010).

There have also been projects to promote reading at primary school through digital tools. Shen (2014), for example, investigated primary English L2 learners reading online storybooks on tablet PCs and writing their own digital stories using Android applications. Brunsmeier and Kolb (2017) examined young English learners using story apps and found that reading comprehension was supported if the multimodal features provided by the technology related to key elements of the story. Suggestions for shared digital picturebook sessions are also available online (Ellis et al. 2018). The PEPELT21 project offers video clips of authors and teachers reading picturebooks, shares ideas for story-based activities and information on what picturebooks are, how to use them and how to organize online read-alouds (see https://pepelt21.com/overview/). It has become a valuable source in the pandemic and the experiences that are gained from such resources can inform our understanding of how asynchronous digital storytelling can work successfully (see Chapter 3 by Ellis and Mourão and Chapter 4 by Summer in this volume for additional information on this project).

Although the abovementioned projects are mostly individual initiatives that do not reflect the reality of most classrooms, they nevertheless show that digital technology has started to become a part of primary L2 education. It follows that students on teacher education programmes should be offered an opportunity to experience these tools and learn how to use them effectively in classrooms. Lenkaitis, Hilliker and Roumeliotis (2020), in a study with TESOL students who were asked to reflect on their synchronous meetings with university ESL learners in Mexico, have already suggested that modern technology can support student teachers' understanding of their learners' L2 abilities and improve their teaching skills.

The question arises as to how modern technologies can also be applied to the context of primary L2 teacher education that prepares students to work with much younger L2 learners, who require a contextualized learning environment and a holistic learning experience, which includes activities that involve physical interaction. L2 learning at primary level involves story-based activities for creative, emotional, musical and physical development, such as singing, dancing, arts and crafts, games – most of these carried out in close collaboration. For such activities, children need to physically interact with one another.

As I noted above, however, the lack of a shared physical space in online programmes means that only those activities that do not involve any physical interaction with others can be carried out. This has implications for courses that aim at improving skills for which physical interaction is essential, which is undoubtedly the case for primary teacher education programmes. Therefore, the research questions I explore in this study are:

1. Which affordances and limitations can be observed on delivering traditional seminar content in a synchronous online format?
2. How can traditional face-to-face seminar content be adapted to make effective use of digital tools?

The Study

This study involved students on the primary education degree programme at the University of Koblenz-Landau who attended their obligatory module on TEYL during the MEd phase of the programme. Students take this class either after they have studied English as one of their main subjects in the BEd phase or, if they did not choose English as one of their main subjects, after they have completed two courses on language practice and phonetics.

The TEYL module consists of a weekly lecture, which develops student teachers' understanding of second language acquisition, including characteristics of very young L2 learners as well as appropriate activities for that age range, and a weekly seminar, which focuses on cultural studies or children's literature. Students either attend lectures and seminars in the same semester or sequentially, one semester after the other. The lectures always run over eleven weeks and the seminars over twelve to fourteen weeks (depending on bank holiday arrangements). Students can choose between four different seminars, one of which I teach myself to two groups of students.

In the two identical ninety-minute seminars that I normally offer in the summer term, I introduce future primary school teachers to literary texts such as nursery rhymes, legends, fables, folk tales and picturebooks. I encourage student teachers to analyse texts on the basis of genre characteristics and to identify entry points for their young learners (Cameron 2001). They develop their expertise not only in presenting these texts but also in planning story-based activities, such as creative writing, artwork and singing.

Due to the Covid-19 pandemic in 2020, the whole module had to be held in a virtual delivery mode. Within our team of teachers, we decided to offer regular Zoom meetings. This synchronous format was chosen in order to provide real-time interaction that we perceived as essential for student teachers' language practice. Thus, I replaced the face-to-face seminar with weekly ninety-minute web-conferencing sessions. This weekly Zoom session was complemented by an asynchronous element: all texts as well as further reading for weekly assignments were available on the university's online learning platform.

Over the course of two semesters, between April 2020 and February 2021, the design of the virtual seminar was adapted in response to an evaluation of the digital format. In the summer semester 2020, between April and July, the course content was the same as in the traditional face-to-face seminar, encouraging students to carry out activities with the relevant language: regular joint singing of nursery rhymes with accompanying actions, such as 'Incy Wincy Spider', or miming actions for stories, such as *The Hare and the Tortoise* fable (Reilly and Ward 1997). There was also creative writing in connection with the King Arthur legend and artwork in connection with *Goldilocks* (Kaminski 2018). However, some of these activities, such as singing and miming, were experienced as problematic by students due to the lack of a shared physical space. Therefore, in the winter semester of 2020–21, between October and February, I decided to decrease the number of activities that relied on a shared physical space and focus instead on activities that relied on tools that students had commented on positively, in an attempt to make more effective use of digital technology. One of these tools was screen sharing that could be applied for joint discussion as well as group and pair work, both of the latter facilitated through breakout rooms.

In order to do that, I decided to concentrate on one literary text that was available in different adaptations and easily accessible online – the well-known story of *Goldilocks and the Three Bears*. Open access online literature archives were used to study old and new versions of the tale, such as Mure's handwritten manuscript (1831), Southey's version in *The Doctor* (1837/1865), Nicol and Southey's versified story (1839), Cundall's (1850) and Brooke's (1900) Goldilocks's tale, as well as various picturebooks (Delmege and Scott 2012; Sharratt and Tucker 2004; Baxter and Pichon 1999). Video clips that were accessible online were also used, such as YouTube clips for modernized versions of Goldilocks (Playalong 2014), the Goldilocks song and instructions for cooking porridge. This meant that students could still be introduced to different genres and literary devices, and they could also still discuss narrative structure. Moreover, they were able to develop awareness of peritextual features by comparing different versions of the same text. The seminar still featured some artwork, creative writing and cooking, conducted or shared synchronously in one of the weekly sessions on follow-up activities.

In each of the two semesters, the seminar was taught in two parallel groups. Places in the first virtual semester in summer term 2020 were limited to twelve per group due to the fact that it was difficult to envisage which issues would arise from the change of delivery mode; within our team of teachers on the module, it was thought that problems that occurred with emergency remote teaching could more easily be addressed and solved in a smaller learner group. As this implementation was successful, the number of participants per class was increased to sixteen in the following semester, the winter term 2020–21. Between April 20 and February 21, a total of fifty-five MEd students took part in my seminars and completed them.

After students had taken exams and received their results, I invited them to give feedback on the digital seminar. Mirroring the informal feedback system where students are sometimes asked to write anonymously on blank pieces of paper at the end of a semester, this was done in the form of a very simple online survey that contained five items using the free version of *survio*. Since students receive regular requests for comprehensive questionnaires via their university email account, I thought it was important to use a completely different approach in order to encourage response and to avoid fatigue. Students were asked four open-ended questions about the expectations they had when they heard about the change of delivery mode, in how far these were confirmed, aspects that worked well and others that did not. They were also invited to make any additional comments. A total of 27 questionnaires were completed, equalling an overall return rate of 49%. Students produced 127 responses, which ran to a total of 3,451 words. The questionnaire was written in the language of instruction, that is, English, but students were told that they could also reply in German, which is what the majority of respondents opted for.

Using thematic analysis techniques (Braun and Clark 2006), individual student responses for each of the four questions were analysed and broken down into sections if more than one aspect was mentioned. They were then categorized and grouped according to code for further analysis. The aim was to identify prevalent themes in student response that would inform an understanding of what students experienced as challenging or enriching about the digital seminar.

During the implementation, there was an ongoing email discussion with colleagues who taught other online seminars on the same module in order to share insights, and the reflective notes that I produced on a weekly basis provided a form of self-observational data that was later available for triangulation.

Findings

Below I present the findings for each of the two cohorts separately, since the learning context changed over time. Whereas the first cohort (I) had never experienced a situation where all their regular university education was moved online, with different teachers in their modules applying asynchronous and synchronous elements in various ways, the second cohort (II), although still confronted with similar restrictions in their daily lives due to the pandemic, had already gained some experience with digital learning.

First Cohort

Within the first cohort who attended the digital seminar in spring 2020 and were confronted with a one-to-one digital implementation of the traditional face-to-face seminar, student response is characterized by apprehension about the change of delivery mode and also by a need for belonging to a learning community and sensitivity to the lack of physical presence.

From the first cohort, a total of 13 completed questionnaires are available for analysis. When asked about their expectations, 62% of respondents (8) reported that they were worried about the fact that the face-to-face class would be held as a digital seminar. Out of a total of 13 extracts signalling apprehension, the largest number (5, equalling 38%) concerned course organization, with students expecting a 'bumpy start' and 'chaotic' classes (respondents I/J and I/I, respectively). Some comments (3, equalling 23%) also expressed worry about student presentations, which had to be held in the form of a mini teaching session and were a requirement for successful completion of the module. To a lesser extent, students were apprehensive about technical difficulties and the level of difficulty of seminar content, both of which were expressed in 15% of comments, respectively (2 each).

However, in response to question 2 (In how far did the digital seminar turn out to be as you had expected – in how far was it different?), not one student stated that their concerns were confirmed. Instead, comments indicate that their initial apprehension proved unnecessary. Almost 50% (6) of students reported that they had been positively surprised about the digital format of the seminar. Of interest here is the fact that 38% (5 respondents) compared the digital seminar to the conventional delivery mode. Of these, 4 explained their satisfaction by the fact that it had felt almost like a face-to-face seminar, and one commented that the only downside had been that students could not be in the same physical space with one another. The aspect that is mentioned most often in all extracts of student comments (6 equalling 46%) was a sense of 'togetherness' that was established through weekly synchronous meetings allowing for real-time student-student and teacher-student interaction. Students stressed that 'it felt like real uni and not just like working on your own at home', that they enjoyed meeting 'regularly at the same time as in a normal class', that it was 'easy to get in touch with others' and that 'interaction with others was really good' (respondents I/A, I/B, I/G and I/M, respectively). To a lesser extent, extracts from comments to question no. 2 also referred to course organization (5, equalling 38%) with remarks on the seminar 'working without problems', as respondent I/J stated.

When asked about the element of the digital seminar that worked well, comparing work via screen sharing was mentioned most often by students in the first cohort. Forty-six per cent of them (6 students) commented positively on the fact that the screen-sharing tool allows students to show their notes to every participant in class, explaining that as they were sharing their screen with others 'everyone could see and comprehend' and 'when comparing homework, you could look at others' notes and therefore understand it much better' (respondents I/L and I/D, respectively). Thus, screen sharing seemed to enhance the opportunities for engagement and interaction. This additional visual support appears to be a very helpful feature, especially in an L2 learning context. Other positive aspects that were mentioned referred to the choice and provision of material, the organization of group work in breakout rooms (both mentioned by 5 respondents each i.e. 38%) and, again, but to a lesser extent, establishing a sense of 'togetherness' (mentioned by 3 students i.e. 23%).

With reference to aspects that did not work well in a digital format, 6 respondents (46%) mentioned activities that relied on real-life interaction or physical presence. For example, student teachers referred to joint singing and TPR activities, such as *Simon says*, as being less enjoyable via Zoom due to 'acoustic feedback' and the sound being 'distorted' (respondents I/A and I/H, respectively). The fact that it is more difficult 'to evaluate how the others take in what you say and then respond to that' was also mentioned, as well as to use 'your whole body' to mime something (respondents I/C and I/I, respectively). Of course, body posture and gestures are not necessarily visible for the presenter who might have limited space on their screen to see all participants and who can only rely on facial expressions. There was also the realization that participants cannot be addressed directly by looking at them or gesturing towards them (respondent I/I). This suggests that student teachers in this study were aware of the role of teachers' presence, using eye contact and gesture to enhance communication with learners, which has been found to impact positively on learners' motivation and attention (Liu 2021).

This sensitivity to the lack of physical presence was also reflected in students' comments on presentations, which were mentioned by 5 respondents (38%). The general notion expressed here is that it would have been 'easier' to conduct a mini teaching session for young learners that incorporates games or TPR activities in a shared physical space.

Second Cohort

When this is compared to the responses given by students attending the adapted digital class in the winter term, between October 2020 and February 2021, one can say that some of the issues described by the first cohort are no longer as prominent. This is most obvious for expectations students had before taking the class. In the second cohort, 50% of respondents (7/14) expressed apprehension producing a total of 9 extracts explaining their concerns compared to 62% of respondents (9/13) detailing their worries in a total of 13 extracts in the first cohort. The aspects that respondents felt apprehensive about have changed as well. Concerns about technical issues (3 students, equalling 33%) are more prevalent in proportion to concerns about course organization (2 students, equalling 22%), and concerns about group presentations and logistical issues have disappeared. However, there is a new concern that is being voiced which relates to problematic communication and insufficient interaction with other course participants, mentioned by 22%, that is, 2 students. While some students in the first cohort also stated that they had 'no idea' of what to expect, this can no longer be observed. Instead, there is a sentiment not expressed before, and that is frustration. One student reported that their expectation was that this would be another seminar where 'you just had to work through tasks on your own until a certain deadline' (respondent II/H, my translation). This student seemed to refer to previous experience of online classes that were mainly asynchronous and did not provide sufficient teacher-student and student-student interaction.

When asked how their expectations were fulfilled, students' responses are now more varied than after the first semester. Although 'togetherness' and organization are still referred to by 29% (4 respondents) each, these aspects are mentioned more often alongside statements about level of difficulty and the balance of theory and practice (both by 21% equalling 3 respondents). With reference to the former, for example, one student (II/E, my translation) noted that 'live seminars meant that one did not have to be overly self-disciplined'; and regarding the latter, another respondent (II/M) felt that they 'could learn so much' for their future profession. There is also a new theme appearing, namely a sense that this type of digital format might actually have some added value, mentioned by 14%, that is, 2 students. Respondents remarked that they thought the digital format 'worked out better' for them 'than in a normal semester' (II/D), and that they had the feeling that they 'benefitted from the digital delivery mode a lot' (II/F, my translation).

As for aspects that worked well, screen sharing is now mentioned explicitly by only 1 respondent. However, group work in breakout rooms is commented on even more often than before, by 50% (i.e. 7 students). Presentations, mentioned by 43% (6 respondents), are also found to be working well in a digital format. Togetherness appears again in remarks of 36% of respondents (5), and it refers to spending time in changing groups, as well as opportunities for communicating with others and sharing the experience of cooking porridge online, with everyone in their own kitchen.

When it comes to aspects that did not work as well, a few more students now state that there is nothing to comment on (29% as compared to 8% before). When they make critical remarks, however, respondents most often refer to presentations (36% or 5 respondents) which they describe as more challenging with regard to presenting material in front of the camera or interacting with fellow presenters as well as the audience, maybe because they were expecting it to work more smoothly after having gained some experience with web-conferencing. The fact that they had to present their mini teaching session in a digital format is also commented on as 'less authentic' (respondent II/H, my translation). However, explicit remarks on the lack of physical presence impacting negatively on presenting and interacting are no longer made. Instead, one respondent concludes that because one had to adapt how to present material, presenters came up with creative solutions (respondent II/F, my translation).

Discussion and Implications for Research

Going back to the research questions presented in the second section above, findings related to the first question (the affordances and limitations of digital delivery) suggest that students in both semesters showed a great concern for interaction within the learning community. They articulated relief about the fact that synchronous online classes provided a platform for regular contact with other participants for sharing ideas about topics and texts, which is in line with suggestions for establishing presence and creating a learning community (e.g. Moore 1993; Palloff and Pratt 2011; Yamagata-Lynch 2014). Students repeatedly identified screen sharing and group work in breakout sessions as valuable digital tools.

The fact that screen sharing allows all participants to follow more closely what is being talked about, whether the teacher or fellow-students are presenting, is recognized as an affordance by students in this study, implying that additional visual support was provided to an extent they had not previously experienced in a traditional classroom. The management of group work in the weekly web-conferences injected a dynamic element into the meetings, more so than in a face-to-face setting. This is because allocation to breakout rooms was random, and students could not plan who to talk to by choosing where to sit and the grouping was not dependent on the logistic set-up of a physical space. This created surprise and a more authentic communicative situation.

However, especially in the first term of digital teaching, students were acutely aware of a lack of physical presence and how this impacted on activities such as joint singing, miming, orchestrating material during the presentation of a picturebook, cooperating with fellow presenters and addressing individual members of the audience by walking or gesturing towards them and using eye contact.

In order to address these limitations, the number of activities that involved physical interaction was reduced in the second term, which might explain why students were less aware of the lack of physical presence. Furthermore, they had probably become accustomed to less physical contact due to social distancing, which had been in place for more than six months. It may appear as if adapting the class to avoid physical interaction and increasing the use of effective digital tools, such as screen sharing and breakout sessions, resulted in a more successful digital seminar, as illustrated in students' response in the second term. However, it has to be highlighted that this came at the expense of experiencing a number of popular classroom activities that require physical interaction, such as joint singing, miming actions and games involving moving about. At the same time, the constraints imposed by the lack of a shared physical space during their mini teaching lesson also meant that student teachers were forced to plan more carefully how to orchestrate talking and making use of additional visual as well as acoustic support. This is likely to have improved student teachers' awareness of how to use facial expressions, hand gestures, illustrations and sound effectively during shared picturebook sessions or when giving instructions for artwork or games.

The findings of this study, although comprising only a small sample of student teachers over a relatively short period of time, indicate that digital seminars can be a valuable element in the education of language teachers. It seems that traditional course content can be adapted to benefit from the digital delivery mode insofar as student teachers are given the opportunity to focus on and develop one particular aspect of teaching expertise, namely using peritextual features and multimodal elements more effectively. However, more research is needed to better understand how specific digital tools can improve student teachers' skill in applying and orchestrating visual, acoustic, as well as gestural support in primary EFL classrooms, and how student teachers, after realizing how various modes transport meaning, can be encouraged to foster multi-literacy also in their learners.

And yet it has to be noted that physical presence is needed for many cross-curricular activities that help to create a holistic and multisensory learning atmosphere, and that a lack of physical interaction in teacher training would, in the long term, lead to a lack of expertise in student teachers of how to organize and conduct such activities. After all, the idea that young children learn through interaction with their environment, and that therefore the physical learning context needs to be carefully designed in order to allow for activities that foster overall cognitive, social and physical development is a well-established notion within educational research (Gordon Biddle et al. 2013). Thus, digital classes in language teacher education should always be complemented by face-to-face seminars to outbalance these shortcomings.

References

Primary Literature

Baxter, N., and L. Pichon (1999), *Goldilocks and the Three Bears*, London: Ladybird.

Brooke, L. L. (1900), *The Story of the Three Bears*, London: F. Warne. https://archive.org/details/storyofthreebear00broouoft/page/n9/mode/2up (accessed 5 May 2021).

Cundall, J. (1850), *Treasury of Pleasure Books for Young People*, London: Grant & Griffith. https://archive.org/details/treasuryofpleasu00cundiala (accessed 5 May 2021).

Delmege, S., and G. Scott (2012), *Goldilocks and the Three Bears*, Bath: Parragon.

Mure, E. (1831), 'The Story of the Three Bears Metrically Related'. https://static.toron topubliclibrary.ca/da/pdfs/37131062568829d.pdf (accessed 30 April 2021).

Nicol, G., and R. Southey (1839), *The Story of the Three Bears*, 2nd edn, London: Wright, 60, Pall-Mall. https://www.google.de/books/edition/The_story_of_the_three_bears_by_R_Southe/yZUNAAAAQAAJ?hl=de&gbpv=1&kptab=overview (accessed 13 May 2021).

Playalong (2014), 'Goldilocks and the Three Bears – Nursery Rhyme'. https://www.yout ube.com/watch?v=lm3Xjp_ga6E (accessed 13 May 2021).

Sharratt, N., and S. Tucker (2004), *Goldilocks*, London: Macmillan Children's Books.

Southey, R. (1837/1865), *The Doctor*, London: Longman, Rees, Orme, Brown, Green & Longman. https://digicoll.library.wisc.edu/cgi-bin/Literature/Literature-idx?id=Lit erature.RSouthey5 (accessed 13 May 2021).

Secondary Literature

Arnold, J., and T. Murphey, eds (2013), *Meaningful Action: Earl Stevick's Influence on Language Teaching*, Cambridge: Cambridge University Press.

Bernard, R. M., P. C. Abrami, E. Borokhovski, C. A. Wade, R. M. Tamim, M. A. Surkes and E. C. Bethel (2009), 'A Meta-analysis of Three Types of Interaction Treatments in Distance Education', *Review of Educational Research*, 79 (3): 1243–89.

Bland, J. (2013), 'Fairy Tales with a Difference: Creating a Continuum from Primary to Secondary ELT', in J. Bland and C. Lütge (eds), *Children's Literature in Second Language Education*, 85–94, London: Bloomsbury.

Braun, V., and V. Clark (2006), 'Using Thematic Analysis in Psychology', *Qualitative Research in Psychology*, 3 (2): 77–101.

Brewster, J., G. Ellis and D. Girard (2002), *The Primary English Teacher's Guide*, Harlow: Pearson Education.

Brunsmeier, S., and A. Kolb (2017), 'Picturebooks Go Digital – the Potential of Story Apps for the Primary EFL Classroom', *Children's Literature in English Language Education Journal*, 5 (1): 1–20. https://clelejournal.org/article-1-picturebooks-go-digital/ (accessed 14 May 2021).

Cameron, L. (2001), *Teaching Languages to Young Learners*, Cambridge: Cambridge University Press.

Cameron, L. (2004), 'Challenges for ELT from the Expansion in Teaching Children', in G. Ellis and K. Morrow (eds), *ELT Journal: Year of the Young Learner Special Collection*, 9–17, Oxford: Oxford University Press.

de Oliveira Dias, M., R. de Oliveira Albergarias Lopes and A. C. Teles (2020), 'Will Virtual Replace Classroom Teaching? Lessons from Virtual Classes via Zoom in the Times of COVID-19', *Journal of Advances in Education and Philosophy*, 4 (5): 208–13. doi: 10.36348/jaep.2020.v04i05.004.

Dunn, O. (2014), *Introducing English to Young Children: Reading and Writing*, London: Collins.

Dziuban, C., J. Hartmann, F. Juge, P. Moskal and S. Sorg (2006), 'Blended Learning Enters Mainstream', in C. J. Bonk and C. R. Graham (eds), *The Handbook of Blended Learning: Global Perspectives, Local Designs*, 195–208, San Francisco, CA: Pfeiffer.

Edelenbos, P., R. Johnstone and A. Kubanek (2006), 'The Main Pedagogical Principles Underlying the Teaching of Languages to Very Young Learners'. https://ec.europa.eu/assets/eac/languages/policy/language-policy/documents/young_en.pdf (accessed 13 May 2021).

Ellis, G. (2018), 'The Picturebook in Elementary ELT: Multiple Literacies with Bob Staake's *Bluebird*', in J. Bland (ed.), *Using Literature in English Language Education*, 83–104, London: Bloomsbury.

Ellis G., T. Gruenbaum, S. Mourão and A. Sadowska (2018), 'PEPELT21'. https://pepel t21.com/ (accessed 13 May 2021).

García Bermejo, M. L., and M. T. Fleta Guillén (2013), 'The "Art" of Teaching Creative Story Writing', in J. Bland and C. Lütge (eds), *Children's Literature in Second Language Education*, 195–204, London: Bloomsbury.

Ghosn, I.-K. (2013), *Storybridge to Second Language Literacy: The Theory, Research and Practice of Teaching English with Children's Literature*, Charlotte, NC: Information Age.

Golonka, E. M., A. R. Bowles, V. M. Frank, D. L. Richardson and S. Freynik (2014), 'Technologies for Foreign Language Learning: A Review of Technology Types and Their Effectiveness', *Computer Assisted Language Learning*, 27 (1): 70–105. doi: 10.1080/09588221.2012.700315.

Gordon Biddle, K. A., A. Garcia-Nevarez, W. J. Roundtree Henderson and A. Valero-Kerrik (2013), *Early Childhood Education: Becoming a Professional*, Los Angeles: Sage.

Graham, C. R., W. Woodfield and J. B. Harrison (2013), 'A Framework for Institutional Adoption and Implementation of Blended Learning in Higher Education', *Internet and Higher Education*, 18: 4–14. doi: 10.1016/j.iheduc.2012.09.003.

Henderson, M., N. Selwyn and R. Aston (2015), 'What Works and Why? Student Perceptions of "Useful" Digital Technology in University Teaching and Learning', *Studies in Higher Education*, 42 (8): 1567–79. doi: 10.1080/03075079.2015.1007946.

Hockly, N. (2015), 'Developments in Online Language Learning', *ELT Journal*, 69 (3): 308–13. doi: 10.1093/elt/ccv020.

Hodges, C., S. Moore, B. Lockee, T. Trust and A. Bond (2020), 'The Difference between Emergency Remote Teaching and Online Learning', *EDUCAUSE Review*. https://er.educause.edu/articles/2020/3/the-difference-between-emergency-remote-teaching-and-online-learning (accessed 13 May 2021).

Kaminski, A. (2018), 'Goldilocks and the Three Bears: ein Märchen aus der Schatztruhe des englischsprachigen Kulturraumes', in B. Smieja and O. Weyrauch (eds), *Fächerübergreifender Grundschulunterricht: Beiträge aus Theorie und Praxis*, 157–80, Frankfurt/Main: Peter Lang.

Kaminski, A. (2020), 'Creating a Multimodal and Holistic Learning Experience with Catherine Rayner's *Augustus and His Smile*', *Children's Literature in English Language Education*, 8 (2): 39–64. https://clelejournal.org/article-2-annett-kaminski/ (accessed 13 May 2021).

Lenkaitis, C. A., S. M. Hilliker and K. Roumeliotis (2020), 'Teacher Candidate Reflection and Development through Virtual Exchange', *IAFOR Journal of Education: Technology in Education*, 8 (2): 127–41. https://issuu.com/iafor/docs/10.22492.ije.8.2 (accessed 13 May 2021).

Liu, W. (2021), 'Does Teacher Immediacy Affect Students? A Systematic Review of the Association between Teacher Verbal and Non-verbal Immediacy and Student Motivation', *Frontiers in Psychology*, 12. https://www.frontiersin.org/articles/10.3389/fpsyg.2021.713978/full (accessed 13 November 2021). doi: 10.3389/fpsyg.2021.713978.

Means, B., M. Bakia and R. Murphy (2014), *Learning Online: What Research Tells Us about Whether, When and How*, New York: Routledge.

Moon J. (2005), *Children Learning English*, London: Macmillan.

Moore, M. G. (1972), 'Learner Autonomy: The Second Dimension of Independent Learning', *Convergence*, V (2): 76–88.

Moore, M. G. (1993), 'Theory of Transactional Distance', in D. Keegan (ed.), *Theoretical Principles of Distance Education*, 22–38, London: Routledge.

Mourão, S. (2013), 'Picturebook: Object of Discovery', in J. Bland and C. Lütge (eds), *Children's Literature in Second Language Education*, 71–84, London: Bloomsbury.

Mourão, S., and G. Ellis (2020), *Teaching English to Pre-primary Children*, Stuttgart: Delta.

Naidu, S. (2017), 'Openness and Flexibility Are the Norm, but What Are the Challenges?', *Distance Education*, 38: 1–4. https://www.tandfonline.com/doi/full/10.1080/01587919.2017.1297185 (accessed 12 November 2021).

Palloff, R. M., and K. Pratt (2011), *The Excellent Online Instructor: Strategies for Professional Development*, San Francisco, CA: Jossey-Bass.

Paran, A., C. Furneaux and N. Sumner (2004), 'Computer-Mediated Communication in Distance MA Programmes: The Student's Perspective', *System*, 32 (3): 337–55.

Phillips, M. (2010), 'The Perceived Value of Videoconferencing with Primary Pupils Learning to Speak a Modern Language', *Language Learning Journal*, 38 (2): 221–38. doi: 10.1080/09571731003790532.

Piaget, J., and B. Inhelder (1969), *The Psychology of the Child*, New York: Basic.

Pinter, A. (2006), *Teaching Young Language Learners*, Oxford: Oxford University Press.

Pritchard, A., M. Hunt and A. Barnes (2010), 'Case Study Investigation of a Videoconferencing Experiment in Primary Schools, Teaching Modern Foreign Languages', *Language Learning Journal*, 38 (2): 209–20. doi: 10.1080/09571731003790508.

Read, C. (2006), 'Supporting Teachers in Supporting Learners', in J. Enever and G. Schmid-Schönbein (eds), *MAFF 14: Picture Books and Young Learners of English*, Munich: Langenscheidt.

Read, C. (2007), *500 Activities for the Primary Classroom*, Oxford: Macmillan.

Read, C. (2020), 'How to Implement a WHOLE Child Approach in the Early Years', *TEYLT Worldwide* 2: 28–32.

Reilly, V., and S. M. Ward (1997), *Very Young Learners*, Oxford: Oxford University Press.

Selwyn, N. (2020), 'Online Learning: Rethinking Teachers' "Digital Competence" in Light of Covid-19', *Lens*. https://lens.monash.edu/@education/2020/04/30/1380 217/online-learning-rethinking-teachers-digital-competence-in-light-of-Covid-19 (accessed 13 May 2021).

Shen, C.-H. C. (2014), 'An Investigation of Young EFL Learners' Use of Online Reading Strategies', *Official Conference Proceedings: The Inaugural European Conference on Technology in the Classroom 2013*, 251–9. http://papers.iafor.org/wp-content/uplo ads/conference-proceedings/ECTC/ECTC2013_proceedings.pdf (accessed 13 May 2021).

Yamagata-Lynch, L. C. (2014), 'Blending Online Asynchronous and Synchronous Learning', *International Review of Research in Open and Distance Learning*, 15 (2): 189–212. doi: 10.19173/irrodl.v15i2.1778.

Part 4

Tools and Concepts for Teaching Literature Online

7

Implementing a Collaborative Reading Project Online: Solutions for a Pedagogically Meaningful Virtual Workshop

Jennifer Schumm Fauster

Introduction

In March of 2020, the country of Austria, like many other European countries, went into lockdown due to the Covid-19 pandemic, which resulted in educational institutions moving their teaching to online platforms practically overnight. At the time of the lockdown the fifty pre-service English as a foreign language (EFL) teachers attending parallel classes of my course 'Teaching Literature and Promoting Intercultural Competence' in the English language teaching (ELT) programme at the University of Graz had just begun a collaborative reading project with two fourth-form classes of approximately fifty pupils at a local secondary school. Uncertain as to how the school year would continue and whether we would have the opportunity to go back to the classroom, my colleagues from the local secondary school and I had to make a quick decision as to whether we would continue with the collaborative reading project, and if yes, how we could implement the final stage of the project, the Crossing Borders Workshop, in case we had to carry it out virtually.

In this chapter, I will first describe the context of the collaborative reading project and how it is carried out under 'normal' circumstances. Then I will turn to the various aspects which were taken into consideration when we moved the Crossing Borders Workshop online, specifically how we included both synchronous and asynchronous learning. This chapter will conclude with a reflection on lessons learned for future online teaching in general and the collaborative reading project in particular as well as implications for research in teaching literature online.

Context

The collaborative reading project has been a component of my ELT course 'Teaching Literature and Promoting Intercultural Competence' for eight years. Approximately twenty-four students take part in the course, which is offered every semester. The ELT programme is based on a loose modular structure, which gives students considerable freedom concerning the order in which they complete their coursework. As a result, some pre-service EFL teachers may already have practical teaching experience and be further along in the teaching programme than others attending the course.

The purpose of the course 'Teaching Literature and Promoting Intercultural Competence' is to introduce pre-service EFL teachers to ways in which they can integrate literature into their language classrooms and address intercultural issues. Therefore, the main objectives of the course are

- to develop thoughtful and principled approaches to using literature and promoting intercultural competence in the language classroom,
- to provide opportunities for developing classroom materials for teaching literature and enhancing intercultural competence and
- to present ways of using literature which will help learners to improve their English.

In addition to weekly in-person classes, the pre-service EFL teachers also work with fourteen-year-old pupils from local secondary schools on a collaborative reading project, which includes a workshop that takes place at these schools (see section titled 'Collaborative Reading Project under "Normal" Circumstances' for detailed information about the Crossing Borders Workshop). Participation in the collaborative reading project provides these pre-service EFL teachers with the unique opportunity to design materials for teaching literature with a specific focus on intercultural issues and to try them out with pupils. As many of the students who take part in the course have had only limited experience with working with literature during their schooling and their internships as pre-service teachers, they perceive this part of the course as very useful for their future teaching. A reason for their limited experience may be what Dalton-Puffer, Boeckmann and Hinger (2019: 216) refer to as 'the progressive marginalisation of literature in the Austrian FL curriculum, where it is mentioned as one in a row of possible "topics" along with family, food, or adolescence at lower and as one "text type" among many at upper secondary level'. Thus, the collaborative reading project plays an important role in showing pre-service teachers that literature has a place in the language curriculum by providing them with the opportunity to experience how literature can be integrated into the language classroom.

The first objective of the collaborative reading project is to enhance pupils' intercultural competence, which is in line with the Austrian curriculum for secondary schools (BMBWF 2018). According to the Austrian curriculum, this transversal principle should be included across the curriculum, thus underlining its interdisciplinary nature (BMBWF 2017). 'Intercultural education' is defined as a principle which should help learners develop an open-minded attitude towards otherness, raise their awareness of Eurocentric and ethnocentric beliefs and provide them with the skills to explore different perspectives in heterogeneous societies (BMBWF 2017).

The second objective is to provide pre-service EFL teachers with the opportunity to design classroom materials which can be used with literature in order to enhance learners' intercultural understanding. The materials should consider the objectives as described in Byram's (1997) model of intercultural communicative competence, thus particular attention is paid to attitudes, knowledge, skills of interpreting and relating and critical cultural awareness. An advantage of working with Byram's model is that it provides pre-service EFL teachers with a set of teaching objectives which they can draw on when designing their materials.

Finally, the third objective of the reading project is to provide pupils and pre-service EFL teachers alike with the opportunity to share their reading experiences in an atmosphere where everyone can express themselves freely. This approach to working with literature is in line with what Rosenblatt (1995) refers to as aesthetic reading, which is one aspect of her reader-response theory. Rosenblatt describes this approach to reading as one that emphasizes 'the personal associations, feelings, and ideas being lived through during the reading' (292). Taking an aesthetic approach to literature can be particularly effective when working with young learners as it allows them to form opinions about what they have read and learn to support these views with concrete examples (Rosenblatt 1995). As one of the goals of the collaborative reading project is to share reading experiences of both pupils and pre-service EFL teachers, an aesthetic approach to reading facilitates this.

Collaborative Reading Project under 'Normal' Circumstances

The collaborative reading project takes place in three main stages.

Stage 1 usually lasts approximately four to six weeks. During this stage, all participants (pre-service EFL teachers and pupils) choose from a list of pre-selected multicultural young adult novels (see Appendix A for a list of books used in the project) and work with the same reading booklet, which is divided into pre-, while- and post-reading activities designed to support the reading process. The three pre-reading activities focus primarily on the learners' personal (inter)cultural experiences and identity in order to activate schemata and prepare them for reading their books. The activities require them to write a cultural autobiography; consider the role that the languages they speak have concerning their identity; and reflect on previous intercultural encounters. The while-reading activities help to support the reading and focus more on the theme of the reading project, namely crossing borders. These include activities such as finding places in the reading where the characters cross borders both physically and metaphorically; comparing key concepts in the novels, such as hope, dreams and being a stranger with their own views and experiences; and reflecting on their understanding of stereotypes and the role they play in their books. The post-reading activities require readers to consider the whole reading experience. They are required to draw a Venn diagram in which they compare their culture(s) with those of the main character; fill in a story pie which summarizes the main points of their book; design sociograms showing the relationships among the characters of their books; and take part in literature circles (see Schumm Fauster and Pölzleitner (2013) for more detailed information about the individual tasks). It is important to note that this part of the project takes an extensive reading approach as the pupils and pre-service EFL teachers can choose their books, read more for information and general understanding, read at their own pace and do most of the reading as homework (Bamford and Day 2004). In this first stage, there is a considerable amount of independent work; however, teachers do make periodic checks in order to ensure that everyone is keeping up with the reading and the tasks in the booklet.

During stage 2, which normally lasts approximately two weeks, pupils prepare interactive presentations of their books with an emphasis on plot, setting, characters, themes, personal evaluations and overall message. These may be in the form of PowerPoint presentations. However, they often consist of pupils acting out key scenes from their books, presenting their books in a talk-show format and/or doing 'Novel Museum' presentations during which they display a number of items that play a role in their given books and then act like museum tour guides who present the artefacts to the class and explain the importance of each item. At the same time, the pre-service EFL teachers design interactive materials focusing on intercultural issues addressed in the books and try out these materials within the framework of their university course. In this way they receive oral feedback from their peers on their materials based on criteria prepared by their teacher and can make any required changes before doing the tasks with the pupils.

In the final stage of the project, the four-hour Crossing Borders Workshop takes place. It begins with a fifteen-minute ice-breaker in which pupils and pre-service EFL teachers mix and mingle and introduce themselves by using realia that represent them culturally. After this, pupils give ten- to fifteen-minute interactive presentations on the books that they have read. The presentations provide information about the plot, setting, characters, themes, personal evaluations and overall message of the books. The purpose of the presentations is to provide all participants with information about the books, since everyone has read only one of the pre-selected books. In this way, the presentations prepare participants for the second part of the Crossing Borders Workshop where intercultural aspects raised in the books are discussed as they are provided with important information about them. The second part of the Crossing Borders Workshop lasts approximately two to three hours. During this time, the pre-service EFL teachers set up stations for each of the respective books and the pupils move from station to station working on activities that address intercultural issues raised in the books. This method is often referred to as the 'World Café method' (The World Café 2020). Pupils usually stay at each station for approximately twenty minutes. The Crossing Borders Workshop ends with a debriefing activity, which lasts approximately fifteen minutes, during which pupils and pre-service EFL teachers are asked to reflect on the workshop and their takeaways.

Moving the Crossing Borders Workshop Online

The decision to implement the Crossing Borders Workshop online required a number of considerations, including whether it was actually doable. However, there were certain aspects that were important for my colleagues at the secondary school and me. For example, the first important aspect was to ensure that the virtual Crossing Borders Workshop would be an experience, not just a transfer of information, thus keeping in line with Moore (2020) who states that 'the most important principle for designing lively eLearning is to see eLearning design not as information design but as designing an experience'. Another important consideration was to ensure that the objectives of the collaborative reading project were met. Finally, we wanted to provide our learners with a large choice of learning options (Ocriciano 2020a).

Although my colleagues and I were clear about our overall aims, moving the Crossing Borders Workshop to an online environment still posed a number of challenges. Firstly, we had to consider what platform would be best suited for the workshop. Secondly, we needed to devise a timetable which was flexible and gave everyone involved enough time to be able to take part in the online activities. Finally, we had to consider how the transitional changes would be most effectively communicated to all participants as our only form of communication was online.

Choosing the Appropriate Platform

One of the 'four pillars' necessary for online learning is 'adopting a user-friendly learning environment and flexible online technical support' (Roddy et al. 2017: 6). With this in mind, my colleagues and I quickly decided on the platform: Microsoft Teams. The platform itself is user-friendly as there is a clear distribution of content to users. In addition, the pupils involved in the reading project were already using it in their virtual English classes, which meant that they were familiar with the platform's functions and knew how to navigate it. Many pre-service EFL teachers attending my course also had experience with the platform due to their internships in schools and online teaching practice. For this reason, the platform was not completely new to them. As a result, those pre-service EFL teachers who had less experience with the platform could ask their more experienced colleagues for help. This turned out to be very helpful as there was no opportunity to provide any professional training due to time constraints. Thus, there were fewer 'technical-based hurdles', which Roddy et al. (2017: 6) find particularly important in order 'to increase student retention and engagement' especially in online learning environments which are used only over a shorter period of time. According to Roddy et al., in intensive learning environments, 'there is less available time to acclimatize to new tools and operating environments' (2), which makes it even more vital that the choice of platform is carefully considered. If working with the online tools becomes too cumbersome, interest and engagement are likely to suffer (Roddy et al. 2017).

In addition to most participants having experience with Microsoft Teams, another advantage is that the platform provides a variety of functions which allow for interaction between everyone involved in the project (e.g. pupils, pre-service EFL teachers and instructors). One of the findings of Bailey and Card's (2009) study of effective online instruction, conducted amongst e-learning instructors at the tertiary level, was that engagement is essential for productive online learning. The various functions on the Microsoft Teams platform allowed for engagement in a number of ways. Firstly, the chatroom function gave participants the opportunity to discuss their reading experiences in real time. Secondly, participants could share their work, be it in the form of presentations prepared by the pupils or as materials devised by the pre-service EFL language teachers. In addition, Microsoft Teams has a function which allows participants to give each other feedback on their work. Finally, all of the instructors involved in the online Crossing Borders Workshop could monitor the work and thus 'establish presence' (Spataro 2020: 11). According to Spataro (2020), one way to best utilize online platforms is to ensure that instructors are visible by providing support and motivation where necessary. This was done by writing reminders to everyone about online assignments, providing feedback on materials that had been uploaded and leaving encouraging messages to motivate everyone to continue to do the online activities.

Planning the Online Crossing Borders Workshop

After deciding on the platform, the next step when moving the collaborative Crossing Borders Workshop online was to consider the timeline and also which mode the workshop would occur in: synchronous and/or asynchronous learning. Ocriciano states that 'planning, prioritising and defining are key elements when building e-learning' (2020b: 8). We quickly noted that the learning objectives and priorities of the collaborative reading project and, more specifically, the Crossing Borders Workshop did not need to be adapted to the online format that we had chosen. Therefore, our main focus was on planning the online workshop.

'Flexibility' is a term often used to describe effective online teaching (Bailey and Card 2009; Ocriciano 2020b). When it came to organizing the online Crossing Borders Workshop, it was very important for everyone involved to be flexible by 'keeping an open mind and having the ability to adapt' (Bailey and Card 2009: 154). This was especially the case concerning time issues as the various schedules of the pupils, pre-service EFL teachers and their instructors needed to be considered as did the time needed to design the online activities and complete them. Therefore, we decided to turn a four-hour workshop into a four-week online workshop in order to provide participants with enough time to properly design and engage with the online activities. This meant that in comparison to the learning objectives of the online Crossing Borders Workshop, a major change in the time frame was made due to the online format.

When planning online learning, Ocriciano advises combining both synchronous and asynchronous activities 'to offer a more complete learning experience' (2020b: 8). Synchronous learning means that teachers and learners meet virtually in real time. For this reason, 'it is inextricably tied to classroom instruction'; thus, according to Bernard et al., 'it may be viewed as an extension of, or as a special case of classroom instruction' (2004: 102). Ocriciano (2020b) notes some of the advantages of this form of online teaching are that it allows for exchange of information, including answering questions and discussions. Typical tools include online classes, chatrooms and webinars. In contrast to synchronous learning, during asynchronous learning, 'students in remote locations work independently' and the instructor does not need to be present in real time (Bernard et al. 2004: 102). According to Ocriciano (2020b), this approach to online learning can enhance learner autonomy and allows for more flexibility. Online tools often used are email, online forums and pre-recorded classes.

As the pupils and pre-service EFL teachers had very different schedules, we decided to include more asynchronous learning opportunities when planning the Crossing Borders Workshop. However, to provide all the participants with an opportunity to interact with each other in real time and share their reading experiences, we did include one synchronous element in the final week of the project. The following is the final shape of the online Crossing Borders Workshop (see Appendix C for the information provided to pre-service EFL teachers about the changes).

Week 1: The online mode of working for the first week was asynchronous. The pupils were required to upload the presentations of their books (e.g. voiced-over PowerPoints; videotaped presentations of pupils acting out scenes and discussing content) to the Microsoft Teams platform at the beginning of the school week (Monday), and the pre-service EFL teachers were given a week to view all of the presentations and provide feedback for each one in the forum function. The pupils also had the opportunity to respond to the feedback.

As this was the first online contact, the pre-service EFL teachers were instructed to provide feedback that was informal in tone and encouraging by highlighting the positive aspects of the pupils' presentations to cultivate the online relationships. My colleagues and I felt that having the pre-service teachers follow specific guidelines concerning online feedback might give the pupils the feeling that they were being assessed and thus have a negative influence on the online relationships. In this way, we hoped to promote a 'sense of belongingness and community' (Roddy et al. 2017: 7), which is considered key for learners' online success. In addition, taking an asynchronous approach provided a rather non-threatening atmosphere for everyone involved as the pupils could prepare their presentations ahead of time under the guidance of their teachers instead of presenting them in real time, and the pre-service EFL teachers had enough time to watch the pupils' presentations and provide feedback.

Weeks 2 and 3: The online mode of working for weeks two and three was also asynchronous. This part of the online Crossing Borders Workshop could be compared to the World Café method which was used when doing the workshop in the classroom. At the beginning of week 2 of the online Crossing Borders Workshop, the pre-service EFL teachers uploaded self-designed worksheets which comprised a variety of activities addressing intercultural issues in the books that all participants had read. It is important to note that the pupils did not only complete worksheets related to the book that they had chosen for the reading project but also worksheets referring to intercultural issues in the other books. This means that the worksheets often addressed more general intercultural aspects such as cultural identity or considering the overall theme 'Crossing Borders' so that all pupils could do the activities regardless of whether they had read a certain book or not (see Appendix B for sample activities). After the pre-service EFL teachers had uploaded their materials, the pupils began working on them. The pupils had approximately two weeks to complete the worksheets and upload their work to the Microsoft Teams platform.

Week 4: The online mode of working for week 4 was synchronous. At the end of week 3, the instructors uploaded sign-up sheets to the Microsoft Teams platform in which two pupils and two pre-service EFL teachers could sign up for synchronous online meetings in chatrooms at designated times. The meetings in the chatrooms lasted ten to fifteen minutes and the pre-service EFL teachers were required to devise questions to facilitate the discussions in case the pupils were reluctant to communicate. Before the pre-service EFL teachers met with the pupils online, they were given some guidelines for running the meetings:

1. The online meetings should be seen as informal reading circles.
2. They should be conducted in English as much as possible.
3. The online meetings should not be seen as 'teaching sessions' but rather as an opportunity for everyone to share their ideas.
4. In preparation for the meetings, some questions should be prepared to facilitate the online discussion. Suggested topics are: (1)

ice-breaker – introduce yourself and then show an object and explain how it represents you culturally; (2) reviews of books – what did the pupils like/ not like and why? Who was their favourite character? What insights did they gain about intercultural issues? What is the message of their book? and so on; (3) reflection on the online experience – how was their online experience? What part did they like the most? Were they happy with the feedback that they received on their presentations? and so on.

The purpose of this final part of the project was to allow all participants to share their reading experiences. This final week was also seen as a way to wrap up the Crossing Borders Workshop and give all participants the chance to meet and discuss their books in chatrooms. The pupils and pre-service EFL teachers worked in pairs so that there were four participants in each chatroom, which my colleagues and I hoped would enhance everyone's willingness to communicate as more people were involved in ensuring that the discussions were successful.

Communicating Changes to the Collaborative Crossing Borders Workshop Format

Before beginning the collaborative online Crossing Borders Workshop, the pupils and pre-service EFL teachers still needed to be informed about the platform that we intended to use, the time frame and the mode of learning (synchronous or asynchronous). When teaching in the classroom, this most likely would have required an in-class explanation via a PowerPoint presentation and a handout as a reminder. As I was only meeting with my students virtually, communicating the changes required much more thought. According to West, when teaching online, 'communication is key' and 'more attention needs to be focused on how we express ourselves clearly and effectively' (2020: 15). The importance of clear and timely communication was also highlighted as one of the most important elements of effective online teaching in Bailey and Card's (2007) study on effective online teaching.

In order to communicate with the EFL pre-service teachers, the information for the online Crossing Borders Workshop was presented both synchronously and asynchronously. Concerning the latter, an information sheet outlining the time frame and stages was sent to all participants via email so that they could process the information at their own pace and consider any questions that they might have about the online Crossing Borders Workshop (see Appendix C for the outline). After that, a synchronous Q&A session was held where once again the virtual Crossing Borders Workshop was presented, and participants had the opportunity to ask the questions they had prepared. While more time-consuming, this two-pronged approach to communicating changes proved to be quite effective as the questions that occurred during the actual four-week online Crossing Borders Workshop did not refer as much to the activities and time frame, but more to technical difficulties with navigating the platform and breakdowns in internet connections during the online chats.

Lessons Learned: Key Takeaways

Moving the Crossing Borders Workshop to an online platform required flexibility and adaptability for everyone involved. Below are some of the key takeaways based on our observations.

Choosing the Right Learning Platform Is Vital

Based on teachers' observations and feedback from the participants, Microsoft Teams was an effective learning platform for the Crossing Borders Workshop as the learning objectives could be achieved by using it. For the most part, it was easy for everyone involved to navigate, which Spataro sees as the 'golden rule' of online learning (2020: 10). It was naturally an advantage that many of the participants were already acquainted with the platform, but it seemed to pose very few difficulties for those who were not, including me.

As I have explained above, the Microsoft Teams platform provided tools for both synchronous and asynchronous learning and thus offered multiple opportunities for working with literature while at the same time ensuring that the overall objectives of the Crossing Borders Workshop were met. For example, although the pupils' presentations of their books were not held in real time, taking a time-independent asynchronous approach proved to be just as effective. The pupils were still able to fulfil the task of presenting their book. In addition, since the presentations were recorded they had the opportunity to rerecord parts they were unsatisfied with, which seemed to improve the overall quality of their presentations. In fact, the pupils seemed more invested in ensuring that the overall quality of their online book presentations and the comments and insights they shared about their books was higher than when they were held in real time. This may be due to the permanency of asynchronous online work, which can be viewed again and again compared with synchronous work, unless it is recorded. The quality of feedback from the pre-service EFL teachers was also very high. A reason for this may be that they could view the presentations when it was convenient for them, as the assignment was time independent. This meant the pre-service EFL teachers had more time to formulate constructive feedback on the pupils' presentations, which is not always possible when presenting in real time. Another reason may be that they were aware of the fact that their feedback would be read not only by the pupils but also by everyone who had access to the platform, including the instructors.

The Role of Good Pedagogy Should Not Be Underestimated

While the form of media is obviously important in order to teach effectively online, the actual level of effectiveness seems to depend on the pedagogy underlining it. This observation is also supported by the findings of Murphy, Rodríguez-Manzanares and Barbor's (2011) study of synchronous and asynchronous teaching in Canadian high school distance learning. Their findings showed that pedagogy played a more important role in online environments than the types of media used for both modes of teaching. Therefore, while the choice of media is important, it is only as good as the pedagogy behind it.

While preparing the online Crossing Borders Workshop, it was important that the instructions were clearly expressed and presented in a timely manner. In addition, it was important that activities done under 'normal' circumstances could still be carried out in a way that ensured the overall objectives were met. While moving the Crossing Borders Workshop online was certainly an achievement, especially under the given circumstances, we would not have been as satisfied with the outcome if we had not been able to use the Microsoft Teams platform in a pedagogically sound way. For example, the importance of participants' interaction and sharing understandings has always been an important aspect of the Crossing Borders Workshop as this seems to provide deeper insights into the books read and intercultural concepts. For this reason, the instructors tried to design an online workshop which aimed to achieve this by providing pupils and pre-service EFL teachers with as many opportunities to interact with each other. This seemed to have been achieved with the book presentations and online feedback as well as the meetings in chatrooms. In both cases, the pedagogical considerations informing the activities seemed to help us reach the objectives of the project.

In contrast, we may need to reconsider our decision of taking an asynchronous approach to replace the activity of the Crossing Borders Workshop where the pupils move from station to station and take part in activities dealing with intercultural issues addressed in their books. While the pre-service EFL teachers did their best to design interesting activities, the lack of interaction in real time, due to the asynchronous approach, meant that most pupils did the worksheets on their own and submitted them like homework. When the Crossing Borders Workshop takes place in real time, the pupils and pre-service EFL teachers work together on the given activities to construct meaning and thus gain deeper insights into the intercultural issues discussed. In addition, the pre-service EFL teachers can provide guidance where needed. This personal contact was missing. Therefore, while the objectives of this part of the Crossing Borders Workshop could still be met in the online format, the lack of real-time interaction seemed to affect its overall effectiveness in dealing with intercultural issues raised in the books in more depth.

Importance of Establishing Teaching Presence

For Anderson (2004), teaching presence is vital for effective online teaching. This includes 'design and organization, facilitating discourse, and direct instruction' (291). Anderson's observation is also in line with our online experience, especially concerning the following points: facilitating discourse and direct instruction. While design and organization were certainly important to ensure that the Crossing Borders Workshop ran smoothly, the online presence of the instructors of the workshop seemed to play a decisive role in ensuring that pupils and pre-service EFL teachers stayed engaged and active until the very end. This did not only mean answering questions about the workshop in a timely manner but also being present on the Microsoft Teams platform, taking part in the asynchronous tasks and being available for questions that came up during the week of synchronous teaching where the pupils and pre-service EFL teachers chatted with each other. Concerning the synchronous online meetings in the chatrooms, we observed that we could have taken an even more active role by being present at the start of the meetings, especially in cases where pupils and pre-service EFL teachers required a bit more prompting. Thus, our experience as instructors is very much in line with Anderson's (2004) assessment of the role of the teacher in online settings when he states that seeing the role of a teacher as only that of an online facilitator devalues it. Just like in a classroom setting, a teacher working online needs to take an active role in instruction not only concerning the topic at hand but also regarding pedagogical aspects.

Good Communication Is Imperative for Online Learning

In the case of our collaborative online Crossing Borders Workshop, good communication was necessary not only between the teachers and their classes of pre-service language teachers and secondary level pupils but also amongst the teachers involved in the project. In addition, it was essential that the communication was effective and timely (Bailey and Card 2009). For example, initially, the instructors involved in the planning of the online Crossing Borders Workshop communicated via email; however, we soon turned to using Microsoft Teams to avoid misunderstandings due to communication lines often crossing. A similar tendency could be found when communicating with participants in the project. While email was useful for informing participants about general planning, a quick online meeting often cleared up issues which would have required a number of emails to clarify.

However, while communication to impart information seemed essential for the online Crossing Borders Workshop, how that information was communicated was also important. This is in line with the findings of Bailey and Card, who note that instructors 'have to be very attentive to their communicating styles and the words they use' as paralinguistic aspects such as tone of voice and body language may play less of a role in virtual learning environments (2009: 154). Naturally, this aspect is important for everyone involved in the communication, but as one participant in Bailey and Card's study noted, teachers 'have to be careful with [their] wording so that they [learners] don't take things the wrong way' (154). The importance of how information is communicated could particularly be noted in the first activity where pre-service EFL teachers were required to provide feedback on the pupils' presentations. As this was the first interaction between the pupils and pre-service EFL teachers, we stressed to the latter how important it was to provide constructive and more informal feedback in order to establish rapport. This type of feedback did not only result in more discussion between the pupils and pre-service EFL teachers about the presentations and books but also seemed to contribute to all participants' willingness to take part in the activities planned for the following three weeks, because a positive atmosphere had been established. Therefore, the good communication did not only lead to more exchange concerning the literature read but was also instrumental in contributing to the overall success of the online Crossing Borders Workshop.

Learners' Need for Human Interaction

A final key takeaway is that when working online, learners still require human interaction. This point has already been alluded to when referring to the teacher's presence and the importance of good communication, but based on my colleagues' and my own observations throughout the four-week online Crossing Borders Workshop, it seems to go beyond this. This chimes with West's observations of her students' changing online communication behaviour, where learners seemed 'to be craving increased human interaction with an appetite for everyday discussions' (2020: 15). For this reason, she suggests reserving time for 'authentic conversations' (15).

Our online observations appeared to be quite similar. One example of this is the constructive feedback that the pre-service EFL teachers provided for the pupils' presentations. According to the teachers at the secondary school, their fourth-form pupils particularly enjoyed this part of the online Crossing Borders Workshop as they had invested quite a lot of time in their presentations and received very positive and constructive feedback. The pupils responded to all of the pre-service EFL teachers' comments and lively discussions occurred concerning various details of the presentations of their books and issues related to their readings. In addition, the synchronous meetings in the chatrooms, in which two pupils and two pre-service EFL teachers met, were also seen in a positive light as everyone had the opportunity to not only share their reading experiences with real people but also talk to them in real time. Based on feedback from the pre-service EFL teachers, the pupils sometimes needed prompting. However, after the preliminaries, they were generally very willing to discuss their books. The pre-service teachers were particularly impressed by the pupils' interest in talking about social issues, in particular the Black Lives Matters movement and migration, which were addressed in many of the books they read.

Implications for Future Collaborative Reading Projects

As previously mentioned in the section titled 'Collaborative Reading Project under "Normal" Circumstances', stages 1 and 2 of the collaborative reading project are carried out for the most part with limited interaction between the fourth-form pupils and the pre-service EFL teachers. This is due, in part, to conflicting schedules and the fact that organizing meetings in real time involving between fifty and one hundred people has always seemed unfeasible. For this reason, pupils and pre-service EFL teachers have generally had their first encounters with each other on the day of the Crossing Borders Workshop. The instructors involved in organizing the reading project have always felt that it would be even more effective if there was communication between pupils and the pre-service EFL teachers before this event.

To give participants more opportunities to discuss their books, share their reading experiences and enhance overall communication, my colleagues at the secondary school and I are considering organizing a number of meetings in online chatrooms on Microsoft Teams. To ensure that the online meetings are meaningful for the collaborative reading project, a topic will be suggested for each online meeting, such as requiring participants to introduce themselves by choosing an object that says something about their cultural backgrounds, sharing intercultural insights obtained while reading their books and reflecting on the messages of the given books and passages that hold a particular meaning either for the overall plot and/or the reader. By including virtual online meetings as a part of our collaborative reading project, we hope to facilitate the participants' reading experience and interaction at the Crossing Borders Workshop.

As far as making changes to the actual Crossing Borders Workshop based on our online experience, we are considering giving the fourth-form pupils the choice between recording their presentations ahead of time or doing them in real time. During the online Crossing Borders Workshop, pupils had no option but to record their videos, and this resulted in them acquiring useful skills such as preparing interactive voiced-over PowerPoints and recording themselves acting out various scenes and/or presenting certain aspects of their books while talking into the camera. By providing the pupils with this option, we would also address some issues that arise during the Crossing Borders Workshop. These include saving time setting up pupils' interactive presentations, the nervousness that some pupils experience when having to present in front of a live audience and scheduling conflicts that lead to pupils being unable to take part in their book presentations. Therefore, pupils will be given the option to present in the format they prefer because some may find it to be more natural to present face-to-face rather than provide a video as this will be done in real time. Regardless of their choice, the pupils will still have the opportunity to gain useful experience for giving presentations.

Implications for Research

This chapter has shown that working with literature in collaboration with other institutions is possible on an online platform and can have similar results to running such a workshop in real time (see also Chapter 11 in this volume for an online creative writing project). In the future, research could be designed to compare the learner and teacher experiences of this course in the online and face-to-face formats. Such a comparative case study approach could contribute to a better understanding of the gains in linguistic and literary terms but also in terms of intercultural understanding, engagement, social connection and student experience. Detailed comparative research could help inform future pedagogical decisions and offer valuable insights into how educators could make the best of both formats when working with literature in the ELT context.

Appendix A: Multicultural Books Used in the Project

Abdel-Fattah, R. (2009), *Ten Things I Hate About Me*, New York: Orchard.
Alexie, S. (2007), *The Absolutely True Diary of a Part-Time Indian*,
    New York: Little, Brown.
Budhos, M. (2007), *Ask Me No Questions*, New York: Simon Pulse.
Creech, S. (1994), *Walk Two Moons*, New York: HarperTrophy.
Crew, L. (1989), *Children of the River*, New York: Laurel Leaf.
Flake, S. G. (2007), *The Skin I'm In*, New York: Hyperion.
Gallo, D. R., ed. (2007), *First Crossing Stories about Teen Immigrants*, Somerville,
    MA: Candlewick.
Gleitzman, M. (2003), *Boy Overboard*, London: Puffin.
Jaramillo, A. (2006), *La Línea*, New York: Square Fish.
Myers, W. D. (1999), *Monster*, New York: HarperTempest.
Thomas, A. (2017), *The Hate U Give*, New York: HarperCollins.
Woodson, J. (1998), *If You Come Softly*, New York: Puffin.

Appendix B: Adapted Sample Online Activities

The pre-service EFL teachers designed the following adapted sample online activities, and the pupils completed them during weeks 2 and 3 of the Crossing Borders Workshop. The instructions were provided in English.

Activity 1: Crossing Borders

1. Think back on the book you read and draw a picture of one of the borders the main character encounters. Then write three–four sentences about why you chose to draw this border and its importance for the book.

2. In your book, the character(s) cross many borders both visible and invisible. Think about the borders that you have to cross in your everyday life. Are they similar to those the characters in your book have to cross? How are they different? What could be reasons that a border cannot be crossed? In the space below, brainstorm whatever comes to your mind. Feel free to use bullet points to list your points, make a mind map, sketch some pictures and so on. When you are done, share your ideas with someone who has read a different book.

Activity 2: My Identity Iceberg

In the novel *The Hate U Give*, Starr struggles a lot with her identity – not only in her school but also at home. Her identity is not only about what other people can see. It is so much more.

1. Think of an iceberg. You can see only the tip of the iceberg. You cannot see what is under water. Draw an iceberg in the space provided below. Then draw a clear waterline that divides the visible part of the iceberg from the invisible part.

2. Now:

- think about all the different roles you take on in different areas of your life (son/daughter, brother/sister, student, friend, athlete, musician …);
- think about how you see yourself and how others see you. What are the things your close friends and family know about you?

3. Place the roles in your identity iceberg: Are they visible to others? Or are they hidden underwater? When you are finished, reflect on this activity and write two–three sentences about what it tells you about your identity.

Appendix C: Schedule for Pre-service EFL Teachers

Due to the present situation, we have had to move our Crossing Borders Workshop online. The following information is designed to give you an overview of how we will proceed this semester.

Group Organization

We will work with the 4a and 4b classes. The Crossing Borders Workshop will take place on Microsoft Teams. In order to access Microsoft Teams, you will need a student guest account and password, which I will send you via email. To have access, you just have to go to Microsoft online https://www.microsoft.com/de-at/microsoft-365/free-office-online-for-the-web and type in the student guest account and then password.

Duration of Project

We will work on the project over a four-week period.

1. *In week 1*, the pupils will upload their presentations of their books. You will have a week's time to view them and give feedback on Microsoft Teams.
2. *In weeks 2 and 3*, you will upload the materials that you have designed for your respective book to Microsoft Teams under Datein. The pupils will then complete the activities and upload their finished work to the platform.
3. *In week 4*, you will meet on Microsoft Teams in chatrooms at designated times to talk about your reading experiences and the project. These meetings will last approximately fifteen minutes. A sign-sheet for this activity will be uploaded to the platform during this week.

Note

I would like to thank Michaela Blumrich, Gerhard Fröhlich and their fourth form classes, and the pre-service teachers who attended my ELT course, for their commitment and enthusiasm, without which the online Crossing Borders Workshop would not have been possible.

References

Anderson, T. (2004), 'Teaching in an Online Context', in T. Anderson (ed.), *The Theory and Practice of Online Learning*, 1st edn, 273–94, Edmonton, AB: Aupress Athabasca University.

Bailey, C. J., and K. A. Card (2009), 'Effective Pedagogical Practices for Online Teaching: Perception of Experienced Instructors', *Internet and Higher Education*, 12: 152–5.

Bamford, J., and R. R. Day (2004), *Extensive Reading Activities for Teaching Language*, Cambridge: Cambridge University Press.

Bernard, R. M., P. C. Abrami, A. Wade and E. Borokhovski (2004), 'The Effects of Synchronous and Asynchronous Distance Education: A Meta-Analytical Assessment of Simonson's "Equivalency Theory"', in M. Simonson and M. Crawford (eds), *Annual Proceedings of Selected Research and Development Papers Presented at the National Convention of the Association for Educational Communications and Technology (27th, Chicago, Illinois, 2004)*, 2: 102–9, Washington, DC: Association for Educational Communications and Technology.

BMBWF (2017), 'Bundesministerium für Bildung, Wissenschaft und Forschung: Interkulturelle Bildung – Grundsatzerlass 2017'. https://www.bmbwf.gv.at/Themen/schule/schulrecht/rs/1997-2017/2017_29.html (accessed 15 July 2021).

BMBWF (2018), 'Bundesministerium für Bildung, Wissenschaft und Forschung: Gesamte Rechtsvorschrift für Lehrpläne – allgemeinbildende höhere Schulen'. https://www.ris.bka.gv.at/GeltendeFassung.wxe?Abfrage=Bundesnormen&Gesetzesnummer=10008568&FassungVom=2018-09-01 (accessed 9 July 2021).

Byram, M. (1997), *Teaching and Assessing Intercultural Communicative Competence*, Clevedon: Multilingual Matters.

Dalton-Puffer, C., K.-B. Boeckmann and B. Hinger (2019), 'Research in Language Teaching and Learning in Austria (2011–2017)', *Language Teaching*, 52: 201–30.

Moore, C. (2020), 'Design Training That Matters'. https://blog.cathy-moore.com/ (accessed 9 July 2021).

Murphy, E., M. Rodríguez-Manzanares and M. K. Barbour (2011), 'Asynchronous and Synchronous Teaching and Learning in High-School Distance Education: Perspectives of Canadian High School Distance Education Teachers', *British Journal of Educational Technology*, 42 (4): 583–91.

Ocriciano, M. (2020a), 'Considerations When Building e-Learning Courses, Part 1', *IATEFL Voices*, 275: 8–9.

Ocriciano, M. (2020b), 'Considerations When Building e-Learning Courses, Part 2', *IATEFL Voices*, 276: 8–9.

Roddy, C., D. L. Amiet, J. Chung, C. Holt, L. Shaw, S. McKenzie, F. Garivaldis, J. M. Lodge and M. E. Mundy (2017), 'Applying Best Practice Online Learning, Teaching, and Support to Intensive Online Environments: An Integrative Review', *Frontiers in Education*, 2 (59): 1–10.

Rosenblatt, L. M. ([1965] 1995), *Literature as Exploration*, 5th edn, New York: MLA.

Schumm Fauster, J., and E. Pölzleitner (2013), 'Crossing Borders', *Modern English Teacher*, 22 (1): 25–30.

Spataro, C. (2020), 'Moving an EFL Undergraduate Course Online: Tips and Tricks with Moodle, Zoom and Meet', *IATEFL Voices*, 275: 10–11.

West, C. (2020), 'Community and Well-Being in the Online Classroom', *IATEFL Voices*, 275: 15–16.

The World Café (2020), http://www.theworldcafe.com/key-concepts-resources/world-cafe-method/ (accessed 11 November 2020).

8

Digital Storytelling as a Pedagogical Approach for Meaningful Learning: Alternative Implementations of Technology in the Libyan EFL Context

Fatma Abubaker and Hana A. El-Badri

Introduction

Digital technologies are often considered as tools with the potential to create engaging and collaborative learning environments. The impact of technology in language education has inarguably been most positive when it comes to enhancing students' repertoire of knowledge and skills (Rhema and Miliszewska 2010). Research (Honey, Culp and Carrigg 2000; Earle 2002) has indicated that the integration of technology enhances students' engagement, critical thinking, autonomy and motivation to learn. How best to address the academic rigour of educational standards and engage students in meaningful uses of educational technology is therefore a topic of great interest to both researchers and practitioners.

In Libyan higher education, initiatives have been taken in the past decade to introduce and implement technology in university classrooms, but these have been cut short because they were premature and under-planned (Rhema and Miliszewska 2010). They did not seem to value pedagogy over technology, thus failing to proclaim the importance of technology as a tool for learning rather than the goal of learning. This may be due to the initial problem in which Libyan university classrooms operate as a vehicle for passively consuming knowledge rather than as an environment for developing productive skills. This is especially true in English as a foreign language (EFL) classrooms where much of the focus is on developing language skills and the accumulation of knowledge, not on developing critical and creative thinking (Elabbar 2011; Mohsen 2014).

The potential for changing the way in which EFL classrooms in Libya operate in this digital age means that suitable sources of information and interaction ought to be implemented. This means that Libyan EFL classrooms need to invest in technological tools which can be integrated across different subjects of the curriculum and which can draw on an array of skills and literacies. This is especially true for Libyan literature classrooms where technology has not had any significant existence in instruction. An investigation conducted by the second author (Mohamed 2017) on Libyan learners' interactions with technology when reading short fiction online has shown its potential for enhancing collaboration and understanding. However, Mohamed's research did not provide tools which could be implemented to develop students' understanding of literary texts.

Among those technological tools with potential in the area of English language arts is digital storytelling (DST). This view is mainly based on the body of literature indicating its effectiveness for strengthening students' understanding of content and encouraging reflection (Jenkins and Lonsdale 2007; Ohler 2008), which points to its particular benefit for language learners. As a modern expression of the ancient art of storytelling, DST uses multimedia technology, including computer-based tools such as graphics, video clips, audio recording, music and text, to tell stories (Robin 2008). It is a task-based project that makes use of multimodal and multi-literacy skills to construct knowledge, reflect on learning and help learners make sense of the world around them. Abubaker (2017) recommended using student-led group projects (as a post-reading activity) that use digital tools to extend students' understanding of literary texts, develop imagination and creativity in reading (meaning making) and therefore language skills. Creating a digital representation of the text can serve this particular purpose. During these activities, group members get to share ideas and establish a purpose for the story using specialized language to discuss literary features, digital moviemaking software and technology.

Storytelling (ST) and learning are inseparably intertwined because the process of making stories is a process of making meaning (Miller and Kim 2015), and researchers have observed the potential of DST in helping learners interact deeply with a text and construct meaning (Sadik 2008; Sylvester and Greenidge 2009). The very fact that 'storytelling' can be integrated into academic content development provides opportunities for learning (Matthews-DeNatale 2008), and the pairing of ST with digital technology provides better prospects for meaningful learning (ML).

In this chapter, we argue for the power of DST as a pedagogical approach for ML in the Libyan EFL literature classroom. This chapter therefore explores the potential of implementing DST to develop Libyan EFL students' understanding of and response to short stories. The following research questions were postulated:

1.   How can DST raise students' understanding of short story elements?
2.   How can DST provide students with opportunities for actual ML?

The chapter starts with a discussion of the literature on DST and its benefits in the language classroom followed by a description of the attributes of ML. We then present a case study on the implementation of DST in Libya. Drawing on the findings from this study, pedagogical and research implications are offered.

Review of Related Literature

Digital Storytelling and Its Role in Language Education

DST has only recently made its way into instructional settings. Using multimedia technology, DST combines digital graphics with audio narration, video and music to present a story. The use of digital resources to tell stories can range from the simple use of slides with pictures corresponding to the narrative, to the complex effects of using sounds and visual aids. Put simply, DST combines the uses of multimedia, including computer-based tools such as graphics, video clips, audio recording and music, to tell stories (Robin 2011).

From the original model which mostly relied on providing personal narratives using graphics, video, soundtrack and animation (Davis 2002; Bull and Kajder 2004), digital stories (DSs) have become more innovative as a pedagogical approach to specific subject areas and themes. Topics can range from the telling of personal tales, to the recounting of historical events, to instruction on a specific topic.

Research suggests that DST can be an effective tool in EFL classrooms. It can develop students' language learning (Robin 2008) and critical thinking (Normann 2011) skills. As a multimedia tool, students use technology to tell the story using their own words and voice, therefore making use of their knowledge of the language and encouraging their engagement and reflection (Normann 2011). Michalski, Hodges and Banister (2005) indicate that in this multimodality associated with DST, language learners combine visual and verbal functions which are essential for language understanding. They add that, as learners collect information to create their own stories, they can also enhance their comprehension of the content. Additionally, the process of creating DSs allows language learners to collaborate and brainstorm ideas, reflecting on what they have internalized and understood from any subject.

Most of the research on DST presents it as a cutting-edge educational and communicative tool (Ohler 2008). Normann (2011) found that teachers implementing DST in their learning activities reported higher levels of learner engagement and as a result language use. Learners will most likely be able to engage with the different aspects of a story, including presenting a coherent storyline and interesting characters. The very fact that learners can engage in telling stories would then benefit their abilities to meaningfully communicate their ideas and frame them by their understanding of the world around them. This way learners not only focus on the meaning they aim to communicate as they reflect on the topic or idea but also on the language they use in their DSs.

When used to impart content knowledge, DST can be a constructive and collaborative process in which students take responsibility for their own learning (Liu and Hsueh 2016). Students engage in authentic situations as they work together to create a multimodal project. They negotiate meanings and use their language skills to create meaningful storylines and plots using their background knowledge and experience. The participation in such group projects is inherently interesting and engaging to most students because they get to create their own DS. This level of engagement can raise language learners' motivation and hence their learning (Dörnyei 1997). Through the process of selecting words and producing multimodal representations in groups, learners can gradually assume responsibility for their own comprehension, interpretation and understanding, guided by the roles they assigned to themselves (Tobin 2012). Therefore, it can have great potential for teaching more complex, abstract or aesthetic content that requires imaginative visualization and creative representation.

English language arts classes in the first language (L1) have already started to make use of DST as a classroom or home-learning activity (Bull and Kajder 2004; Maddin 2014; Tobin 2012). It has been indicated that DST can help students construct meaning during reading and interact more deeply with texts (Sadik 2008; Sylvester and Greenidge 2009) and can therefore be effective for teaching literary analysis (Maddin 2014). Therefore, in a second language (L2) literature classroom, DST could be used at the end of a lesson to create digital adaptations of a text, showcasing students' understanding and interpretations of it. This will help them understand literary devices, reflect on what they have learnt and produce a multimodal representation of it.

Additionally, DST can be used as a tool for self-expression. Using images to represent ideas and emotions – both symbolically and literally – is an element which makes DST more valuable in the literature classroom (Ohler 2008). Known as 'non-linguistic representation' (Pitler et al. 2007: 86), the selection of story images to represent and elaborate on knowledge can be seen as a strategy that increases reflection and recall; a way for readers to reflect on different issues and characters in a story by relating them to their own lives and experiences to create meaning.

DST can also facilitate cultural and intercultural understanding, which can facilitate meaning making. Storytelling in general is a powerful pedagogical approach to enhance learning outcomes in any form of education (Smeda, Dakich and Sharda 2014). It has always been used to pass on knowledge from one generation to the other, both written and oral. Stories (written or digital) are therefore a way of transferring history, tradition, values and cultural heritage. The value that literature holds within cultures, and Arab cultures in particular, makes storytelling a medium where ideas, problems and cultural issues are discussed and dealt with.

Therefore, DST incorporates the benefits of storytelling (selecting, comparing, inferring, arranging and revising) into the creative process where learners interactively turn a one-dimensional task into a digital narrative that can be shared to the external world (Sylvester and Greenidge 2009). DST can therefore be a unique and effective approach to develop students' critical thinking and, if used as a post reading activity, critical reading skills. As learners create DSs, they engage in the issues and problems of the text. They become sensitive to the different elements of a story, how it links to the story events and to the world around them. This way of thinking facilitates creativity in learning (i.e. meaning making) because it draws on both cognitive and affective qualities (Abubaker 2017). Learners make associations between their lives and that of the story, making sense of the world around them.

Lambert (2010), in a discussion of the elements of DSs, suggests that a good DS is one which has a point of view; a dramatic question; emotional content; voice (perspective); the power of effective soundtrack; economy (simple, precise and concise); and good pacing. Robin (2011) adds the quality of images (which can affect the quality of the DS), good grammar and language usage and, more importantly, purpose (moral). Alexander (2017) extends this by demonstrating the evaluative purposes of DSs. He asserts that they should provide a compelling narration of a story; present a meaningful context to understand the story; use visual aids to capture emotions in the narrative; and use other sound effects to promote ideas and encourage reflection from the audience(s).

What can be inferred from this discussion is that integrating storytelling into academic content (such as literature) can strengthen learning (Matthews-DeNatale 2008) and as a result create better opportunities for meaning making.

Meaningful Learning

The theory of ML revolves around the idea that learnt information needs to be fully understood and connected to previously acquired knowledge to aid further understanding. Ausubel (1968) stressed that knowledge construction involves the creation of personal interpretations, and therefore meaning making is influenced by one's life and previous understanding because it shapes and modifies one's thinking.

Jonassen (1995), addressing the role of technology in educational settings, suggested that ML happens when five interrelated attributes are present: ML is said to happen when learners are active, constructive, collaborative, intentional and working on authentic tasks. According to Jonassen et al. (2007) these attributes work together but do not all have to be present for ML to happen. Their findings proposed a shift in classroom pedagogy from a focus on technology as an end product to a focus on teaching with technology as a tool for learning, thus changing the way educators conceive of technology use in education.

The first of the five attributes listed by Jonassen (1995) focuses on the importance of the learners being active in learning. They interact with their environment, manipulate the objects, observe the effects of their interventions, construct their interpretations of the learnt phenomena and share those interpretations with others. Such formal and informal apprenticeships of learning communities enable learners to develop their skills and knowledge which can then be shared with others.

The second attribute of ML, the constructive attribute, involves learners in making meaning. According to Jonassen et al. (2007), learning new knowledge often leads to discrepancies between what learners are observing and what they already know. Such discrepancies serve as a catalyst for meaning making. Learners create their own models of understanding using their prior experiences and by reflecting on them and looking for implications in different contexts (Jonassen 1995).

The collaborative attribute in ML is very important for knowledge construction. Collaborative learning requires learners to consider shared ideas that support reasoning, exploration and regulating each other's work. This means that group work is essentially an important aspect of ML.

Intentionality in ML refers to the 'cognitive processes that have learning as a goal rather than an incidental outcome' (Bereiter and Scardamalia 1989: 363). Intentional learners have high levels of self-efficacy and are motivated and responsible. They set learning goals, monitor, evaluate and strategically use their learning as a transformative force (Karki et al. 2018).

Finally, the most meaningful tasks are those which take place in authentic contexts. When learners engage with authentic problems, they not only understand better but also learn to transfer their understanding to new situations where they have more meaning. This means applying learnt skills to similar learning contexts (known as near transfer) or to contexts different from the earlier learning environment (far transfer), such as online learning. With constant practice, transfer becomes an aim of instruction (Karki et al. 2018), as it facilitates adaptation to different learning situations.

For the reasons mentioned above, the five attributes from Jonassen et al. (2007) on ML were used to evaluate the learning that took place using DST. We now describe the methodology and procedure of the study.

A Digital Response to Short Fiction: The Libyan Background

This study aimed to use DST as a pedagogical tool to develop Libyan EFL university students' understanding of and response to short stories to create ML environments. This was driven by the belief that the adoption of technology can, with the right support, provide Libyan EFL literature classrooms with means for constructivist learning opportunities.

Using purposive sampling, the study initially involved ten Libyan second-year English major students from the University of Benghazi, but only eight ended up participating. The majority of students in the English department are females as were most of the students who initially volunteered to take part (with eight females and two males). All eight participants who finally took part were females. The participants were previously taught by the second author. We chose this group because in the second year, students are first introduced to the three main genres of literature, namely poetry, fiction and drama, and are therefore familiar with it but still do not have much experience reading and understanding it.

Based on our experience of the Libyan EFL literature classroom, we suggest that it is still reliant on teacher-centred approaches and traditional methods of teaching and learning. As part of their literature module, second-year students study different literary genres and theoretical knowledge, including different text types. They are not however required to provide their own personal interpretations of the text and are, in most cases, provided with ready-made interpretations. A large part of the responsibility lies with the teacher. Importantly, there are no opportunities for making use of technological tools in the classroom. Furthermore, assessment focuses on developing knowledge about literature and developing surface-level reading comprehension skills, and therefore there is very little opportunity for independent meaning-making skills which draw on personal response and creativity. Our goal was therefore to try and make use of a technological tool that could utilize interactive, collaborative and constructive skills to respond to short stories, and DST was our approach to make this shift.

The investigation was conducted virtually during lockdown due to the Covid-19 pandemic. All interactions between the researchers and participants were through Zoom online conferencing and social networking platforms (Facebook, WhatsApp and Messenger). An invitation for participation was sent out on the classroom Facebook page, and interested students were asked to contact the researchers on Messenger with their details. They were then contacted and added to a Messenger group and provided with a plain language statement and consent form before participation. Online recruitment was slow due to the pandemic, as well as due to slow internet connection because of low bandwidth and sometimes complete lack of connectivity because of constant power cuts (caused partly by the political instability and conflicts in western parts of Libya, which have been going on for the past few years). This meant that it took around two to three weeks to reach the intended sample.

It was also very difficult for the researchers and the participants to communicate and proceed with the study (for both technical and emotional reasons). This meant that the study, which was originally planned to take around twelve weeks, was delayed and put on hold for about ten weeks after recruitment. Only then did we manage to send general information about the research to the participants, provide information sheets, get their consent and proceed with the data collection phase.

Methodology and Research Procedure

This study used qualitative methods to determine how well Libyan EFL students engage with DST to understand short stories. After getting participant consent, the students were provided with a timetable showing the main stages of this study. Essentially, this involves three main phases: a process, production and evaluation phase distributed across a four-week period. The process phase involves all procedures for preparing and scaffolding the students to produce their DSs. To scaffold the process, students attended a workshop during week 1. After the workshop, they were provided with follow-up resources, including a handout, a video tutorial and self-evaluation criteria (see Appendix A). The production phase (weeks 2 and 3) included the process of producing the DSs. The eight participants were asked to put themselves in small groups of three or four; there were two groups of three, and one group with only two students, giving a total of three teams. Finally, in the fourth week, students were interviewed. This evaluation phase aimed at determining the quality of the DSs and of the students' experiences with DST.

The Process: The Student Workshop

A two-hour workshop was delivered by the researchers via Zoom to introduce the students to DST, what it involves, the elements of a DS and how it can be used in the literature lesson. We first presented DST by giving a definition and showing visuals of what a DS looks like. A DST software called 'Storyboard That' was introduced, and a short tutorial about how to use this tool was given. Unlike other DST tools which make use of videos, 'Storyboard That' mainly uses text and still images, as well as recordings of voice narrations.

Two activities were demonstrated, both for 'The Story of an Hour' by Kate Chopin. Students had already studied this story, but they had not engaged in activities related to it, and certainly not using digital technology. The first activity dealt with plot structure while the other focused on teaching irony (situational and dramatic). In the first activity, the students were asked to work in pairs to arrange the cells in the digital storyboard into the correct order by organizing the pictures according to the five main stages of a plot (exposition, rising action, climax, falling action and resolution). Then they had to match the pictures with the appropriate text. The purpose of this activity was to teach plot and help students understand how storyboarding could be used to present plot structure. The second activity included two pictures with two textual descriptions of the situational and dramatic irony in the story and definitions for these two types of irony. In pairs, students had to name the type of irony and match it to the situation. Finally, in groups students were given two questions to discuss what the story meant to them, what they found most interesting, and why. Then they were asked to share their answers with the rest of the group.

The final part of the workshop introduced the students to the research process, including data collection, and their assignment (task). Students were then given criteria which covered the important aspects of creating a 'good' DS (see Appendix A) and a checklist with Robin's (2011) elements of a DS. A classroom account on 'Storyboard That' was set and the assignment was uploaded with an open access link to create their DSs.

The Product: The Digital Stories

Students were asked to create a digital representation of a story they had read, either one they had previously studied or one they were familiar with. A total of three DSs were produced, all of which were storyboards which only made use of images and text narrations, with no voice-over.

DS1, 'The Obstacle in Our Path', shown in Figure 8.1, describes a situation in which an obstacle can be turned into an opportunity to improve one's circumstances, and while the lazy complain, others create opportunities to get things done.

DS1 was set in a small town in ancient times. The story starts with a wise king who wanted to reward anyone who could move a big boulder which he left in the middle of a walking path. While everyone was criticizing the king for not keeping the village roads clear, a peasant decided to move the big rock out of people's path and found a bag of gold coins hidden under it. The DS was arranged in four cells showing the main events.

DS2 (Figure 8.2) was based on an Australian urban legend originally called 'The Dead Kangaroo'. Group 2 replaced the kangaroo with a monkey because they could not find a picture of a kangaroo in the selection of animals in the DST tool. The DS consisted of six cells for the plot and used mainly pictures, with very little text in a speech bubble. Set in the wild, this DS tells the story of a driver who runs over an exotic animal (monkey) and wraps it in a coat for a fun photo. The monkey revives and runs off with his jacket, which has his passport, credit cards and $1,000 inside.

DS3, 'The Dinner Party' (Figure 8.3), discusses the idea that both men and women are equally courageous and can have control of a challenging situation. The story describes a situation over a dinner party where there was a debate about how women and men act in crises. Although the hostess has a cobra crawling on her foot under the table, she very calmly signals to another person in the room to bring a bowl of milk to the balcony. Realizing that a cobra is present, her husband cleverly asks everyone to play a game where the person

In ancient times, a King had a boulder placed on a roadway. He then hid himself and watched to see if anyone would move the boulder out of the way. Some of the king's wealthiest merchants and courtiers came by and simply walked around it.

Many people loudly blamed the King for not keeping the roads clear, but none of them did anything about getting the stone out of the way.

A peasant then came along carrying a load of vegetables. Upon approaching the boulder, the peasant laid down his burden and tried to push the stone out of the road. After much pushing and straining, he finally succeeded.

After the peasant went back to pick up his vegetables, he noticed a purse lying in the road where the boulder had been.
The purse contained many gold coins and a note from the King explaining that the gold was for the person who removed the boulder from the roadway.

Figure 8.1 Digital story 1: 'The Obstacle in Our Path'.

who moves loses. As the cobra goes out on to the balcony, the husband locks it outside. When asked how she knew about the cobra, everyone realizes that the cobra was crawling over the hostess's foot all along. The students provide the plot structure (in five cells) as well as two extra cells that detail the two types of irony (situation and dramatic) in the story and the theme(s) in the story. It is worth mentioning that the quality of the pictures in this DS was a little poor as the students used the free version of 'Storyboard That' to create their DS rather

Figure 8.2 Digital story 2: 'The Dead Monkey'.

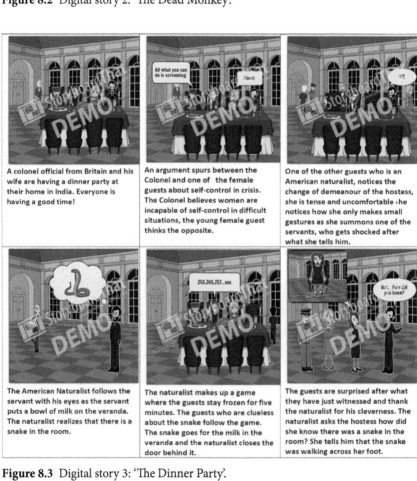

Figure 8.3 Digital story 3: 'The Dinner Party'.

than using the class account (paid for by the researchers), to get full access to its features. This is why there is a logo at the centre of the images in this DS, making it a little difficult to see all the details.

Upon completion, students shared a link to their DSs on the Facebook page for peer review and feedback. However, because of the poor internet connection and long hours of power cuts, no one provided feedback on the DSs. Some responded through Facebook with emojis and likes.

The Evaluation of DST as a Pedagogical Approach

Student Interviews

To capture the students' experiences in the process of creating DSs, we conducted an online semi-structured interview with each group. The interviews took around forty minutes and were conducted in English via Zoom. All student responses were then recorded and transcribed to be analysed.

The Evaluation Rubric

We used a scoring rubric to rate the quality of the created DSs, analysing each DS separately. Our analysis was framed by our understanding of Robin's (2011) elements of a DS. First, a general view of the quality of the DSs as a digital artefact was reviewed using the same self-evaluation criteria given to the students before production (see example for DS2 in Appendix A) evaluated its interpretability, communicative power and whether it was easy to follow. To determine the quality of students' experience of creating a DS, two sets of criteria were used, as suggested by Robin (2011). The first was based on the quality of DS content, including choice of theme/topic, purposefulness, value, accuracy of the information used, formatting and use of details (see example for DS2 in Appendix B1). The second focused on evaluating the process and mechanism of learners' experiences with the DS (see example for DS2 in Appendix B2). The rubric thus covers criteria which correspond to critical aspects of the learners' experience with DST, including interaction, knowledge construction, collaboration and negotiation in the selection and organization of a DS (see Jonassen et al. 2007).

Data Analysis

We first examined each set of data independently, then against Jonassen's (1995) attributes of ML. The analysis started with determining the active modes which construct the DS and segmenting it into analysable units. This was then followed by an examination of both modes (visual and textual). To rate the quality of the DSs, we reviewed the pictures and the narrations (written/oral), including the speech bubbles. None of the groups used oral narrations with their DSs. The analysis also included content analysis of the interview responses. Based on both DSs and interviews and the associated evaluation rubrics, aspects of ML were examined and highlighted in the form of codes to determine the most relevant themes.

DST in the Libyan EFL Literature Classroom: A Shift in Perspective

Although the DSs created in this study use basic narrative lines and only images, text and narration, different modes collaborate to make them special. Aspects of this multimodal representation of meanings not only capture students' understandings but with the appropriate images and words, students were able to communicate their visualizations of the different elements of a story. We structure this section around our two research questions to examine the effectiveness of DST for understanding short stories and creating an ML opportunity for Libyan EFL learners.

How Can DST Raise Students' Understanding and Awareness of Short Story Elements?

The content analysis of DSs, with support from the interviews, revealed that the story purpose and theme were the most prominent elements in the students' selection and production of content. The plot structure, characters and setting were the elements that helped communicate that message of the moral and issues of the theme(s), making it more concrete (visible).

Didactic Purpose (Moral)

All three DSs focused mainly on communicating and exploring a story that entertains the readers and teaches them about the real world, drawing on the first aspect of the criteria. It is a combination of instructional and personally and emotionally rich content which has come to inspire the learners with their selection of DS. DS1 (Figure 8.1) addresses the life issue of confronting obstacles and people's perception of them. Although the DS was short and had only four cells, the message is clearly communicated in the scenes through text narration, the character's physical appearance and the ending. In the interview, the creators of DS1 talked about the importance of not only communicating purposeful stories that teach but also the significance of effective communication for both sender and audience. As S1 puts it, students can 'understand fiction easily and get the meaning of the story by themselves' (S1), and as S2 indicates, focus on communicating the message eventually plays an important role in learning and creating it. Demonstrating the importance of purpose/moral, they suggested that it was the moral that made them choose this particular story. They explained that creating the storyboard 'made this message come to life' (S2).

In DS2, 'The Dead Monkey' (Figure 8.2), the moral becomes concrete through the choice of pictures. The combination of text and images (with the help of facial expressions), along with surprise ending, indicates that 'what goes around comes around', demonstrating that Karma or Godly punishment is the natural consequence of wrongdoing or inhumanity.

In DS3, 'The Dinner Party', the participants had a powerful message that portrayed their critical stance of what it meant to be a young woman, especially in their culture, therefore shaping their own identities as females, which is supported by their responses in the interview and their determination to make a statement about gender equality. This is shown by the strong language of opinion used in scene 2 and admiration in the final scene, thus revealing the importance of the message conveyed through dramatic irony. DS3 with its textual and visual representation, though of average quality when it comes to the production and selection of visuals (e.g. in character positioning, size and gestures), managed to clearly communicate the moral behind the story, which is the need to lose stereotypes perpetuated in our societies about gender qualities and traits. Taking a pluralistic look onto the meaning of courage and wisdom, the creators argue for the need to re-evaluate gender roles in general, and more precisely in Arabic societies, therefore making purpose or/and moral a key element in the art of DST.

Theme(s)

Through the multimodal elements of DST, the theme in DS3, 'The Dinner Party', as shown in Figure 8.3, was handled well with a good choice of scenes to portray the most relevant ideas. The title does not give much of an indication about the topic of the story. Text and image show a dialogue between a man and a woman in the second cell. In the speech bubbles the man says, 'Women will always panic in times of crises.' The woman in the picture is shown with an angry face, saying 'Nooo! Women are like men.' A separate cell (Figure 8.4) was added by the creators to summarize the theme by placing emphasis on character behaviour,

The theme(s) of this story is control in situations of both men and women. This story tells us that in times of crises, we must take control, remain calm, and make make the best we can, and this story gives us an example.

Figure 8.4 Theme for digital story 3: 'The Dinner Party'.

and as they put it, 'There is no better way to show this, than when a deadly snake is crawling on your foot' (S8). Although they were not asked specifically to create a separate scene (cell) for story theme, it was their interpretation of the self-evaluation criteria (see Appendix A) that led them to choose a scene they believed contributes to the intended message. They therefore focused on the discussion that took place between the hostess and the man on the different responses of men and women to crises, and revealed through a written summary, along with the man's speech and facial expression, as he finds out how the hostess reacted to the situation calmly. The contrast between text and image is an indication of the sort of stereotypes in the story. This is supported by the creators' explanation that this issue was a universal one, especially in their culture.

The Plot Structure

The students were able to focus their attention on maintaining the flow of the stories while keeping them short and putting the most relevant ideas in cells. This could be because, as they indicated in the interviews, they arranged the plot according to its main stages (exposition, rising action, climax, falling action and resolution). The creators of this DS (Figure 8.2) were keen on making the events easy follow by putting more weight on the pictures (not the text) and presenting their own visualization of it with as few words as possible. One student explains: 'I was keen on the plot of the story and the characters present in it so that my story is clear and everyone who watches it can understand the dialogue that took place in my mind as if he/she designed it' (S4). This story draws heavily on visual literacy, which is one of the important benefits of DST. The dialogue in this DS compensates for the minimum use of text. The creators expressed their worry about the quality of pictures because of their unfamiliarity with the digital tool and how to accurately place the visual items in the scenes. We analysed the pictures and realized that some aspects of the visual content were less accurate, for example, the size of characters based on angles of the visual shot, the distance between characters and background, and positioning of items (like the mobile phone). This however did not negatively affect the DS, as we found that the meaning was portrayed well. This indicates that the representation of meaning of plot structure was more important than accuracy of the use of the digital tool, which as the creators explain is a little challenging to master when it is new and unfamiliar.

Setting

Students took advantage of the features of the DST tool to carefully choose the setting. The creators of DS1 decided to provide a digital representation of a fable that they had heard before but had not read until they had started working on this task. They read it online before transforming it into digital mode. DS1 (Figure 8.1) was set in a traditional town in early times. According to the creators of this DS, there is no detailed description of the setting in the text they read, but they were able to infer from the context what it might have looked like, including the characters' appearance, because they were able to rely on their prior knowledge of stories that often take place in that era.

To better help the audience picture the story and show the abstract emotional content, students made use of the many features of 'Storyboard That', including character types, different colours, backgrounds, facial expressions and the use of different items to describe the setting. Speech bubbles, combined with facial expressions, were used to show the characters' emotions, including dissatisfaction and astonishment (DS1), shock (DS2) and anger and fear (DS3). This provides a better aesthetic experience not only for the creators of the DSs but also for the audience, which is one of the strengths of DST.

The goal of DST is to allow a writer to experience the power of personal expression (Bull and Kajder 2004), which is why students' DSs were interesting as they were able to reflect their own experience and understanding of the stories. Although students' point of view was not quite apparent in those DSs by, for example, using words of opinion or the personal pronoun 'I' to show what they think, they portrayed instances of this in their selection of scenes and use of language (as in DS3). This is more explicit in their responses to the interviews where they express more of the attributes associated with ML as they reflect on the DST experience and their DSs.

How Can DST Provide Students with Opportunities for Meaningful Learning?

Despite the challenging conditions presented in this study, including lack of electricity and poor internet connection, and the fact that it relies heavily on digital technology for both research and communicative purposes (which can ultimately have an impact on the outcomes of a research investigation), findings point towards some features of ML.

Our data shows that students were able to construct the meaning of the story by being active thinkers as they initiated and engaged in discussion, showing instances of criticality as they analysed characters' actions and thought about the meaning of the text. S8 explains how they selected the pictures for DS3 by saying:

> We discussed how the characters looked, about the appearance of the characters, and the setting. Each one of us gave her opinion, because the story was set in the 20th century, so we didn't want something modern, it had to be a little older.

The creators of DS2 were engaged in a constructive process as they expressed their ideas on the importance of having a monkey in the story, rather than the original kangaroo, because of the funny ending, indicating that a monkey was more suitable because they are usually 'cheeky' (S4). They also shared their concerns about the world nowadays and how the main characters' actions were unacceptable, therefore concluding that he deserved punishment, when the monkey left with his jacket and wallet. Based on the events, S5 says: 'I think the monkey is good at acting and has been able to deceive the man easily.' She reflects on her own understanding of the world by adding that 'it reminds me of wisdom and the moral consequences. I mean when someone does something bad, he gets what he deserves at the end'.

Students also engaged in reflection as they talked about their own learning process. S1 explains her understanding of the purpose of the task (to create a visual representation of a story) and reflects on her learning by evaluating her (and her teammates') ability to achieve this goal by saying, 'I succeeded in showing the images that have been going into my mind to others by translating it to group of pictures that tell a complete story.' S2 adds her reflection on the importance of this task for their learning when she comments that 'it was an interesting experience; you can be creative … I think that creativity is very important now'.

DST provides a social context where students use multimodal tools to create personal interpretations of a text and externalize their interpretations through collaboration. Group work was an important aspect of the DS project because learners could work together to negotiate meaning, build on each other's understandings and regulate each other's work. This was one of the main aspects which the students felt was an advantage when undertaking this task. The students did face some challenges creating their DSs because they had to have access to the internet, which was not possible with constant power cuts that sometimes lasted for up to eight hours a day. This of course made it challenging to access the digital tool 'Storyboard That'. In addition, not all participants had a laptop or computer, and most features of 'Storyboard That' could not be accessed with a mobile phone. In each group, however, there was at least one person who had a computer and students compensated for the lack of access to laptops/computers with their ability to work in groups, assign specific roles and take on specific responsibilities during the production of the DSs, such as writer, director and producer/editor. This cooperation, however, took place online only because Libya was in lockdown at the time. S8 (DS3) explained how this was done:

> Well, I was the one to put the girls in their positions. I chose to write the story, and Hanna put the storyboard together, and I told Hend that she can determine the elements of the story, because it was easier for Hend because of her weak internet connection, and because she doesn't have a laptop.

This also helped them become organized and assume a sense of intentionality as they thought about their tasks and how to carry them out to reach their aim. They relied on different skills to regulate their learning, by analysing, managing and evaluating ideas about the selected scripts and images to create a meaningful story which communicates these meanings clearly to the audience. S8 shows this as she describes how they negotiated things in DS3:

> I first wrote the story in the cells on the storyboard, to see how much space is there to put in one cell, then I finished the story … She (Hanna) told me to write

the story first and then she would put the images together. She was the one who told me that I need to skip one cell and change the structure of the story. She thought that one part doesn't require to be in a cell on its own as separate cell.

This, however, does not mean that there were no challenges in reaching the intended aim. To become intentional means to plan out and manage information that needs to be included and evaluate its relevance for communicating the main ideas of a story. S1 describes these challenges by saying: 'I think it was a bit challenging (translating all the story elements into visuals), because I had to leave a lot of details out.' The students do therefore realize the complexity of not representing meaning in visual mode but also in writing. S1 further explains the importance of achieving the task objectives and particularities by stating: 'There were other characters that I wanted to put in the storyboard, but I had to leave them out.' Compared with the other two DSs which were both fables, DS3 had probably more details, including more characters. This makes it more challenging to organize and design the cells for the storyboard, and of course there is more information to summarize.

DST provides students with real, contextualized language. This contextuality also included the cultural and intercultural context and how it could be interpreted through DSs. Although the DSs were based on stories the students had previously read, the task of writing additional speech to accompany the pictures (in speech bubbles) and the narration in the scenes also required in part previous knowledge of what happens in similar situations by drawing on what they felt about a particular topic or issue. This is shown in DS3 ('The Dinner Party'); that women and men are 'equal', drawing on how cultural and intercultural ideas can be communicated through this text-images combination. To S7, this idea was not just about the meaning of the story but also what it means to her as a young woman. She says:

> It was interesting for us as female students too, because we (our culture) demonstrate women like this, that women belong in the kitchen, that women are weak, that they are not as strong as men, whereas in this story they showed that women are capable of *doing things and being as calm as men in difficult situation*. (Her emphasis)

We mentioned earlier that ML also requires learners to successfully transfer their learning to other similar contexts (Liu and Hsueh 2016). Transferability might be one of the things that the students found challenging when creating DSs, not only because they were required to present their understanding of a written text into a visual production online but also because DST requires an array of literacies, including both digital and visual skills. It seems that students were reluctant to make use of other features of DST (such as voice-over or sound/music), mainly because they felt it demanded a certain level of digital proficiency, familiarity and even mastery in using the tool itself. Still, students were able to successfully transfer their learning online through digital media. This transferability becomes clear as they communicate complex ideas, such as irony in DS3, demonstrating how prior learning was positively supported by the new digital context, making the experience, easy, engaging and enjoyable. S4 explains the benefit this multimodality by explaining: 'I made the pictures and I enjoyed to transfer the information into a DS to be understood by just looking at the pictures.' S5 concurs by saying that it is a good way of understanding literary elements 'because some people find it not easy to read and visualize the story', therefore drawing on the importance of not only making meaning of a story but also communicating that meaning through pictures.

Conclusion: Lessons Learnt and Implications for Research

This study explored the effectiveness of using DST as an approach to teach Libyan EFL students to make sense of short stories. What we discovered in the short time working with DST in the Libyan EFL classroom is that effective teaching practices paired with powerful technologies provide student readers with unique ML experiences to transform their understanding of short stories. Hence, creating and communicating meaning becomes the main goal of creating a DS. That said, this approach should remain grounded in the curriculum where literature should be in the foreground and technology in the background. The focus should be on the communication process rather than technical effects: students and teachers should centre their efforts on the practice of the storyteller, with the digital media serving as a tool.

As promising as this approach may be, there are some barriers that need to be considered and therefore mitigated when using DST in the classroom. These barriers might include not having the necessary technical support, insufficient teacher expertise and training, time for planning or the lack of pedagogical applications. Challenges presented in this study relate to online instruction, including availability of electricity, internet access and access to computing resources (laptops and computers). There are also some barriers that can arise due to the extra expenditure involved in getting a tool like 'Storyboard That'.

Although students' lack of response when asked to provide feedback on other DSs was mostly due to lack of access to the internet, another reason which we posit is that Libyan students are used to teacher-centred methods, and therefore feedback is not something that they are encouraged to do; therefore, they do not have a positive attitude towards it and no awareness of its importance for knowledge construction.

There are some steps which can be taken to overcome barriers when using DST in contexts like Libya. Recommendations to teachers using DST would be: to use it as a student-led group project where students divide responsibilities between themselves, to provide coordination of the activity, to give each student a directed purpose and to draw on their strengths. Also, we recommend using DST in addition to written assignments/tasks. It is also recommended to use tools which are free and accessible to students. Finally, it is important to provide feedback (from both teachers and peers) on students' DSs to help them build on each other's ideas and construct meaning and also improve their DSs.

What this research shows is that even though technology integration offers teachers novel ways of instruction, it can present limitations in contexts like Libya. This points back to our quote at the beginning of this chapter and the importance of making pedagogy the focus when integrating technology into teaching practice.

Additionally, we came up against other issues that the use of technology might posit when conducting research in contexts affected by crises, including conflict and/or the pandemic, which can influence the research process itself (including time management, communication, flexibility of resources, as well as internet connection). This is why awareness of the impact of conflict on such educational systems and the importance of education to move beyond these circumstances is vital (Smith 2014). By sharing our experiences of undertaking research and teaching in such conditions, we aim to not only share content but also inspire others. We also hope to share good practice and highlight aspects of teaching that value the need for teacher's agency. As Smith (2020) states, it is important that problems are converted into questions and that teachers take on enquiry and experimentation as a main goal in challenging contexts.

According to Alexander (2017), capturing sound effects is important. Further research could be done using other software which make use of video to determine ways in which these multimodal skills interact when producing DSs, and how students negotiate meaning when producing them. Investigations can be conducted on using DST with struggling readers and writers, and with those who have not yet experienced the power of personal expression. Personal expression is something we have come to value through this research; therefore, we encourage investigative qualitative research that explores the role of DST as an educational tool which reflects students' experiences and responses to conflict and its impact on their education. Finally, investigations of how DST could be used to teach other subjects would be worth exploring.

Through this investigation we confirm that students' appreciation of DST came from the opportunities it provides for interaction, engagement, autonomy and, more importantly, collaboration. Simply put, DST can help Libyan EFL literature instruction shift towards interactive, student-centred approaches.

Appendix A: Criteria for Creating a Good Digital Story

The overall quality of the digital story:

Criteria	Yes/no	Comment
Was it able to communicate the logic of the intended idea? (plot/events)	Yes	The sequence of events is clear. A story with a surprise ending and a message behind it.
Are the ideas easy to follow? (plot/events)	To some extent, yes	The ideas of the story follow the main structure of a plot.
Are readers/audience able to interpret the message behind the story?	Yes	The main idea can be generalizable, and audience can relate to it. However, some may respond differently, which is a good thing as it is open for different interpretations.
Do the scenes contribute to the intended message?	Yes	Some scenes more than others.
Do the text, pictures and audio complement each other?	To some extent, yes	Needed more text, to support the pictures. There is no audio and no narrations. The relationship between text and picture seems to be more reliant on one element more than the other in the first five scenes and more on the text in scene six.
Are the pictures clear?	Yes	The general aim of the use of the pictures has been reached, which is to convey a message. Some detail is unclear. Size and angle need work.
Is the language used grammatically correct and appropriate?	Yes	Capital letter missing.

Source: Adopted from Robin (2011).

Appendix B: Evaluating the Students' Experience of Creating a Digital Story (DS2: 'The Dead Monkey')

B1: The quality of the DS content.

Criteria	Yes/no	Comments
Title	Yes	'The Dead Monkey' The original name of the story was changed from 'The Dead Kangaroo' to Monkey because the storyboard did not have a kangaroo picture to choose from. The choice of a monkey adds more to the humorous aspect, thus providing readers with a connotation for deception and cheekiness.
Interesting theme/topic	Yes	The idea of deception behind the story is universal and interesting. What makes it more interesting is that the main character is a monkey (animal) which provides it more humour and at the same time highlighting a lesson to be learnt.
Purposefulness of the story (aim/moral)	Yes	The main aim was to teach a lesson while maintaining a sense of humour and lightened mood.
Plot structure	Yes	Although it seemed that the final scenes could have been arranged in a way that better describe the final events in more details.
Value of information included	Yes	Some details are relevant but need more clarity in terms of the objects used and text.
Accuracy of information included	Yes	Text is needed to provide more accuracy, in addition to use of objects.
Details	No	Needs more detail to reach full potential and clarity of cause and effect more accurately (e.g. how the monkey got on the jacket and what was it for). Some details need clarification. It was important to show in the pictures that the jacket belongs to the driver; this leads the readers/audience to eventually respond differently, thus changing the overall mood and tone. The point of view could have been clearer through detail in the pictures and text to highlight how the driver deserved what happened to him.
Format	Yes	With less text, formatting is less problematic. Pictures need to be adjusted with correct angles and sizes.

Source: Adopted from Robin (2011).

B2: The process and mechanism of learners' experiences with the DS.

Criteria	Yes/no	Comments
Interaction with the real world	Yes	The selection of topic addresses more than one idea and is therefore based on how the creators see the world around them.
Knowledge and personal experience included	Yes	Based on prior knowledge and experience the selection of a monkey to replace a kangaroo was smart, as it made it clear to the readers that the ending, though surprising, is what you can expect from a monkey (cheekiness).
Internal conflicts (if any) revealed and solved in the choice of theme/topic	Yes	The DST tool did not have a picture of a kangaroo. Collaboration and negotiation when addressing the theme and the role of replacing the kangaroo with a monkey had a positive effect on depicting the theme. It also provides some reference to life in the twenty-first century, discussing aspects relating to sensitivity and morality while aiming towards an understanding of spiritual principles of cause and effect (karma) or godly punishment. It depicts the ideas present in this time according to which technology has in one way or another revealed two sides of who we are as humans, tells what is interesting in the solution or ending is how it is important to make sure that we maintain our human nature, and shows consequence for inhumanity. It is rich with metaphor and symbolism which all make the theme powerful.
Types and extent of negotiations for choices of titles, details, format and structure of the story (selectiveness, extensiveness, rigorousness of search and choices)	Yes	There was negotiation in terms of changing the title of the story based on the main characters 'Kangaroo' into 'Monkey'. The choice of a monkey' was smart and purposeful as it provides more opportunity to derive a lesson behind it as well as make sure that it attracts the readers because of its comedic and rather humorous theme while teaching an important lesson.
		There was negotiation in terms of what to select for a DS and how to create something that was relevant to all.

References

Primary Literature

Chopin, K. (1894), 'The Story of an Hour'. http://archive.vcu.edu/english/engweb/webte xts/hour/ (accessed 7 December 2021).

Secondary Literature

Abubaker, F. (2017), 'The Road to Possibilities: A Conceptual Model for a Program to Develop the Creative Imagination in Reading and Responding to Literary Fiction (short stories) in Libyan English as a Foreign Language (EFL) University Classrooms'. PhD thesis, University of Glasgow, Glasgow.

Alexander, B. (2017), *The New Digital Storytelling: Creating Narratives with New Media*, Santa Barbara, CA: Praeger.

Ausubel, D. P. (1968), *Educational Psychology: A Cognitive View*, New York: Holt, Rinehart and Winston.

Bereiter, C., and M. Scardamalia (1989), 'Intentional Learning as a Goal of Instruction', in L. B. Resnick (ed.), *Knowing, Learning, and Instruction: Essays in Honour of Robert Glaser*, 361–92, Hillsdale, NJ: Lawrence Erlbaum Associates.

Bull, G., and S. Kajder (2004), 'Digital Storytelling in the Language Arts Classroom', *Learning and Leading with Technology*, 32 (4): 46–9.

Davis, J. E. (2002), *Stories of Change: Narrative and Social Movements*, New York: State University of New York.

Dörnyei, Z. (1997), 'Psychological Processes in Cooperative Language Learning: Group Dynamics and Motivation', *Modern Language Journal* (81): 482–893.

Earle, R. (2002), 'The Integration of Instructional Technology into Public Education: Promises and Challenges', *Educational Technology*, 42 (1): 5–13.

Elabbar, A. A. (2011), 'An Investigation of Influences Affecting Libyan English as Foreign Language University Teachers' (LEFLUTs) Teaching Approaches in the Language Classroom'. PhD thesis, University of Glasgow, Glasgow.

Honey, M., K. M. Culp and F. Carrigg (2000), 'Perspectives on Technology and Education Research: Lessons from the Past and Present', *Educational Computing Research*, 23 (1): 5–14.

Jenkins, M., and J. Lonsdale (2007), 'Evaluating the Effectiveness of Digital Storytelling for Student Reflection', in *ICT: Providing Choices for Learners and Learning*. Proceedings ASCILITE Singapore 2007. http://www.ascilite.org.au/conferences/singapore07/procs/jenkins.pdf.

Jonassen, D., R. Marra, J. Howland and D. Crismond (2007), *Meaningful Learning with Technology*, 3rd edn, New Jersey: Prentice Hall.

Jonassen, D. H. (1995), 'Supporting Communities of Learners with Technology: A Vision for Integrating Technology with Learning in Schools', *Educational Technology*, 35 (4) (July–August): 60–3.

Karki, T., H. Keinänen, A. Tuominen, M. Hoikkala, E. Matikainen and H. Maijala (2018), 'Meaningful Learning with Mobile Devices: Pre-service Class Teachers' Experiences of Mobile Learning in the Outdoors', *Technology, Pedagogy and Education*, 27 (2): 251–63.

Lambert, J. (2010), *Digital Storytelling Cookbook*, Berkeley, CA: Digital Diner.

Liu, K. S., and S. L. Hsueh (2016), 'Effects of Digital Teaching on the Thinking Styles and the Transfer of Learning of the Students in Department of Interior Design', *Eurasia Journal of Mathematics, Science and Technology Education*, 12: 1697–706.

Maddin, E. (2014), 'Teaching Literary Analysis with Digital Storytelling: An Instructional Approach', *Kentucky Journal of Excellence in College Teaching and Learning*, 11 (11): 105–22.

Matthews-DeNatale, G. (2008), *Digital Storytelling: Tips and Resources*, Boston, MA: Simmons College.

Michalski, P., D. Hodges and S. Banister (2005), 'Digital Storytelling in the Middle Childhood Special Education Classroom: A Teacher's Story of Adaptations', *Teaching Exceptional Children Plus*, 1 (4), Article 3. http://escholarship.bc.edu/education/tecplus/vol1/iss4/3.

Miller, J., and S. Kim (2015), 'Digital Storytelling as an Integrated Approach to Language Learning and Teaching', *Language and Communication Quarterly*, 4 (3): 41–55.

Mohamed, H. (2017), 'Intercultural Interactive Processing Model of Reading English as a Foreign Language Short Fiction in the Libyan Context'. PhD thesis, University of Aberdeen, Aberdeen.

Mohsen, A. S. (2014), 'Teaching English as a Foreign Language in Libya', *Scientific Research Journal (SCIRJ)*, II (XI): 2201–796.

Normann, A. (2011), 'Digital Storytelling in Second Language Learning: A Qualitative Study on Students' Reflections on Potentials for Learning'. MA dissertation, Norwegian University of Science and Technology, Trondheim, Norway.

Ohler, J. (2008), *Digital Storytelling in the Classroom: New Media Pathways to Literacy, Learning, and Creativity*, Thousand Oaks, CA: Corwin.

Pitler, H., E. Hubbell, M. Kuhn and K. Malenoski (2007), *Using Technology with Classroom Instruction That Works*, Denver, CO: Mid-Continent Research for Education and Learning.

Rhema, A., and I. Miliszewska (2010), 'Towards E-Learning in Higher Education in Libya', *Issues in Informing Science and Information Technology*, 7 (1): 423–37.

Robin, B. (2011), 'Educational Uses of Digital Storytelling'. http://digitalstorytelling.coe.uh.edu.

Robin, B. R. (2008), 'Digital Storytelling: A Powerful Technology Tool for the 21st Century Classroom', *Theory into Practice*, 47 (3): 220–8.

Sadik, A. (2008), 'Digital Storytelling: A Meaningful Technology-Integrated Approach for Engaged Student Learning', *Educational Technology Research and Development*, 56 (4): 487–506.

Smeda, N., E. Dakich and N. Sharda (2014), 'The Effectiveness of Digital Storytelling in the Classrooms: A Comprehensive Study', *Smart Learning Environments*, 1 (1): 1–21.

Smith, A. (2014), 'Contemporary Challenges for Education in Conflict Affected Countries', *Journal of International and Comparative Education*, 3 (1): 113–25.

Smith, R. (2020), 'Teaching and Learning in Difficult Circumstance'. Presentation for Nepal Scholars' Association, University of Warwick, UK. Slides available online, https://warwick.ac.uk/fac/soc/al/people/smith/san/ (accessed 7 December 2021).

Sylvester, R., and W. Greenidge (2009), 'Digital Storytelling: Extending the Potential for Struggling Writers', *Reading Teacher*, 63 (4): 284–95.

Tobin, M. (2012), 'Digital Storytelling: Reinventing Literature Circles', *Voices from the Middle*, 20 (2): 40–8.

9

Simple and Engaging Fiction for Adult Beginners

Pedro Malard Monteiro, Margaret Wilkinson and
Martha Young-Scholten

Introduction

The dearth of engaging and accessible fiction for beginning-level adult readers motivated the writers of this chapter to take up the challenge of producing books which mimic children's early readers in their brevity but whose narratives appeal to adults and whose text is readable by those at the lowest levels of linguistic competence in a new language. To produce such books, the Simply Cracking Good Stories project uniquely applies what we know as creative writers about the craft of writing fiction for adults and what we know as linguists about the earliest stages in the acquisition of a new language to guide potential writers in their creation. In this chapter we discuss the processes involved in guiding writers with a particular focus on support provided in various ways, including online since 2013.

The target readership of Simply Stories books includes immigrant adults with limited or no formal schooling in their home language and whose literacy in this and other languages they might know is limited or non-existent. Theirs is a dual burden: they are acquiring the language of the country of resettlement while learning to read for the first time in that language. Not surprisingly, they can take up to eight times longer than educated, literate immigrants to reach comparable proficiency levels in a new language (Schellekens 2009; Tarone, Bigelow and Hansen 2013). Their slow progress remains a concern for educators, particularly in countries like the UK where provision for language classes for this lowest level is inadequate due to funding cuts (£245.9 million in 2008, reduced to £105 million in 2018; see e.g. http://actionforesol.org/).

Insufficient exposure to the new language slows learners' progress. One way to increase exposure is through engagement in individualized, extracurricular reading, that is, pleasure reading (also referred to as extensive reading, free voluntary reading, reading for gist, sustained silent reading). This practice entails reading what, when, where and how the reader chooses, and research dating back decades shows this sort of reading is superior to intensive reading in building reading fluency, expanding vocabulary and, for learners of a new language, aiding acquisition of morphosyntactic competence (Elley and Mangubhai 1983; Krashen 1993; Nation 1997). When compared to other sources of language input, including other media, reading compelling fiction is more likely to result in vocabulary expansion and acquisition of linguistic aspects of a text, resulting in more exposure to the language (Coady 1997; Birch 2002; Zunshine 2006; Lee 2009). Pleasure reading also produces psychological and social benefits such as autonomy, civic involvement, existential self-information, motivation, self-confidence, self-development and well-being (Clark and Rumbold 2006; Spiegel and Sunderland 2006; Mar and Oatley 2008; Djikic et al. 2009; Duncan 2014). It is, however, uncommon in immigrant language programmes, whose emphasis is on functional literacy for daily survival rather than on critical literacy (Freire 1970; Graff 1983; Williamson 2013). In contrast, a critical literacy approach is more likely to make time for practices such as pleasure reading. Pleasure reading also has the welcome benefit of not requiring extensively trained practitioners, which means the practice will appeal to the unpaid volunteers upon whom countries such as the UK increasingly rely for supporting the language and literacy development of adult beginners. However, there are currently too few fiction books at their level to support the practice of pleasure reading for this population of readers.

Appropriate Books for This Readership

What Is Required for Beginning Readers

It has long been recognized that pleasure reading requires an ample amount of books at readers' linguistic and reading levels which cater to a range of interests and preferences (Jose and Brewer 1984; Anderson et al. 1987). Calculating the amount of books required can be based on class size. Rodrigo et al. (2007), for example, adopted a ratio of six books per reader in their semester-long study of pleasure reading by forty-three native and non-native English-speaking adults at a mid-primary school reading level. This meant over two hundred books were made available to readers for several months. However, for adult second language learners at lower levels, there are very few books available.

What Is Available for Beginning Readers

Teachers and tutors of adult beginners often draw on the wealth of story books for children just starting to read on their own (see Martin 2015; Young-Scholten 2017; Filimban et al. 2022). At first glance such books might be the best solution to address the paucity of adult beginners' pleasure reading books: they are short, their text is limited to a few lines per page and the text is supported by images. However, a closer look reveals the limitations of children's books for adults starting to read on their own in a new language. This is because children's linguistic competence, as reflected in the texts of these books, is by age four approaching that of adult native speakers. This means that the complex morphosyntax and extensive vocabulary children's books use renders them inaccessible to adult immigrant beginners when independent reading is the aim (Harrington-Bragg 2018). Equally important here is that children's fiction concerns themes and situations of interest to them. In targeting the young mind, children's books involve clear-cut moral schematism tinged with optimism, fanciful ideas without much concern for reality, and characters who may be non-human creatures that take a child's point of view (while acknowledging their still disempowered status). Plots are predictable, story lines are optimistic and style is dialogue and incident (see Cass 1967; McDowell 1973; Rudd 2005; Wallace 2008).

Mainstream publishers do produce beginners' books for adolescents and adults, but while their books are plentiful, even the lowest levels are too advanced linguistically for our readership. Several publishers of reading materials for adults also produce series (e.g. Gatehouse Books and Grassroots Press) which are at suitably low levels and which treat topics of interest to adults. However, more books than are currently available are needed to embed the practice of pleasure reading for this readership. To fill the gap, teachers and tutors also make use of books that they, or their students, have written.

Simply Stories are short, between fifty and three hundred words (see below), and while they necessarily dispense with the description and introspection of novels, the aim in writing them is to draw on the characteristics of books for educated, literate adults. Unlike children's books, there should be real or realistic situations with real characters who demonstrate agency and the complexities of adult motivation;

plots are unpredictable, and their unfolding entails moral ambiguity; meanings can be hidden; ideas about the world can be challenged; viewpoints other than the reader's own can be presented. This makes Simply Stories comparable to literary fiction. By drawing on sophisticated literary techniques, the Simply Stories writer can produce short narratives appropriate to the age and experience of adults. In the next several sections, we describe these techniques.

Workshops to Produce Simply Stories Books

A writer interested in writing a Simply Stories book typically starts by participating in a workshop. Workshop participants include Newcastle University creative writing students and language and linguistics students as well as those in Newcastle and elsewhere who work with adult immigrants with limited education and literacy. Guidance is provided in a variety of ways, as shown in Table 9.1. After participating in a workshop and being guided in the writing process, the next step for the aspiring Simply Stories writer is to submit what they have written to the editors (the authors of this chapter). If the draft shows promise and if the writer

Table 9.1 Guidance Provided for Writing Simply Stories

Context and participants	Type, mode and timing of guidance
Catherine Cookson Foundation funded contest for Newcastle creative writing postgraduate students and undergraduate language acquisition students	Single face-to-face workshop to launch the Simply Cracking Good Stories project (2010)
Newcastle University creative writing MA and PhD students	Face-to-face workshops and meetings (2011–present)
Newcastle University language and linguistics undergraduates on Immigrant Second Language and Literacy Acquisition module (taught by third author)	Workshops in the seminars supporting the module (2011–19) Online pre-recorded PowerPoints with subsequent access to module leader (2020–21)
British Council ESOL Nexus funding for the general public	Videoed online writing workshop with access to Simply Stories editors (2014)
Teachers and tutors of immigrant adults	Hour-long face-to-face workshops at conferences Online recorded PowerPoints with subsequent access to presenter Hour-long live online webinars followed by access to workshop leader Half-day online workshop (2013–present)

commits to a further editorial process, the text is developed until it is ready for publication, whereupon artists are sought to provide images.

Applying Linguistics to Simply Stories

During a workshop, whatever its length, a potential Simply Stories writer receives information (in handout form if face-to-face or on the workshop PowerPoint if online) detailing what must be considered for a text to be accessible to a reader who is only able to sound out individual words. Participants are introduced to the principles presented in Table 9.2. For longer workshops (especially on the undergraduate students' module), time is set aside to apply these criteria to simplify the writer's text. If participants are not linguists, however, they will need to work with the editors on simplification. This is a collaborative process because changing syntax or vocabulary can easily change a narrative. The goal is to produce a book of between fifty and three hundred words (slightly longer books can be divided into chapters). Each page of text will have one to four sentences, and each page will be accompanied by an image.

Writing a Text at the Reader's Level

The aim of linguistic simplification for Simply Stories books is to make sure that each word and each sentence can be easily processed by an adult beginning to

Table 9.2 Simply Stories Linguistic Criteria

Nouns, verbs and prepositions
Use words beginning readers already know

Syntax
Use this simple word order: subject, verb, object
Do not join sentences

Inflectional morphology
Write in simple present tense

Pronouns
Instead of personal pronouns such as 'he' and 'she', use names
Do not use pronouns without semantic content such as 'there' and 'it'

Phonology
Use words with a single consonant-vowel-consonant syllable

Orthography
Do not use words that contain silent letters or whose spelling is irregular

---

Note: The information given to writers described here is available in distilled form on the Simply Stories website, which also serves as a means of book distribution: http://simplystories.org/simply-stories-guide/.

read in a new language when their linguistic competence in this language is at a low level. Table 9.2 presents the criteria for writing at the appropriate level.

Independent reading for pleasure is more likely to be successful when the reader knows the meanings of the nouns, verbs, adjectives, adverbs and prepositions in the text. This is the first simplification criterion, which is most easily met by those who teach or tutor the intended readership. When this is not the case, workshop leaders provide or generate a list of words readers are likely to know.

The second and third criteria concern syntax and inflectional morphology. Sentences also involve function words and morphemes and in writing simple text with respect to these, writers are asked to apply the lowest stage of Organic Grammar. This stage is based on what learners, regardless of their level of formal schooling and literacy, consistently produce when starting to learn a new language. It excludes all functional elements, and what learners at this stage produce may be ungrammatical (see Vainikka and Young-Scholten 2013). Writing Simply Stories therefore entails adjustments to produce a grammatical text for a Simply Story book. Writers are expected to write sentences with only a main verb, for example, 'Mo drives to Newcastle', rather than an auxiliary verb + main verb, for example, 'Mo is driving to Newcastle'. But when the writer opts for simple present tense in third-person singular, this still involves using a functional element, the inflectional suffix -s for agreement with the subject. There are indications from observation of learners reading Simply Stories aloud that they ignore functional suffixes that they have not acquired and which would therefore have no meaning for them. That is, the suffix -s seems unlikely to impede their reading. Accessible morphosyntax also means downplaying words with minimal semantic content, including pronouns, and avoiding idioms.

Ideally, the writer will use words which are easy to read because they only comprise a single syllable which begins with a consonant followed by a vowel and may or may not end with a consonant such as 'Mo', 'lip' or 'book'. This is because learners' home languages may lack the consonant clusters of English. In addition, the spelling of words should be regular. With minimal guidance, aspiring Simply Stories writers find it straightforward to apply the first two criteria. Application of these criteria along with the first criterion might lead to trade-offs when there is a conflict between words known and the phonology and orthography of these words. A source for words meeting these criteria and the first criterion (words known) is the 300-word set of nouns, verbs and adjectives compiled for the Digital Literacy Instructor for beginning reading software (https://eninfo.diglin.eu/; see Vainikka (2013) on the principles of orthographic regularity upon which this software relies).

Writing a Simply Story: The Writer's Brief

Subject Matter

Readers of Simply Stories come from various cultural and religious backgrounds and live in various countries, yet there are enough situations common to all adults to result in books of wide appeal. Specific but familiar situations and settings can explore universal topics and themes such as love, health, work, family, loss, betrayal, temptation, loneliness and spirituality. Genre is also a consideration and when Simply Stories was begun in 2010, focus groups were conducted with immigrant adults on programmes in the north-east of England. Two of the three groups preferred crime, history, real-life stories and biographies. The third group, all women, preferred comedy and crime. Romance, adventure, fantasy and science fiction were at the bottom of all learners' lists.

Character

When reading independently, the reader can stop and turn to something else if a book does not engage them (Birch 2002). Among the components of fiction that engages the reader is character. When the reader identifies with or cares about the characters, this increases their engagement with the text. At the minimum characters should be recognizable types who elicit sympathy from the reader. It is complex characters whose behaviour is ambiguous, however, who most reliably motivate the reader to keep turning the pages. The writer creates a sympathetic main character, a protagonist, not by making her good but by placing her in a plausible situation and giving her a strong desire that is unfulfilled or obstructed. The stakes for fulfilling this desire should be high and the protagonist's need to fulfil the desire should heighten as the writer introduces obstacles. When the protagonist attempts to fulfil an obstructed desire, her attributes, even in a short book, are revealed. Toolan (2012) considers how a character in short fiction elicits sympathy and describes how the writer accomplishes this by presenting a situation or a state of mind the reader easily recognizes. The brevity of short stories and of books like Simply Stories leaves no time or space for gradual building towards a climax typical of novels, and so at the start of the story, the writer must establish a situation and a narrative arc and then move quickly towards a point where the reader feels most engaged.

Pragmatics and Inferencing

The ambiguous behaviour mentioned in the preceding section relates to the cognitive sophistication adults have that enables them to interpret the world around them. They also have a wealth of life experience and – just as in daily life – when reading a text they can deploy their inferencing skills when a written text leaves things unsaid. Grice (1989) introduced a set of maxims to account for how humans converse: one should be informative, truthful, clear and relevant. Regardless of literacy level or linguistic competence in their new language, all adults are able to deal with the common violation of Grice's maxims, prompted by a human dislike of being told things they already know or can work out or processing extraneous information. And as we have seen above, the writer should keep processing load low for the beginning reader.

With respect to pragmatics, communication involves responding to a speaker's intentions rather than to the surface level of what has been said. Listeners use their skills in pragmatics to make inferences by reasoning, by working out what their interlocutor intends to communicate (see Sperber (1995) on implicature). Clark (2018) illustrates this with the following exchange:

Billy: Did you enjoy the film?
Annie: I always love a good cry.

Annie does not answer Billy's question straightforwardly with 'Yes, I did.' Although this answer would comply with Grice's maxims by being informative, truthful, clear and relevant, she instead responds to what she thinks Billy really wants to know by referring to a seemingly unrelated reaction, assuming that he is familiar with such a reaction to a film, and that he will be able to infer that she did, in fact, enjoy it (Clark 2018; see also Clark and Owtram (2012) on teaching writers to think like readers).

Writing the Text

The initial aim of our workshops is to bring potential writers to an understanding of what Simply Stories are and what underpins writing these short books. The ideas above are presented during a workshop (or similar; see Table 9.1) by the workshop leader and discussed. This occurs live if face-to-face or live or asynchronously as a PowerPoint or in other documentation if online. The next aim is to apply well-honed methods of working with creative writing students to guide workshop participants in writing a draft of a text for a short book. This involves the exercises in each section below.

We have been using 'pleasure reading' to indicate individualized reading, but we have not been explicit about what gives adult readers pleasure. Our view is that adults derive pleasure by reading books that engage them by requiring them to interpret the text based on their own life experiences and by applying what they know about how the world works. The writing of such a text requires the writer to apply subtext and innuendo, and this is important not just in novels for literate readers but also in books for beginning-level adult readers. The writer has to conceal and delay information and not directly or explicitly convey information to reveal the heart of the story. Fiction that does not draw conclusions for the reader, that does not spoon-feed information even when linguistically simple, not only enhances reader involvement but also boosts the adult reader's confidence in ways that fiction for children does not. When the reader is required to interpret a text, when there is some work to do, engagement increases and because the reader's interpretation is needed to complete the story, he or she becomes part of the story. Interpretation is individual; one reader's interpretation may differ from another's and thereby inspire conversation among readers as they discuss and debate their interpretations with each other. This has the additional benefit of building beginning readers' desire to read more as well as developing their oral language.

Meeting these narrative criteria is difficult for new writers and requires training in the techniques described further below. The first step is planning the story.

Story Structure

A Simply Stories book, however short, starts with a status quo immediately disrupted by a trigger which could be anything, from a change in the weather to a murder. The trigger alters the character's circumstances. It is this change of circumstance that creates a desire or problem to solve.

The first exercise applies a standard three-part dramatic structure: beginning, middle and end. Even for a very short narrative, these are: desire – obstacle – outcome; or problem – attempted solution – outcome. In the middle, one or more obstacles (or failed solutions) impede the protagonist, and the book can be lengthened by drawing out the middle when obstacles mount. At the end of the narrative, something has changed for the protagonist, for example, their circumstances, relationships, understanding or world view, but not necessarily fulfilment of their desire or solution to their problem. In some narratives, the protagonist is left desiring something new or confronting a new problem. Adding final surprises or twists (reversals) also enhances the reader's experience.

In the first exercise, the workshop leader asks the workshop participants, the prospective Simply Stories writers, to think of and write down a situation – the 'status quo' – and to place a protagonist in this situation. Whether face-to-face or online and depending on the length of the workshop, writers are given time to complete this activity. The workshop participants then write the middle of the book based on this situation in terms of the desires or problems involved and the protagonists' attempted solutions. In considering the end of the book, writers are encouraged to avoid a highly resolved happy ending and think about endings that are left open for the reader to interpret. How much time they are given depends on the length of the workshop and whether it is face-to-face or online. This also applies to writers reading their work aloud to others in the group, a typical feature of creative writing workshops.

Concealing Information and Writing in Scenes

Writing in scenes requires effort from the writer but serves the reader well by prompting them to make inferences from description of actions, by showing rather than telling (see below). The reader is required to interpret the text to complete and/or understand the story. The writer must also refrain from providing complete information and/or delay its release. The practice of doing so keeps the reader turning the pages of a story in order to try to find this withheld information. The argument could be made that requiring inferencing and interpretation is too cognitively challenging for adult beginners, particularly those who have had little or no formal education and whose literacy in both their new language and home language is limited. Writers are admonished to keep in mind that the notions of pragmatics, as described above, are invariably applied by adults during their interactions with others to make inferences. Beginning readers simply need to transfer to reading what they automatically do while listening.

The novice writer may need to practice leaving things unsaid, to under-describe or to describe in such a way as to invite the reader to see some of the setting, characters, situation or emotions for herself. Mariani (2007) admonishes thriller writers not to tell the reader that a character is bad but to show it to them. Writing in scenes also often creates an immediacy which draws the reader in. This involves focusing on what the character is doing moment by moment, in time and place, using concrete details which impart a sense of reality. Writing in scenes is a technique which discourages novice writers' natural tendency to summarize events and draw conclusions for the reader. 'Telling' in writing uses adjectives and adverbs and because using them impedes the reader's personal visualization of the situation and characters, the writer is advised to avoid them. 'Showing' in writing not only dispenses with adjectives but also reduces use of copula 'be', with its low semantic content, and verbs such as 'think', 'feel', 'want' and 'like', which refer to inner states rather than paint a picture in the reader's mind. Applying this advice has the additional benefit of producing more easily processed sentences. Consider, for example, these explicit statements:

John is vain.
John thinks he should work harder.
John feels sad.
John would like a better job.

Each of these tells us about John, but each could be replaced by writing that shows the same thing. Showing that John is vain, for example, uses verbs that depict action:

John looks in the bathroom mirror.
John combs his hair.
John puts gel in his hair.
John sprays his hair.
John smiles.

There is also a trade-off in length of text; where there was a single sentence telling the reader that John is vain there are now six sentences showing this. Each, however, is short and they combine to paint a picture of John that a single adjective referring to him does not.

The following exercise, used in our writing workshops, guides participants in practicing concealing information. The amount of time spent on this exercise will vary, as noted above. The workshop participant is asked to choose one of these jobs: carer, dishwasher, hairdresser, taxi driver, cleaner, doctor, dentist. They are then asked to write several sentences in first person from the point of view of the character who has that job, responding to each of the following questions. The participant should not reveal the job. Instead, they should go through the day, building hints. Adjectives and adverbs that impede the reader's visualization of the situation and characters should be avoided.

It's 9 am, what are you doing?

It's 12 noon, what are you doing?

It's 6 pm, what are you doing?

It's midnight, what are you doing?

The following is a Simply Stories book by Ian Patterson (2015) which uses delayed information. In addition, the writer delightfully misleads by deliberately encouraging the reader to infer that violence is taking place. It is only at the very end that something rather different is revealed.

THE KNIFE
The knife cuts.
The children scream.

One cut.
Drip.

Two cuts.
Drip. Drip.

Three cuts.
Drip. Drip. Drip.

Sue eats a slice.
Ben eats a slice.
Josh eats a slice of the orange.

The workshop leader then directs participants to turn to the plan for their own story and select a scene to write by answering the questions shown below. After having practiced concealing information in the exercise above, they should be prepared to do so in writing their own narrative.

What is the protagonist seeing and hearing?

Where are they? (What is under his/her feet? Above their head)?

What time of day (year, etc.) is it?

What is the protagonist holding in his/her hand or touching?

Who else is in the scene?

Effort is required at the editing stage, as Clark (2014) points out: after production of a first draft, subsequent drafts involve removing text to leave the reader to work out what is unsaid. Depending on the length and nature (face-to-face or online) of the workshop, writers can share what they have written and at least one additional round can be added during which the writer edits their scene and then shares it again. To produce a complete Simply Stories book, the writer will – either on their own or in a follow-up workshop – follow the instructions in the exercise just above, adding the rest of the scenes needed for the entire story they have planned in the first exercise.

Concealing Information and Using Dialogue

Concealing information and writing in scenes often prioritizes dialogue because it encourages reader interpretation where much must be inferred. Simple dialogue between two people can be most effective. The first example below illustrates what not to do. Diane and Joe leave nothing unsaid in what is an unnatural conversation. Note that the text is not linguistically simple, with long, often multi-clausal sentences and abstract verbs. In the final sentence, Diane bluntly expresses her feelings rather than employing indirectness as a vehicle for politeness (Brown and Levinson 1987).

Joe:	How is your mother? I know she has been really ill because you told me last time we met. You were so worried.
Diane:	I think she is getting better. I am so relieved.
Joe:	Yes, you must be relieved.
Diane:	I am very close to my mother.
Joe:	I know that because we are good friends. But now that she is better, let's spend some time alone together. How about going to the cinema?
Diane:	No. That's not possible. We are friends, but I do not want anything more. Going to the cinema would be like going out on a date and I don't want to.

The reader, not required to engage with the text by making inferences, is likely to become bored when reading such a dialogue. The best dialogues are driven by conflict. But conflict need not entail argument; it can be just a difference of opinion. Conflict keeps the action vivid and immediate and is yet another means of increasing reader engagement.

In the second example, below, the two characters do not talk directly about their real wants, their relationship or their attitudes towards each other. This is implied as they discuss something else, again Diane's mother. But Diane's responses to Joe are brief as she conceals information about herself from him. The reader might wonder whether she is taking advantage of her mother's health as an excuse to decline Joe's advances, prompting further reading. In addition, good dialogue can result in less text than bad dialogue.

Joe:	How is your mother?
Diane:	Better.
Joe:	Now we can go to the cinema.
Diane:	Well … um … not that much better.

Brief, well-written dialogue helps to create a scene in which time and place are implied; linguistically speaking, this dispenses with adverbs and can result in shorter sentences. However, it is more difficult for the novice writer and can require additional guidance from the workshop leader.

The next exercise builds the participants' dialogue-writing skills. One character is about to go on a journey and the other character is seeing them off. Instead of talking about what they really want to say (their hidden subtext), they might discuss the weather, what the traveller is wearing or what they have brought with them to eat. This workshop exercise involves two people at an airport, train or bus station who are saying goodbye. Character A is leaving home. Character B is a partner, best friend or family member. The participants need to write a dialogue to show one of the following conflicts through what they say to each other:

> Option 1: A wants to leave quickly, but doesn't want to admit it; while B wants to postpone A's leave-taking for as long as possible, but doesn't want to admit it.
>
> Option 2: A doesn't want to leave and tries to postpone the inevitable, while B wants A to leave without a fuss.

Both narrative demands and the need for linguistic simplicity (as in Table 9.1) can be met by using dialogue in which the writer can choose from imperatives, admonishments and salutations as well as a range of elliptical utterances, where phrases or sentences are not spoken, for example, as in single 'wh' words instead of full questions (see e.g. Culicover and Jackendoff 2005).

> Hey, Phil!
> Yoo hoo, Mrs. Goldberg!
> Seatbelts fastened!
> Everyone in the car!
> Books open to page fifteen!

In considering the nature of compact writing in short stories, Toolan (2012) argues that elliptical utterances heighten emotional immersion (see also Booth 1961; Bal 1985; and on ellipsis, Merchant 2002). While this may be so, linguistic simplicity is the main reason for their use in Simply Stories books.

The Wedding, by Azad Maudaressi (2015), is an example of a Simply Stories book which requires the reader to make inferences from the dialogue. Note how the writing is effective despite many repeats. These are natural in conversation, and they also help the beginning reader process the text.

THE WEDDING
'I love you,' Jalil says.
'I love you too,' Katie says.
'Marry me,' Jalil says.
'Yes!' Katie says.

'I want a big wedding,' Katie says.
'A big wedding?' Jalil says.
'A big church wedding,' Katie says.
'A church wedding?' Jalil says.

'Are we alone?' Jalil says.
'Mother and father are out,' Mahmud says.
'Katie wants a big wedding,' Jalil says.
'A big church wedding.'
'A big church wedding?' Mahmud says.

Katie's family come to the wedding.
Katie's friends come to the wedding.
Mahmud comes to the wedding.
Jalil's mother and father stay home.

From Workshop to Finished Simply Stories Book

As we have pointed out above, a Simply Stories book involves a character that the reader cares about, whose life is disrupted by a succession of obstacles. This creates page-turning dramatic tension. Writing in present tense in scenes and using dialogue keeps the text linguistically simple while requiring the reader to interpret the text, encouraging them to make inferences from their own life experiences, which further enhances their involvement with the story and the characters (Wilkinson and Young-Scholten 2010). In the Appendix we provide an example of the outcome of the workshop process, demonstrating the points crucial to writing a good Simply Stories book. The underwritten text allows the reader to infer information yet there is still narrative build, change, desire, frustration of desire, growing problems, complications and conflict written in a linguistically simple way.

Production of Books Face-to-Face and Online

The Face-to-Face Process

A face-to-face process of writing a Simply Stories book is the ideal. Writing starts with a workshop which focuses on writing the outline of a story. Several subsequent workshops are each devoted to writing the synopsis as scenes, writing the actual story, then editing and applying linguistic simplification techniques to the text. Each workshop includes sharing these pieces of writing with other participants to receive and then discuss feedback from them and from the workshop leader.

The undergraduate language and linguistics students have been taking a module with the third author, Immigrant Second Language and Literacy Acquisition, half of which is devoted to reading, including pleasure reading. When the module was first offered, only one optional workshop on writing a short book was offered and few students wrote books. To address this situation, workshops were made compulsory, taking the place of the one-hour seminars attached to the module for the twelve-week semester. These included both fiction writing and linguistic simplification exercises on which students worked in small groups, and out of which emerged a book which they field-tested with adult learners at local English language providers. They then donated these books to these providers. Crucially, students were not marked on the narrative aspects of the books themselves. It was unrealistic to expect that even with extensive training, language and linguistics students would devote the time required to develop creative writing skills and work with the editors (the second and third authors) to produce a Simply Stories book. However, training was not entirely dispensed with but shifted to the last two seminars of the module and writing a book became optional.

The above also applies to practitioners who work with our target readership to support their acquisition of a new language. Honing the writing skills to produce a Simply Stories book requires more than a single workshop.

Online Processes

'Depending on the length of the workshop' is a phrase that has appeared a number of times in the descriptions of the workshop steps above. Writing in a quiet room, even with others, is a positive experience and sharing what one has written in a face-to-face workshop, an important part of the process, can be less daunting in person than online. In conducting workshops online with potential contributors to Simply Stories we have discovered that the process requires multiple workshops/meetings. The chance to write a short fiction book has wide appeal, but producing a book that meets the criteria described above requires a high level of dedication by the writer.

The British Council Nexus–funded workshop, which took place in 2014, was spearheaded by a journalist and media specialist who recruited an actor to produce an online video-based version of the above workshop ideas. The idea was for a non-linear, flexible approach that would attract aspiring writers from around the world. The workshop was widely marketed in English-speaking countries via social media and search engine advertising, but almost no prospective writers contacted the Simply Stories editors. Some of the British Council funding and the Newcastle University funding in 2015 was then used to support the delivery of a series of face-to-face workshops with MA and PhD creative writing students at Newcastle and several others who expressed an interest in participating. These sessions produced over twelve books which met Simply Stories criteria because the participants were committed to meeting them and were willing to engage in a lengthy process of editing and re-editing.

When teaching shifted to online during the pandemic both in 2020 and 2021, students regularly expressed concern about less contact time with module leaders. For the Immigrant Second Language and Literacy Acquisition module, an online workshop on creative writing with post-workshop availability of the workshop leader was offered both in spring 2020 and spring 2021. This did not address students' concerns; uptake was minimal.

In addition, online workshops have been delivered to teachers and tutors who work with immigrant adults. For the online workshops shown in Table 9.2, a PowerPoint-based, one-hour workshop was delivered, and the presenter (the third author) then made herself available for post-workshop consultation. In the spring of 2020, the initial workshop was delivered as a well-attended webinar across multiple time zones as part of a six-week online, non-credit-bearing module for those who teach or tutor these adult learners.[1]

Participants taking the module were from all over the world and were already used to interacting with others on the module across time zones. Based on awareness that participants hoped to produce a book, at least for their own learners, and based on the discovery that those who are not aspiring creative writers are unlikely to commit considerable time to writing a Simply Stories, no additional webinars were offered. Instead, participants were invited to submit book drafts by the end of the summer. These were then checked for linguistic accessibility only. This resulted in fourteen books in English as well as in Arabic, Bosnian, Italian and Spanish. Writers added images. None of the participants, however, expressed an interest in committing to working further with the Simply Stories editors to apply the narrative criteria discussed above for writing literary fiction. Books were therefore shared only with each other and with their learners in much the same way as the undergraduates donated their books to local English providers.

Conclusion

We have worked with creative writing and language and linguistics students at Newcastle University and second language practitioners around the world, both face-to-face and online, to guide them in producing very short fiction books which would give adult beginners a better chance to develop the habit of reading for pleasure. This involves working closely with potential Simply Stories writers to convey to them what the craft of writing fiction for adults involves. Teaching online is a challenge we have now met, and we hope to move forward to apply what has succeeded in face-to-face workshops to produce books that meet the Simply Stories criteria. Aspiring creative writers are more likely than others to dedicate the time to hone their skills regardless of workshop mode.

Appendix

Protagonist: Katie. Trigger: marriage and moving in with in-laws, a familiar situation which immediately presents obstacles. In confronting these obstacles, Katie introduces an obstacle herself. This 244-word book can be laid out as nine chapters to indicate to the reader that these are separate scenes.

Chiko

Katie's mother smiles.
Katie's father smiles.
Katie and Jalil kiss.
They are married.

Katie and Jalil drive and drive.
They see many buildings.
They see many houses.
They see a big house.
Jalil stops the car.
Katie sees Jalil's mother, father and grandmother.

'Welcome!' Jalil's mother says.
'Come in,' Jalil's father says.
'Welcome, come in, come in,' Jalil's grandmother says.
'Thank-you. You have a lovely home,' Katie says.
'What?' Jalil's mother says.
'No English,' Jalil says.

Katie sits alone in the bedroom.
No TV. No phone. No internet.
No Jalil. Jalil is at work.
Katie looks out the window.
Katie sees a dog.
'Woof, Woof,' the dog says.
Katie goes outside.

'Shoo, shoo,' Jalil's mother says.
Jalil's father gets a broom.
'Please,' says Katie.
'Not in the house,' Jalil's grandmother says.

Please, Jalil. The dog is alone,' Katie says.
'No dogs in this house,' Jalil says.
'Please,' Katie says.
'No,' Jalil says.

'The dog needs a name.
'Chiko,' Katie says.
Katie and Chiko walk outside.
Katie and Chiko play.
Katie loves Chiko.

Chiko barks.
'Go away,' says Jalil's grandmother.
Jalil's father gets a broom.
'Shoo, shoo,' says Jalil's mother.

'Come eat,' Grandmother says.
'Eeeeeeeeeek! Snake in the salad!' grandmother screams.
The snake is on the table.
The snake is on the floor.
'Chiko! Chiko!' Katie says.
Chiko runs inside.
Chiko sees the snake.
The snake is in Chiko's mouth.
Jalil opens the door.
Chiko and the snake go out.
'Good dog,' Jalil's mother says.

Note

1 The module is part of a suite of six online modules designed for teachers and tutors who work with adult immigrants with little or no home language literacy. These modules run for six weeks and upon occasion involve additional, post-module workshops. They are not credit-bearing. See https://research.ncl.ac.uk/eu-speak/.

References

Primary Literature

Maudaressi, A. (2015), *The Wedding*, Newcastle University: Simply Stories.
Patterson, I. (2015), *The Knife*, Newcastle University: Simply Stories.
Wilkinson, M., and M. Young-Scholten (2015), *Chiko*, Newcastle University: Simply Stories.

Secondary Literature

Anderson R., L. Shirey, P. Wilson and L. Fielding (1987), 'Interestingness of Children's Reading Material', in R. Snow and M. Farr (eds), *Aptitude, Learning and Instruction, Vol. III, Conative and Affective Process Analysis*, 287–99, Mahwah, NJ: Erlbaum.

Bal, M. (1985), *Narratology: Introduction to the Theory of Narrative*, Toronto: Toronto University Press.

Birch, M. (2002), *L2 English Reading: Getting to the Bottom*, London: Erlbaum.

Booth, W. (1961), *The Rhetoric of Fiction*, Chicago: University of Chicago Press.

Brown, P., and S. Levinson (1987), *Politeness: Some Universals in Language Usage*, Cambridge: Cambridge University Press.

Cass, J. (1967), *Literature and the Young Child*, London: Longman.

Clark, B. (2014), 'Pragmatics and Inference', in P. Stockwell and S. Whiteley (eds), *Cambridge Handbook of Stylistics*, 300–14, Cambridge: Cambridge University Press.

Clark, B. (2018), 'Applying the OG Stages to Create Simple Fiction for Beginning Level Adults. Engaging Books: Pragmatics'. Paper presented at the conference Adults Learning to Read for the First Time in a New Language: New Ideas in Practice, Newcastle, 21 July.

Clark, B., and N. Owtram (2012), 'Imagined Inference: Teaching Writers to Think Like Readers', in M. Burke, S. Czabo, L. Week and J. Berkowitz (eds), *Current Trends in Pedagogical Stylistics*, 126–41, London: Continuum.

Clark, C., and K. Rumbold (2006), *Reading for Pleasure: A Research Overview*, London: National Literacy Trust.

Coady, J. (1997), 'L2 Vocabulary Acquisition through Extensive Reading', in J. Coady and T. Huckin (eds), *Second Language Vocabulary Acquisition*, 225–37, Cambridge: Cambridge University Press.

Culicover, P., and R. Jackendoff (2005), *Simpler Syntax*, Oxford: Oxford University Press.

Djikic, M., K. Oatley, S. Zoeterman and J. B. Peterson (2009), 'On Being Moved by Art: How Reading Fiction Transforms the Self', *Creativity Research Journal*, 21 (1): 24–9.

Duncan, S. (2014), *Reading for Pleasure and Reading Circles for Adult Emergent Readers: Insights in Adult Learning*. London: National Institute of Adult Continuing Education.

Elley, W. B., and F. Mangubhai (1983), 'The Impact of Reading on Second Language Learning', *Reading Research Quarterly*, 19: 53–67.

Filimban, E., A. Middlemas, E. Mocciaro, P. Malard Monteiro and M. Young-Scholten (2022), 'Pleasure Reading for Immigrant Adults on a Volunteer-Run Programme', in A. Norland Shaswar and J. Rosén (eds), *Literacies in the Age of Mobility*, London: Palgrave.

Freire, P. (1970), 'The Adult Literacy Process as Cultural Action for Freedom', *Harvard Educational Review*, 40: 205–25.

Graff, G. (1983), *Beyond the Culture Wars*, New York: Norton.

Grice, H. P. (1989), *Studies in the Way of Words*, Cambridge, MA: Harvard University Press.

Harrington-Bragg, J. (2018), 'Beyond Comprehension: Are Children's Emergent Readers Appropriate Pleasure Reading Materials for LESLLA Learners?' Unpublished ms., Newcastle University. https://www.leslla.org/research.

Jose, P., and W. Brewer (1984), 'Development of Story Liking: Character Identification, Suspense, and Outcome Resolution', *Developmental Psychology*, 20: 911–24.

Krashen, S. (1993), *The Power of Reading*, Englewood, CO: Libraries Unlimited.

Lee, S.-K. (2009), 'Topic Congruence and Topic of Interest: How Do They Affect Second Language Reading Comprehension?' *Reading in a Foreign Language*, 21: 159–78.

Mar, R. A., and K. Oatley (2008), 'The Function of Fiction Is the Abstraction and Simulation of Social Experience', *Perspectives on Psychological Science*, 3 (3): 173–92.

Mariani, S. (2007), *How to Write a Thriller*, New York: How to Books.

Martin, L. (2015), 'Readers at the Margins: Field Testing and Market Research Report'. Unpublished ms., Newcastle University.

McDowell, M. (1973), 'Fiction for Children', *Children's Literature in Education*, 4: 50–63.

Merchant, J. (2002), *The Syntax of Silence: Sluicing, Islands and the Theory of Ellipsis*, Oxford: Oxford University Press.

Nation, P. (1997), 'The Language Learning Benefits of Extensive Reading', *Language Teacher*, 21: 13–16.

Rodrigo, V., D. Greenberg, V. Burke, R. Hall, A. Berry, T. Brinck, H. Joseph and M. Oby (2007), 'Implementing an Extensive Reading Program and Library for Adult Literacy Learners', *Reading in a Foreign Language*, 19: 106–19.

Rudd, D. (2005), 'Theorising and Theories: How Does Children's Literature Exist?' in P. Hunt (ed.), *Understanding Children's Literature*, 15–29, London: Routledge.

Schellekens, P. (2009), 'Cause and Effect: The Impact of the Skills for Life Strategy on Language Assessment', in L. Taylor and C. J. Weir (eds), *Language Testing Matters: Investigating the Wider Social and Educational Impact of Assessment – Proceedings of the ALTE Cambridge Conference, April 2008*, 103–17, Cambridge: Cambridge University Press.

Sperber, D. (1995), 'How Do We Communicate?', in J. Brockman and K. Matson (eds), *How Things Are: A Science Toolkit for the Mind*, 191–9, New York: Morrow.

Spiegel, M., and H. Sunderland (2006), *Teaching Basic Literacy to ESOL Learners: A Teachers' Guide*, London: London South Bank University.

Tarone, E., M. Bigelow and K. Hansen (2013), 'Alphabetic Literacy and Second Language Acquisition by Older Learners', in J. Herschensohn and M. Young-Scholten (eds), *The Handbook of Second Language Acquisition*, 180–204, Cambridge: Cambridge University Press.

Toolan, M. (2012), 'Short Story Passages with High Emotional Impact: An Attempt at Reader-Response Confirmation'. Talk given at Newcastle University, 8 November.

Vainikka, A. (2013), 'English Reading and Spelling for Short Words'. Unpublished ms., Johns Hopkins University.

Vainikka, A., and M. Young-Scholten (2013), 'Stages in Second Language Acquisition', in J. Herschensohn and M. Young-Scholten (eds), *The Handbook of Second Language Acquisition*, 560–80, Cambridge: Cambridge University Press.

Wallace, C. (2008), 'A Socio-cultural Approach to Literacy Instruction for Adult ESOL Learners New to Literacy', in M. Young-Scholten (ed.), *Low-Educated Second Language and Literacy Acquisition. Proceedings of the Third Annual Forum*, 91–8, Durham, NC: Roundtuit.

Wilkinson, M., and M. Young-Scholten (2010), 'Writing to a Brief: Creating Fiction for Immigrant Adults', in C. Schöneberger, I. van de Craats and J. Kurvers (eds), *Proceedings of the Low Educated Adult Second Language and Literacy Acquisition Symposium*, 103–213, Nijmegen: Centre for Language Studies.

Williamson, E. (2013), 'Our Lives Press: Inspiring through the Experience of Others', *National Association of English and Community Language Teaching to Adults News*, 101: 5.

Young-Scholten, M. (2017), 'Taking Stock: LESLLA Learners' Pleasure/Extensive Reading and Access to Materials'. Workshop delivered at the annual LESLLA symposium, Portland, Oregon, 10 August.

Young-Scholten, M., and R. Naeb (2010), 'Non-literate L2 Adults' Small Steps in Mastering the Constellation of Skills Required for Reading', in T. Wall and M. Leong (eds), *Low Educated Second Language and Literary Acquisition. Proceedings of the 5th Symposium*, 80–91, Utrecht: LOT.

Young-Scholten, M., and R. Naeb (2020), 'The Acquisition and Assessment of Morphosyntax', in J. Peyton and M. Young-Scholten (eds), *Teaching Adult Immigrants with Limited Formal Education: Theory, Research and Practice*, 80–104, Bristol: Multilingual Matters.

Young-Scholten, M., M. Sosinski and A. Martín Rubio (2015), 'Undergrads' Involvement in Producing Short Fiction Books for Immigrant Adult Beginners in England and Spain', *Language Issues*, 26: 55–60.

Young-Scholten, M., and N. Strom (2006), 'First-Time L2 Readers: Is There a Critical Period?', in J. Kurvers, I. van de Craats and M. Young-Scholten (eds), *Low Educated Adult Second Language and Literacy Acquisition. Proceedings of the Inaugural Conference*, 45–68, Utrecht: LOT.

Zunshine, L. (2006), *Why We Read Fiction: Theory of Mind and the Novel*, Columbus: Ohio State University Press.

10

Annotating Literary Texts on Conceptboard: Philological Practice in the Digital Classroom

Verena Laschinger

Introduction

My flight to the United States was cancelled when the Covid-19 global pandemic hit in March 2020. Forced to stay put, I had to find my way in virtual space instead of traipsing around the southern edge of the Catskill mountains, where I had been invited to participate in a transdisciplinary, experiential climate change think tank. Rather than inhaling the scents of the forest at Mohonk Preserve, New Paltz, along with the inspirations that its renowned community of artists and scholars supplied, I found myself touring the internet for ten drab hours each day as I would, it later turned out, for months on end.

I established a routine of vanishing through a tiny thirteen-inch screen into the vast netherworld that an assemblage of cables, data and laptop mediated for me in ways I do not comprehend and – if I come to think about it – still perceive as miraculous. I rarely think about it, though. Mostly the effect of immediacy is achieved so seamlessly that 'the presence of the medium and the act of mediation' remain unnoticed (Bolter and Grusin 2000: 11). As the definition goes, 'Virtual reality is immersive, which means that it is a medium whose purpose is to disappear' (21). Fully immersed I effectively distanced myself from others as advised by the World Health Organization. But while I was unimpeded by virus attacks, I came to live a short Mr Duffian distance from my body. At the end of each long day, it took me a moment to recognize as my own and reinhabit the cramped and parched physical shell that painfully reinserted its presence.

No doubt, what mild inconvenience I have been experiencing over the past year and half hardly compares to the drastic physical, psychological and economic effects the pandemic has had on those less bolstered by privilege. And the stories of the dead, the sick and those without access to vaccines are not mine to tell, either. I can only relay the tale of the inconvenienced Western academic, which is, at best, a footnote to the Covid-19 horror story. I do so to report two positive side effects of the pandemic lockdown.

The first concerns the environment. *Not* embarking on a transatlantic flight reduced my ecological footprints in a simple and efficient way. It finally sank in that staying put marks the difference between *acting* on the climate change agenda instead of *debating* it, for example, at a workshop that would have involved – and ironically so – thousands of miles of CO_2-emitting plane trips. The second effect concerns my professional practice as a university teacher, who cherishes small-size, discussion-based, in-person seminars, aiming to personally involve participants and create meaningful exchanges among all parties. In my experience, a democratic, participatory approach fosters students' motivation. I am convinced that their active engagement in the dual processes of information transfer and knowledge production hones the ability to argue cogently and based in critical, independent thinking. In short, I am an advocate of old-school humanities' seminars and the Humboldtian educational ideal.

Forced to change routines and adapt to the virtual environment, I came across a mode of teaching of literature that, surprisingly, turned out to be pedagogically effective and philologically pertinent not despite but because of the medium's constraints on interpersonal exchange as we know it. As Curtis and Lawson point out, 'Online interactions lack the non-verbal cues that are a component of face-to-face contact, and this may reduce the extent of the communication that occurs. Much online conversation occurs asynchronously, with substantial delays in receiving a reply' (2001: 22). Determined to avoid such delays in communication and keep students involved instead of switching off their cameras, muting their mics and drifting off, I employed Conceptboard, a collaborative tool that allows for forms of expression other than verbal. It supplies a remote teaching environment in which students can express themselves simultaneously and spontaneously without having to wait their turn. Given the indispensability of climate-conscious teaching and of higher education's digital overhaul in the post-pandemic future, its simple applicability and usefulness for the teaching of literature make it, I believe, worthy of recommendation.

I wish to thank research affiliates and artists-in-residence at Mohonk Preserve, Andrea Frank, associate professor in art, and Michael Asbill, lecturer in art, SUNY, New Paltz, for introducing me to Conceptboard. In March 2020, Andrea and Michael moved the climate change think tank online rather than

Figure 10.1 Four ways system drawing, 2020. Courtesy of Conceptboard.

cancel it. As the original plan faltered, and we were no longer able to explore ways of healing ruptures and reconnecting with the protected ecosystem in situ, the organizers assembled us on Zoom. They digitally instructed us to explore various states of immersion, through experimental body work and awareness training. Reconnecting on Conceptboard immediately after for spontaneous creative outlet, we silently mapped our experience in synchronous collaborative system drawing sessions (Figure 10.1). On screen we figured as disembodied data, pixelated talking heads and moving cursors only. But thanks to the online application's 'logic of immediacy' which 'dictates that the medium itself should disappear and leave us in the presence of the thing represented' (Bolter and Grusin 2000: 5–6), we actually felt connected with each other, collaborating 'in the same space' (11). This effect was a revelation. Subsequently put to use in my online literature seminars, Conceptboard had a similar effect on the students.

A Case Study of a Philological Teaching Concept

Adjusting methods for the second remote teaching term in winter 2020/21, I designed and implemented an exercise that employed virtual whiteboards in my 'Nineteenth Century American Children's Classics' online seminar. A total of forty-nine students had registered for two consecutive groups of the same course. Five of them were already enrolled in the Master of Education programme and took the course to make up for missing credits. Another twenty were training to become future teachers at the primary and secondary levels. And while children's and young adult literature is a key element for teaching reading and literary analysis, the subject had not yet been part of these students' mandatory programme due to some administrative oversight. Ten other students were enrolled in the English bachelor programme with a focus on specialist content in American literary history and culture, while the remaining four were majoring in literary studies, a theory-laden programme at the University of Erfurt. All of them were given the same task to first read and then collaborate in online annotating the same excerpt from a literary prose text. There was no difference in the implementation of the idea in the two equally heterogeneous groups.

To kick-start the online seminar and engage the students in active collaboration, I instructed them to work on Conceptboard already in week 2. All students accessed the board via the link I shared in the chat on Webex, where the digital class was conducted. Thus far they had only listened to my introductory lecture on the history of children's literature in week 1. Without prior discussion of the primary text, they engaged with the excerpt right away in week 2, spending forty-five minutes reading it closely, registering and recording on the digital whiteboard any fleeting observation, raising every question they had (and would likely pass over in an oral discussion that was less focused on details and less immersive). While everyone jotted down their thoughts on the text, students eventually started to also comment on or expand on someone else's annotations. This way the digital whiteboard filled up quickly with differently coloured sticky notes, freehand commentary, links and tags and images along the margins of the text block that I had copied and pasted on the board in preparation of this session and whose various paragraphs were now highlighted in bright colours, its sentences underlined and words encircled.

Asked to proceed by the steps devised by Wyn Kelley, senior lecturer of literature at Massachusetts Institute of Technology (MIT), students annotated the text synchronously and collaboratively on Conceptboard, 'marking striking passages, unfamiliar words, details that amuse or puzzle or move [them], explicit sources or references, unusual phrasing, words that point to important issues for understanding character or theme in the text' (2014: n.p.). They were free 'to annotate as many details as [they] wish and make [their] comments any length', so we might get 'a variety of different kinds of annotations, from the personal impression, to something that requires looking up information in a dictionary or encyclopaedia, to something more reflective or interpretive' (n.p.). (For detailed information, see Kelley's instruction sheet, available for download from https://www.annotationstudio.org/wp-content/uploads/2014/03/21L000.Essay1-Instructions.pdf.)

While some noted 'all the examples of a certain phenomenon [they] have noticed: words that speak to different sensory images, for example, or place names, or allusions to other authors, or language reminiscent of details from elsewhere in the novel', others felt more inclined 'to cover material from various parts of the chapter or alternatively focus on a particular paragraph or moment' (n.p.). Some searched for 'certain repetitions of sounds, words, or phrases, or conversely significant breaks or changes in a pattern' (n.p.), while others focused specifically on the beginning and/or the ending of the chapter. Given that it was my goal to let students work out from scratch an understanding of the text, every observation was relevant, no question deemed too 'simple' and no inkling too far-fetched. I intentionally let them work at their own pace and without interfering in the process or judging their reading skills. I wanted them to follow their interests, while simultaneously identifying the aspects which they needed to read up on to arrive at a higher level of comprehension.

Ultimately, the goal was to advance their level of competence and acquaint them with a method they could apply to work out the meaning of any, even less accessible texts than *Ragged Dick*. To arrive there, the exercise involved a self-reflective next step which had, again, been originally devised by Kelley. Once students finished annotating the excerpt online, I asked them to consider 'what questions or discoveries annotations inspire' (n.p.), and why they had chosen the approach they did. Discussing students' various considerations on their observations and procedures, we spent the second half of the session identifying topics that required more research, thus further 'developing the data' the group had 'generated' (n.p.).

While I followed Kelley's instructions for this annotating exercise almost to the dot, a number of changes were nonetheless required for the purposes of my course. Originally Kelley had devised the assignment on chapter 4 of Mary Shelley's *Frankenstein* as a first step in the process of writing a five-page essay and for Annotation Studio, an online tool developed at MIT (https://www.annotatio nstudio.org/). Yet I decided to, firstly, substitute the open source web application Annotation Studio with Conceptboard, a company based in Halle (Saale), Germany, which also allows for a-/synchronous online collaboration at no cost. Both tools facilitate free-form, paper-like annotating on digital devices, allowing users to interact with texts intuitively and creatively. Subsequently stored, the virtual whiteboards can be publicly shared or deleted at any point according to the main user's preferences. While Annotation Studio is widely used in the US higher education system, Conceptboard is better suited for the German context. It operates in compliance with the European Union's data security and protection laws, which keep the company liable to protect sensitive user information. Responsible for setting up a teaching environment that protects students from inadvertently giving up data in mandatory class activities, I thus chose Conceptboard. Furthermore, the fact that it also provides both English and German language user interfaces makes it an ideal fit for a teaching environment mandated to operate both in German and English such as a second language American literature programme at a German university.

Secondly, I chose Horatio Alger's coming-of-age novel *Ragged Dick, Or Street Life in New York with the Boot Blacks*, which was more suitable than *Frankenstein* for the purposes of my class. First published serially in *The Student and Schoolmate*, a nineteenth-century children's magazine, Alger's text was republished as a novel in 1868. Even in this closed format, *Ragged Dick* consists of short, self-contained episodic chapters that retain the logic and character of serial narrating. Given the instalment structure of the novel, a single chapter can easily be disconnected from the text body. Read and annotated in isolation it functions *pars pro toto*, yielding results that are pertinent for the complete novel. In other words, fragments of *Ragged Dick* lend themselves particularly well to the reductionist approach of close-reading and annotating in a tightly scheduled survey course designed to introduce the great variety of American children's and young adult literature (see Chapter 2 by Thaler for further approaches to engage with literary texts).

To facilitate synchronous collaborative online annotating I settled specifically on *Ragged Dick*'s opening chapter because it is rich in description. Introducing the main character in terms of appearance, character and his performance in the narrative world, it describes him along the fault lines of age, race, class, sex and gender, which demands critical interrogation. The chapter sketches out the time and narrative setting of the story, making certain buildings such as theatres or hotels function as cultural and socio-economic markers indicative of the protagonist's development in the course of this Bildungsroman. The descriptive mode is further sustained by abounding allusions to specific historical characters and key political and social issues such as child labour, child poverty, homelessness and progressivist reforms, rendering a vivid image of American urban plight in the second half of the nineteenth century. Following up on these historical references, students gain contextual understanding in the process.

Ragged Dick, a staple of children's literature courses and generally a class favourite, functions also as an archive of discourse. It addresses themes such as the American Dream, common motifs such as 'from rags to riches', or 'up the by the bootstraps', and spins intertextually off on the classic *The Autobiography of Benjamin Franklin*, all of which invites a critical discussion of American capitalism. Addressing how the text propagates American capitalism's favourite myth of equal opportunities while facilitating the white male character's formulaic social rise by way of exclusionary classist, racist and sexist practices can even be expanded into a discussion on how twenty-first century's neoliberal capitalism exacerbates climate change and unevenly distributes its effects along the intersecting fault lines of race, class and gender. Given the expanse and complexity of capitalism's systemic implication in pressing global challenges such as climate change and inequality, the issue could be fleshed out in the course of several subsequent sessions.

Needless to say that the text first and foremost warrants an analysis of narrative discourse involving, for example, the chapter's narrative voice, focalization, its humorous tone and irony and its compositional principles such as direct speech or dialogic structure. Addressing young readers, *Ragged Dick* uses simple syntax and language that is accessible to non-native speakers of English in a higher education literature course and in a foreign language environment. The text's style and language are not, however, self-explanatory or free of complexities, because it employs idiomatic speech, slang and sociolect. Displaying, in fact, a diverse set of linguistic, stylistic, narrative, contextual and formal idiosyncrasies, the chapter is suitable for the bachelor student's level of competency and meets the more demanding learning objectives of the master programme. Given the limited time frame of the 90-minute-long, synchronous online session that was allocated to the in-class annotating exercise, a more extensive interrogation of the text's idiosyncrasies has to be undertaken in the following sessions, which explains my last change to Kelley's script.

As already mentioned, I added a step to the exercise that asked students to elaborate in detail on one of their annotations. This way the group got to discuss a number of observations on the text before using them as gateways to raise further questions and stimulate responses. Having thus identified a list of subjects worthy of further interrogation, students grouped up in teams to work together on their favourite subject matter. They were allocated a week's time to effectively research content and decide on a fitting medium and format to present their findings in the next session. While they were at liberty to choose the content, form and medium of their collaborative projects as long as these enhanced the class's understanding of *Ragged Dick*, I restricted the size of the groups to four people at the most mainly to facilitate personal interactions and keep communication between group members manageable.

With community life on campus halted and students isolated, collaborative learning, which entails that 'subjects build synchronously and interactively a joint solution to some problem' (Dillenbourg and Schneider 1995: n.p.), seemed like a good way to foster informal, incidental contact and communication. Better so than cooperation, 'a protocol in which the task is in advance split into subtasks that the partners solve independently' (n.p.). Collaborative learning activities rely less on a 'shared presence, whether such presence is bounded by a classroom or online forum, nor is collaboration synonymous with all joint activity' (Kalir 2020: 3). Collaboration does require, though, that collaborators 'share the cognitive burden implied by the task' (Dillenbourg and Schneider 1995: n.p.). Collaborative learning activities have been found to generally increase overall student engagement while also being instrumental in closing the gap between highly engaged students and those who have trouble getting involved and sustaining it (O'Sullivan, Krewer and Frankl 2017: 15).

Yet, I implemented the collaborative project not only as a means to keep a high level of student engagement and to meet their divergent interests and levels of competency but also to provide an opportunity for students to hone their skills in effective oral communication. In this respect, it seemed only reasonable to also accept artistic approaches to the group projects alongside more conventional formats such as annotated bibliography or PowerPoint presentations. And allowing for artistic approaches meant allowing for a new format 'for gathering information about students' achievements', an alternative assessment seeking 'to serve the welfare of each student' in this time of crisis (Maclellan 2004: 312), with additional pressures such as health issues, job loss, inappropriate work environment at home, caretaking, homeschooling and so on weighing on students. Yet, while the creative approach rendered more playful results than usual in a strictly academic context, students who chose this option still had to expend 'in researching a topic, analysing and synthesizing the gathered information' to present and discuss their projects in class even if their works took the more unusual form of a poster or a drawing, for example (Lemme 1981: 12).

The group projects, for which each student was credited with three ECTS (European Credit Transfer System) or a certificate of attendance, respectively, were indeed unusually varied in form, ranging from written reports, response papers and annotated bibliographies to slides, poster collages, mind maps, podcasts and short films. To name but a few, one group animated two drawings they had made of the protagonist, which dramatically outlined his change from street urchin to respected middle-class citizen in appearance and dress, and underscored their short clip with a sound file. Another prepared a collage of select texts and images, which they used to elaborate on the situation of homeless children in nineteenth-century New York City. A third produced a short podcast on nineteenth-century progressivist politics, which succeeded in making child labour unlawful.

During their seven-minute-long online presentation, each group explained the reasons for the selection of their respective subject, format and medium of representation, and provided a reflection on how the annotating exercise on Conceptboard had promoted their creativity. Participants training to become future teachers also addressed their projects' didactic applicability within a certain teaching environment and its potential to stimulate the acquisition of multimodal literacy. Contrary to regular literary studies classes, considerations on the practical use of the seminar and the didactic possibilities of the material discussed were of central importance, with students continually switching between roles of teacher, student and peer.

Peer assessment followed immediately after a presentation had ended in synchronous class conversation online. So did my feedback on the quality of execution, level of sophistication and relevance, aesthetic appeal, time management, a student's ability to communicate effectively and eloquently in English, and the idiomaticity and range of used vocabulary. Over the next couple of days and on request, I also provided more detailed, individual feedback on students' performances either orally during consultation hours or in written form.

Subsequently uploaded onto Moodle, the projects remained available to all participants. Similarly, the whiteboards stored on the Conceptboard website were accessible at all times and for the duration of the semester. Finally, at the end of the term, some excellent term papers were submitted on subjects such as 'Ragged Dick as a *Kunstmärchen*' (literary fairy tale), or 'Representations of Boyhood and Child Innocence in *Ragged Dick*' by students aiming to altogether receive six credit points for the course. Surprisingly, given the complicated work conditions and increased levels of stress that students had to deal with during the pandemic, their written work met existing criteria of excellence for academic papers in literary studies.

Already during synchronous sessions, many students directly expressed their positive opinion on the exercise. Two voluntary and anonymous surveys – one conducted on mentimeter.com months later and for the purpose of this essay (participation rate of 51.02%), the other during the regular end-of-term evaluation by the university (participation rate of 66.67%) – yielded equally positive feedback. In both, students reported not having engaged in an online annotating exercise before but having enjoyed annotating the literary text synchronously, online and collaboratively. In the open question part of the surveys, they specifically highlighted the dynamic interaction on the whiteboard, the easy pragmatism by way of which observations and information were accrued that were useful for the later assignments as well as the communicative effects of the exercise inside and beyond the remote classroom. On mentimeter.com they agreed, for example, by 4.4 out of 5 points on the rating scale that the exercise increased their understanding of the text. The rate of their agreement that it yielded relevant results was 4.1 points. Yet, apparently some had issues with their internet connections and thus rated the responsiveness of the application and speedy upload times by only 3.9 points.

While it was impossible for me to discern from these anonymous surveys whether there were any significant differences in how the various student groups, literary studies students at bachelor's and master's levels and future primary school teachers at bachelor's and master's level, responded to the annotations tool, this should be investigated in future research. The benefits and challenges of teaching and participating in interdisciplinary courses for university lecturers, students and the respective competence development are further areas of research worth looking at. For now, I am going to discuss the relevance and effects of the annotating exercise from a scholarly perspective.

Discussion of Philological (Teaching) Practice

Media scholar Henry Jenkins has long hailed 'a more participatory culture' that is facilitated by 'shifts in the cultural logics and social practices that shape the ways we interact' due to a 'profound and prolonged media change' (Jenkins et al. 2013: 7). Accelerated by the Covid-19 pandemic this media change made participatory culture enter classrooms across the globe, demanding that even defenders of literary studies as a bastion of analogue teaching embrace new media literacies. These 'build on older print-based literacies, expanding opportunities for human expression, as more and more people pool knowledge and [sic] learning together within online networks' (8). In *Reading in a Participatory Culture*, Jenkins et al. already plead for a 'well-designed curriculum' that 'will help students to develop both the literary mind, as traditionally conceived, and the new competencies required to more meaningfully engage with the new participatory culture' (11). In my view, annotating literature online is one such technology-assisted collaborative activity that pursues both of these learning goals.

Contrary to Jenkins et al., I do not claim that compared with analogue teaching methods online activities ask students 'to reflect *more* deeply on their motives for reading, to take *greater* ownership over the meanings they produce and communicate with one another, and to lay claim to certain kinds of expertise that emerge from their unique engagement with shared texts' (2013: 11, my italics). All of this can and certainly does happen in old-school analogue literature courses. What is to be gained from the active engagement with online media in the literature class, however, is an understanding of how a text is impacted and reconfigured by collaborative properties. Those result from the medium's specific operating of what Friedrich Kittler defined as its 'three basic functions of storing/transferring/processing' (1999: 244). Once the excerpt from *Ragged Dick* is put on Conceptboard, to stick with the example, it becomes itself collaborative, because 'as soon as one converts the printed text to an electronic one, it no longer possesses the same kind of textuality' (Landow 1992: 43). In *Hypertext: Convergence of Contemporary Critical Theory and Technology* Landow explains:

> Once ensconced within a network of electronic links, a document no longer exists by itself. It always exists in relation to other documents in a way that a book or printed document never does and never can. From this crucial shift in the way texts exist in relation to others derive two principles that, in turn, produce [a] form of collaboration: first, any document placed on any networked system that supports electronically linked materials potentially exists in collaboration with any and all other documents on that system; second, any document electronically linked to any other document collaborates with it. (88)

Working together on Conceptboard, the students become active agents in changing the sample's 'kind of textuality' (43), whether they employ standard philological procedures such as markup of select passages, quick notes and commentary that are scribbled on the board like on the margins of the page or implement additional content via links, templates, icons, video- and audio applications (Figure 10.2). From the process of adding marginalia onscreen via typing, tagging, drawing, doodling, drawing, linking, cross-referencing and so on emerges a multimedia-assemblage that both supplements and augments the literary text with digital content such as audio, video, images, charts and so

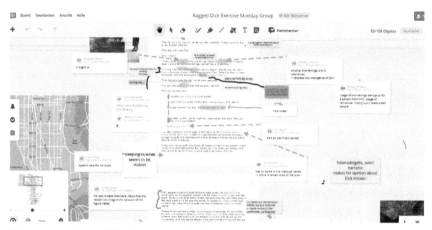

Figure 10.2 *Ragged Dick* exercise Monday group, 2020. Courtesy of Conceptboard.

on. Throughout this process, the online medium's 'basic functions of storing/ transferring/processing' are operational (Kittler 1999: 244).

By adding links and tags and generally putting to use the specific tools that the digital environment provides, the text is reconfigured into a multimedia-assemblage. Assuming the form and functionality of a multimedia-assemblage the literary text not only *looks* different, it can also *do* different things, thus taking on different *meanings*. In the revised edition of *Hypertext*, Landow references Roland Barthes on this account:

> In *S/Z*, Roland Barthes describes an ideal textuality that precisely matches that which has come to be called *computer hypertext* – text composed of blocks of words (or images) linked electronically by multiple paths, chains, or trails in an open-ended, perpetually unfinished textuality described by the terms *link*, *node*, *network*, *web*, and *path*. (2006: 5–6; original emphases)

While the text extends into a potentially limitless, rhizomatic network of processed data that is invisible to the eye, it simultaneously spreads out across the surface of the digital whiteboard. Here the text's manifold nodes of connectivity that are operative in the background are represented in terms of a textual cartography, if you so will. Fulfilling the functions of data transmission, processing and storage in ways that are specific to the medium, the digital whiteboards on Conceptboard render visual the dynamic operations of the text via online annotating. The mapping of the text's activities that appears on the board guides the reader through textual territory while simultaneously propelling her to create multimodal parerga, critical supplements and creative offshoots. In other words, the digital text, itself connected and collaborative in the digital realm and now additionally submitted to the students' synchronous collaborative annotating, renders visible the *process* of reading.

Because 'the practice of annotation is not merely an exercise in note-taking, but is rather a means for sensemaking' (Mehta et al. 2017: 2), the exercise functions to visually display what reading does. Online annotating shows the symbolic work that is performed in any reading operation analogue or digital, how the literary text is extended, reconfigured, changed and moulded in the process of sense-making which really is a creative process of accruing and creating ever-surprising new meanings. It scaffolds that reading keeps the text continuously malleable. In engaging students publicly in the private, personal practice of reading, collaborative online annotating scaffolds 'the breadth of different ways people make meaning from literary texts' in real time and one place (11), which allows for the subsequent storage of the collected interpretative clues to be revisited and followed-up.

By creatively reconfiguring the text into a multimedia-assemblage or multimodal collage, the exercise displays the cultural technique of reading not as a passive procedure of intake but as a dynamic practice of creative output that operates by way of taking cues, establishing connections, tracing developments as well as imagining settings and contexts. What usually happens before the mind's eye only now appears on screen as the result of the public procedure of collective online engagement with the literary text. Ultimately, the exercise fosters 'mid-level reading' (Felski 2015: 741), a term which describes the process of reading literature online as a productive, collaborative operation more appropriately than the term 'close reading'.

In that it stages the process of reading *as* annotating, thus showcasing the productive, proliferating quality of the cultural technique, the collaborative online exercise also harks back to the very beginning of philology. 'Of course, philology as such is initially determined by cultural techniques: it emerges in the margins of pages; it is formed in glossaries and commentaries on the text that generate the text to begin with' (Menke 2020: 219). Executing and technically enhancing the philological practice of annotating in the digital environment brings into view that 'the process of annotating is by no means benign' (Hanna 1991: 179). Annotating has traditionally been heavily regulated by the scholarly community, its practitioners sanctioned to abide by its accepted forms as annotation exists 'deliberately to obscure the aggressive act of controlling audience consumption of the text' (181). Furthermore, the practice itself is 'very old' (179). Profound changes of the practice made annotations gradually appropriate authority over the text: 'On the page, they have taken the place of the text' and as a result 'the annotator has become an author: he is a source of knowledge, his opinions are discussed. What were originally annotations are now cited as independent works' (Mayali 1991: 190).

Collaborative online annotating is hence another step in a long process that has been ongoing since the early Middle Ages. As the practice of annotating developed, the 'political authority of the text' has been contested by the erudite annotator who became ever bolder in taking 'possession of the empty margins' (189). In the digital realm and with text taking the form of codes, erudition (though helpful) is no longer required for the annotator to establish her role as second author. Online the author per se exists in the plural as one actant in the dynamic processes that are performed by and between, for example, the reader, the text, the computer hardware and software. Together they constitute an actor-network, to use a term by Bruno Latour. The online annotating exercise on Conceptboard can hence be used, and this will be my last point, as a doorway to introduce students to actor-network theory (ANT).

Debating in 'Latour and Literary Studies' the reorienting effects ANT has on literary studies, Felski concedes that it 'steers us away from monocausal explanations of what and how a text signifies' as much as it argues against 'a view of meaning as determined only by readers or interpretative communities' (2015: 739). ANT, she states, insists instead 'on the unmistakable pressure and power of the text' (739) to which we 'become attached' both physically and in terms of emotional affect (740). This is mainly because of the 'role granted to non-humans', which are conceived as 'actors' rather than 'simply the hapless bearers of symbolic projection' (Latour 2005: 10). In ANT the materiality of the book, already paramount to Kittler's materialist media theory, or computer hardware, is factored into the meaning-making process as much as the author or reader of a text. ANT accepts 'successive connections' of 'non-social objects' (Latour 2005: 106), which are recognized as having agency. The network, then, is the method that makes connection and interaction of different agents possible.

With the roles and relevance of author, reader, text and other agents thus adjusted within the conceptual frame of ANT, all reading 'becomes a matter of composing and cocreating, of forging links between things that were previously unconnected', and 'to interpret something is to add one's voice to that of the text: to negotiate, appropriate, elaborate, translate, and relate' (Felski 2015: 741). ANT is just a helpful theory to explain all this. With ANT, Felski continues, 'the emphasis is on acts of making rather than unmaking, composition rather than critique, substantiating rather than subverting' (741). In other words, ANT serves to conceptualize the process of collaborative online annotating in such a way that students gain a theoretical understanding of what we commonly call a text as well as literary studies in the digital age.

Conclusion

Having finished the third remote teaching term in a row by now, I am more comfortable in making use of the tools it offers for teaching literature than in the early days of the pandemic. While I would likely not have implemented them under regular circumstances and without Andrea Frank's and Michael Asbill's inspiring use of Conceptboard, I am, however, determined to maintain the practice in a regular classroom setting after the pandemic has ended. Intent to keep the best tools and teaching methods of both the digital and the analogue worlds in my own literature classes in the future, I wish to also share my experience and account for how digital teaching formats may complement our established classroom routines. I do so in the hope of servicing the collaborative effort to garner students' interest in literature in ways that are in keeping with both current literary theory and technology.

References

Primary Literature

Alger, H., Jr. ([1868] 2014), *Ragged Dick, Or, Street Life in New York with the Boot Blacks*, New York: Penguin Signet Classics.
Shelley, M. ([1818] 1963), *Frankenstein*, New York: Airmont.

Secondary Literature

Bolter, J. D., and R. Grusin (2000), *Remediation: Understanding New Media*, Cambridge: MIT Press.
Curtis, D. D., and M. J. Lawson (February 2001), 'Exploring Collaborative Online Learning', *JALN*, 5 (1): 21–34.
Dillenbourg, P., and D. Schneider (1995), 'Collaborative Learning and the Internet'. http://tecfa.unige.ch/tecfa/research/CMC/colla/iccai95_1.html (accessed 8 September 2021).
Felski, R. (May 2015), 'Latour and Literary Studies', *PMLA*, 30 (3): 737–42. doi: https://doi.org/10.1632/pmla.2015.130.3.737 (accessed 21 June 2021).

Hanna, R., III (1991), 'Annotation as Social Practice', in S. Barney (ed.), *Annotation and Its Texts*, 178–84, New York: Oxford University Press.

Jenkins, H., W. Kelley, H. G. Jenkins III, K. A. Clinton, J. McWilliams, R. Pitts-Wiley and E. Reilly, eds (2013), *Reading in a Participatory Culture: Remixing Moby-Dick in the English Classroom*, New York: Teachers College Columbia University Press.

Kalir, J. H. (2020), 'Social Annotation Enabling Collaboration for Open Learning', *Distance Education*, 41 (2): 245–60. doi: 10.1080/01587919.2020.1757413 (accessed 21 June 2021).

Kelley, W. (2014), 'Wyn Kelley Frankenstein'. https://www.annotationstudio.org/portfo lio-view/wyn-kelley-frankenstein/ (accessed 30 June 2021).

Kittler, F. (1999), *Gramophone, Film, Typewriter*, G. Winthrop-Young and M. Wutz (trans.), Stanford: Stanford University Press.

Landow, G. P. (1992), *Hypertext: Convergence of Contemporary Critical Theory and Technology*, Baltimore, MA: Johns Hopkins University Press.

Landow, G. P. (2006), *Hypertext 3.0: Critical Theory and New Media in an Era of Globalization*, Baltimore, MA: Johns Hopkins University Press.

Latour, B. (2005), *Reassembling the Social: An Introduction to Actor-Network-Theory*, Oxford: Oxford University Press.

Lemme, G. D. (1981), 'Poster Display – Alternative Term Project', *NACTA Journal*, 25 (1): 12–14. https://www.jstor.org/stable/43763726 (accessed 18 October 2021).

Maclellan, E. (2004), 'How Convincing Is Alternative Assessment for Use in Higher Education?', *Assessment & Evaluation in Higher Education*, 29 (3): 311–21. doi: 10.1080/0260293042000188267 (accessed 8 October 2014).

Mayali, L. (1991), 'For a Political Autonomy of Annotation', in S. A. Barney (ed.), *Annotation and Its Texts*, 185–91, New York: Oxford University Press.

Mehta, H., A. Bradley, M. Hancock and C. Collins (November 2017), 'Metatation: Annotation as Implicit Interaction to Bridge Close and Distant Reading', *ACM Transactions on Computer-Human Interaction*, 24 (5.35): 1–41. doi: 10.1145/3131609 (accessed 18 May 2021).

Menke, B. (2020), 'Writing Out – Gathered Up at a Venture from All Four Corners of the Earth: Jean Paul's Techniques and Operations (on Excerpts)', in J. Dünne, K. Fehringer, K. Kuhn and W. Struck (eds), *Cultural Techniques*, 219–41, Berlin: de Gruyter.

O'Sullivan, D., F. Krewer and G. Frankl (2017), 'Technology Enhanced Collaborative Learning Using a Project-Based Learning Management System', *International Journal of Technology Enhanced Learning*, 9 (1): 14–36. doi: 10.1504/IJTEL.2017.084085 (accessed 3 May 2021).

11

Writing the Future: Collaborative Creative Science-Fiction Writing in the Virtual EFL Classroom

Christian Ludwig and Elizabeth Shipley

Introduction

Since the 1990s, technology has become a strong force in foreign language education, which offers a yet rarely harnessed learning potential (Buendgens-Kosten and Schildhauer 2021; Lütge and Merse 2021). Connecting technology and writing, Soobin and Warschauer remark that

> the ubiquitous presence of new technology has brought great changes in writing practices and instruction. Technology can have a powerful influence on students' writing; in turn, writing can maximize the potential benefits of digital media for education. (2014: 298)

Indeed, we seem to be spending much more time writing than ever (Kieweg 2009), especially in the new media age (Brauweiler 2021; Dürscheid and Frick 2016). We post on social media such as Instagram, Snapchat and TikTok, write in blogs and wikis and are constantly in touch with people via email, digital gaming and social networking. These technologies not only change the way we communicate in everyday life but also hold vast potential for teaching writing in the English as a foreign language (EFL) classroom, especially if writing education in the foreign language aims to meet the writing needs of the contemporary student generation.

Writing by hand is becoming less common (Neef 2010) as students increasingly use smartphone and computer keyboards, touchscreens and styluses to compose (multimodal) texts which combine abbreviations, symbols and emoticons and may even include images, audio or video files – aspects which also have to be considered in terms of content, genre and audience (Brauweiler 2021). Furthermore, as Ohler points out, 'digital technologies provide one of the greatest imagination creativity amplifiers humankind has ever designed', for example, as we engage in digital storytelling (2007: 13; Skorge 2021).

Last but not least, using modern technologies may be beneficial in that they allow students to work together more during all steps of the writing process, reflecting the fact that writing outside educational contexts, such as on social media or in online game communities (Matz 2014), is becoming increasingly collaborative.

This chapter takes a closer look at the role of technology in collaborative creative writing in the higher EFL classroom through focusing on a practical example. In the summer term 2020, students from two courses, one focusing on science-fiction and fantasy literature (Pädagogische Hochschule Karlsruhe, Germany) and the other on learning with literature in EFL (Freie Universität Berlin, Germany), teamed up to write their own science-fiction and fantasy short stories. The creative writing projects were inspired by Peter Phillips's short story 'Lost Memory' (1952), which explores the future of technology and artificial life from the perspective of the early 1950s. The short story served as a creative writing prompt encouraging students to express their views of technology and reflect the increasing technologization of society. Due to the pandemic, the project was carried out entirely online, allowing students to use whatever platforms and tools they deemed most suitable for their group work. Overall, the project not only strengthened students' writing skills and understanding of the benefits of (online) creative writing for English language teaching but also provided opportunities for them to become world builders themselves. All students were required to write an individual reflection, allowing them to collect their thoughts, questions and ideas and to reflect their own collaborative learning experiences.

The first part of this chapter takes a closer look at second language writing in the age of communicative competence, particularly focusing on both collaborative and creative writing and its potential in the EFL classroom. We argue that fantasy and science fiction are the perfect genres for students to become creative writers, enabling them to reflect on current issues by taking them to otherworldly places, where they can imagine alternative societies (better or worse) and play with imaginary worlds while maintaining an extended sense of anonymity and safety.

The second part of the chapter then concentrates on the project itself, presenting and discussing selected results from the students' writing projects.

The chapter concludes by looking at the participants' feedback and reflections, which not only provide insights into their opinions of the project but also their beliefs about the role of (collaborative) creative writing in their future classrooms.

Collaborative Writing in the Digital Age

Digital media reshape the way we read and write. There are new text formats, many of them born-digital, which take us far beyond the skills and strategies needed to comprehend and compose print texts (Hayles 2004; Thomas 2020; Gibson 2021), as texts which originate in digital format are often non-linear, multimodal, interactive and malleable. Furthermore, we no longer just passively read texts but become prosumers (Toffler 1980), that is, active consumers or, as Landow (1992) says, wreaders. Closely related to this, much of the writing in the digital age is not only technology mediated but also collaborative as we participate in the production of media in today's participatory culture (Jenkins 2006).

If we want to prepare students for effective and appropriate participation in the writing that is 'out there', beyond the classroom, while also bringing their 'in-the-wild' writing experiences (Sauro and Zourou 2019) into the classroom, then we need to create writing situations which allow them to engage in 'participatory practices rather than concentrate on individual performances' (Bear et al. 2014: 146) and where 'students participate in one another's growth as writers' (146). One way of achieving this is supporting writing on digital platforms (Gabel and Schmidt 2017; Brauweiler 2021; Skorge 2021) where multiple writers can work on the same document, either consecutively or simultaneously, manipulate texts easily and engage in written metacommunication about a text which makes digital writing a much more 'dynamic, non-linear and recursive process' (Kirchhoff 2018: 124), and a 'socially situated activity' (Atkinson 2003: 5).

Collaborative writing tasks, whether digital or non-digital, connect various approaches as they help students understand writing as a joint process with the group drawing on the strengths of all group members (Gabel and Schmidt 2017). This can be particularly effective in diverse learning groups with different writing and language skills as all students may feel that they have something unique to contribute.

Writing collaboratively can be particularly fruitful for creative writing tasks where multiple authors share creative control of a text and where 'peer collaboration can resource, stimulate and enhance classroom-based creative writing activities' (Vass et al. 2008: 192). The success of collaborative creative writing, however, may depend on multiple factors, including the task itself but also the quality of collaboration as well as the platform used for collaboration.

Process approaches (e.g. Zamel 1982, 1985) and post-process approaches (e.g. Atkinson 2003; Hyland 2003) have also radically changed the role of the writing teacher, with post-process approaches showing 'how texts and writers and readers are always and inevitably embedded in multiple contexts and cultures' (Tobin 2001: 16). The research of Furneaux, Paran and Fairfax (2007) reveals that differentiated feedback from teachers continues to remain essential and that critical feedback is desired by student writers so that they can work on problems in their writing. However, peer feedback is also valuable, in particular considering the critical role of both teachers and peers as readers. In this role, teachers should 'respond as genuine and interested readers rather than as judges and evaluators' (Zamel 1985: 97).

With all this in mind, future English language teachers, we believe, should engage in digital collaborative writing projects themselves to experience the benefits and challenges of collaborative creative learning.

Creative Writing

Creative writing, as Harper (2015) posits, is not always supported by current institutional and curricular frameworks, especially as creative writing is traditionally a highly individual endeavour which often works outside the boundaries of formal and standardized instruction and assessment. Yet, creative writing offers a special kind of opportunity for learners to develop their writing skills as it allows students to 'engage with the foreign language in a playful way' (Kirchhoff 2018: 125). In the best of worlds, this means to have fun, allowing a freedom of expression and imagination not possible with other writing tasks. As Morley argues:

> Think of an empty page as open space. It possesses no dimension; human time makes no claim. Everything is possible, at this point endlessly possible. Anything can grow in it. Anybody, real or imaginary, can travel there, stay put, or move on. There is no constraint, except the honesty of the writer and the scope of imagination – qualities with which we are born and characteristics that we can develop. (2007: 1)

Consequently, according to Elbow, teachers 'can help [students] like to write' (2000: xv). This happens when they can make their own choices about what and how to write and how to make their writing relevant to their own lives. They learn to enjoy writing by making it their own. This development can be of value both in the L1 and L2 context.

Creative writing gives students leave to explore aspects of language with greater freedom from the critic within and without. Awareness of language develops as a result of these kinds of writing activities. Students can stretch their active productive skills in trying out new vocabulary with less attention to errors. As Elbow (2000) and others (e.g. Hanauer 2011) argue, students improve their writing just by writing. This encourages them to express more openly their need to 'take me as I am!' (Elbow 2000: 19), without 'the drudgery' and imposition of copy-editing (19).

Digital media, as Skorge emphasizes, 'above all web-based media, provide vast, rich resources for creative writing' (2021: 57; cf. also Cornille et al. 2021). There is also a plethora of writing activities for offline teaching which can encourage students to become creative writers in online learning environments. One example is freewriting (also sometimes called fast writing or rapid writing), 'one of the hallmarks of process pedagogy in composition studies' (Matsuda 2003: 76). It is a good warm-up activity for any writing course, a technique often employed to help overcome writing blocks, encourage fluency and spontaneity and release creative energy as expression in words. This technique can be illustrated by the 'First Thoughts' activity from Goldberg's *Writing Down the Bones*:

1. *Keep your hand moving.* (Don't pause to reread the line you have just written. That's stalling and trying to get control of what you're saying.)

2. *Don't cross out.* (That is editing as you write. Even if you write something you didn't mean to write, leave it.)

3. *Don't worry about spelling, punctuation, grammar.* (Don't even care about staying within the margins and lines on the page.)

4. *Lose control.*

5. *Don't think. Don't get logical.*

6. *Go for the jugular.* (If something comes up in your writing that is scary or naked, dive right into it. It probably has lots of energy.) (1986: 8)

Like most writing activities, freewriting can be adapted to contexts where students write on a keyboard as the focus is on spurring output by writing without stopping and editing. In order not to get distracted by red underlines students should be asked to turn off their spell and grammar checkers as well as close any online translators and dictionaries. Moreover, students should be told not to worry about formatting issues such as page layout, fonts, spacing and indents.

Many of these freewriting activities are the first steps of the 'progression from safety to risk' (Elbow 2000: 41), for freewriting is often private writing, not shared with others. In Goldberg's 'First Thoughts' activity, privacy is essential for the activity to be successful in unleashing the writer's raw unconscious creative energy. However, there are also fast collaborative creative writing games and activities, including the collaborative chat poetry activity that we discuss in section 'The Collaborative Creative Writing Project'. Many of these very fast collaborative creative writing activities, though no longer completely private, have the advantages of reducing the risk involved through group responsibility for the shared project and the subsequent safety of the lightening of individual responsibility.

Creative Writing with Science Fiction and Fantasy

Many of today's students are familiar with fantasy and science fiction through famous examples of the genres such as *Game of Thrones*, *X-Men* or *Lord of the Rings*. This establishes a common background knowledge of texts and culture for the classroom, facilitating the generating of new science-fiction and fantasy texts.

Science fiction and fantasy are genres which inspire creativity as they are not limited by reality but deal with futuristic or imaginative concepts such as time travel, parallel universes, new species or magical creatures. Thus, the freedoms of world building within the genres of fantasy and science fiction are immense and have great potential for the foreign language classroom (Ludwig and Shipley 2020).

Many fantasy writers have a map of their world at the very beginning of their works, and the map is a particularly appropriate image for the world-building aspect of creative writing in this genre in general. Maps of real geographical places usually represent that which already exists. Ekman argues that the function of maps of imaginary, or what Tolkien (1947) called secondary worlds is seminal to their creation, that is, 'the world comes into being as it is being mapped' (Ekman 2018: 72). Ursula Le Guin ([1968] 2012) concurs in her afterword to *A Wizard of Earthsea*, in which she describes the process of getting to know her secondary world Earthsea by drawing a map. The map, according to Ekman, 'can tell the reader or critic what is important in its world, what is worth bearing in mind, what readers and critics should pay attention to' (2018: 74).

Another important aspect of world building is that of identity which is outside the ordinary sphere, whether we are talking about little wizards at Hogwarts learning to deal with their magic powers, young people learning the burdens and pleasures of becoming vampires or of mating with aliens, or about your ordinary Android longing to become 'a real boy'. Creating and assuming these identities in a piece of world-building fiction provides a change of perspective and a safe distance to explore real-life issues in the disguise of another world. The project we describe below provides an example of how much the students enjoy the freedoms the genre offers.

The Collaborative Creative Writing Project

Project Concept

Students from two courses participated in the project with thirty students altogether. All of the students were enrolled in a degree programme to become English teachers. The course at the Freie Universität Berlin with twenty participants focused on exploring literature as a tool for foreign language learning, paying particular attention to contemporary and cutting-edge literary texts outside the traditional canon (see Kirchhoff 2019; Sauro and Sundmark 2019). The second major goal of the course was to investigate the role of digital media for reading print literature with primary and secondary learners of English as a foreign language (Ludwig 2021). The course concentrated primarily on learner-centred approaches to working with literary texts, including, among others, reader response and doing literature (Myers 2014; Lütge 2018a, b).

The course at the Pädagogische Hochschule Karlsruhe with twenty-nine participants was a literature course that dealt with both fantasy and science fiction, including Mary Shelley's *Frankenstein*, Ursula Le Guin's *A Wizard of Earthsea*, Isaac Asimov's *The Bicentennial Man* and Philip Dick's *Do Androids Dream of Electric Sheep?* as well as two science-fiction stories by Jonathan Shipley. Unlike the course in Berlin, the project was not required for all course participants but only for those who wanted to do their required module research project credits in this particular course. This was represented by ten of the twenty-nine students in the course. In addition, all students were required to do a number of reader-response papers based on the course reading, which they could choose to do as creative outputs. Seven of the twenty-nine of the course participants chose to do classical creative reader response (e.g. what would the monster's narrative have been like if Frankenstein had accepted and educated his creation?) as well as collaborative world-building narratives in these papers, thus underlining the attraction of creative writing in the fantasy and science-fiction environment. It was no surprise that most of the students who chose the creative writing option for their reader-response papers also joined the collaborative writing project.

Collaborative Lesson

Students from both universities were informed about the project in the first week of the summer term, introducing them to the general structure of the project which, in addition to the thirteen regular course sessions, included one joint session on Webex in the third week of the term. In preparation for the joint session, students were given the task to read 'Lost Memory' by Peter Phillips ([1952] 1986). The story centres around a human astronaut who wakes up in a robot society after the crash of his spaceship. The machines, unable to grasp the concept of a non-mechanical being, kill the pilot in their attempt to help him. The short story can help to develop not only students' linguistic skills but also their inter- and transcultural competence as they explore the robot society, its cultural memory and religious beliefs and the complexities of the human-machine as well as machine-machine relationships. To enhance their engagement with the story and prepare them for the creative writing activities planned for the joint session, students were assigned tasks together with the reading to help them focus on some of the story's main ideas as well as linguistic characteristics (cf. Ludwig 2019).

At the beginning of the ninety-minute joint session, the concept of collaborative writing in the EFL classroom was briefly introduced, particularly focusing on the benefits and challenges of implementing collaborative writing in the classroom, possible stages of writing with a partner or in a group and the role of the teacher in supporting students in their collaborative writing endeavours. The presentation then focused on creative writing in the foreign language classroom, exploring some of the reasons for doing creative writing and ways to help students become creative writers themselves.

The sixty-minute practical part of the session then gave students the opportunity to become creative writers themselves. For this, they were given an excerpt from the short story, the passage in which the astronaut tries to convince the robot reporter Chirik that humans were the creators of robots:

> The mad words flowed on. 'You call me he. Why? You have no seks. You are knewter. You are *it it it*! I am he, he who made you, sprung from shee, born

of wumman. What is wumman, who is silv-ya what is shee that all her swains commend her ogod the bluds flowing again. Remember. Think back, you out there. These words were made by mann for mann. Hurt, healing, hospitality, horror, deth by loss of blud. *Deth Blud*. Do you understand these words? Do you remember the soft things that made you? Soft little mann who konkurred the Galaxy and made sentient slaves of his machines and saw the wonders of a million words, only this miserable representative has to die in lonely desperation on a far planet, hearing goblin voices in the darkness.'

Here my recorder reproduces a most curious sound, as though the stranger were using an ancient type of vibratory molecular vocalizer in a gaseous medium to reproduce his words before transmission, and the insulation on his diaphragm had come adrift.

It was a jerky, high-pitched, strangely disturbing sound; but in a moment the fault was corrected and the stranger resumed transmission.

'Does blud mean anything to you?'

'No,' Chirik replied simply.

'Or deth?'

'No.'

'Or wor?'

'Quite meaningless.'

'What is your origin? How did you come into being?' (Phillips [1952] 1986: 41; original emphasis)

The passage was chosen for this activity because it illustrates the tragic results of pragmatic failure as Chirik is incapable of understanding that humans, not an omnipotent machine, created the robots that inhabit his planet. Furthermore, the excerpt contains a plethora of alternative spellings, for example, *blud* (blood), *deth* (death), *seks* (sex) and *wumman* (woman), allowing students to gain an insight into how science fiction creates and plays with language. The students were then given twenty minutes to write their own individual poems: *Write a poem using only the words in this passage.*

The poems were shared in the chatbox on a voluntary basis and read aloud by the authors. Each of the poems was then briefly discussed with the whole group. As expected, the poems differed in length, form, style and content. While some poems remained rather close to the original by rewriting or altering the conversation between Chirik and the astronaut, for example, through simply shortening it, other poems moved further away from the original text and explored entirely different themes as the following example illustrates:

Wumman hurt in darkness
Disturbing
Wumman in desperation
Horror
Mann by mann for mann
Blud, deth blud
Loss of Wumman
Mann, the wonders of a million worlds
Wumman, meaningless
Do you understand these worlds?

(Hartisch 2020; reprinted with permission)

The untitled poem plays with the words used by the astronaut to convince Chirik that robots were originally created by humankind and that he is the only one who was born in a natural way. The author reduced the original text to a few words and used the remaining words, for example, *wumman, mann, deth, blud* in their original to create a poem which describes how a robot sees human society. He establishes a contrast between the world of men and the world of women who live in two separate worlds, emphasized by how lines five to nine alternate between the male and the female worlds. While in the male world, men admire each other for their masculinity and manliness, the female world is characterized by darkness and desperation. In the last line, the robot expresses his lack of understanding of human society by asking: 'Do you understand these worlds?'

The remaining ten minutes of the joint session were used to explain the next steps of the project and give students the task of dividing themselves into teams in order to write a short story collaboratively out of class. The instructions to the students were as follows:

1. As our last activity of the joint session today, create writing projects in the Google doc and sign up for a team of two to six. If possible each team should have both Berlin and Karlsruhe students.
2. Please submit the first draft of your short story to your lecturer as a word. doc file for proofreading by June 15.
3. An individual written reflection of the process, along with the corrected and revised version of the short story, should be submitted to your lecturer by July 1.
4. The final version of your short story should be uploaded to LMS (stud.IP or Blackboard) a week before the final class. Your texts will be the required reading for class discussion in the final week.

5. With your permission, these short stories will be entered into the literature course archive on stud.IP for reading for future class participants and possibly later published as an e-book.

The eight project groups were formed by the students themselves according to target readership (e.g. if specifically for young or teenage readers) as well as to the kind of story they wanted to write. While most groups decided to compose a written short story, two groups opted for drawing a graphic short story. Soon after this initial meeting, all groups had to send us their working titles for the story, also indicating their target readership and text type. After submitting their penultimate drafts, all groups received both language and content feedback from both lecturers via email and were then given time to revise their stories.

Not surprisingly, the larger groups were more difficult for the students to navigate their collaborative process. Often these larger groups chose to assign each writer a chapter in a basic story that they agreed upon. Although the groups of two were grateful for the relative collaborative ease, there were also benefits from the larger collaborative efforts, as the reflections of the participants showed.

The final results were then read and discussed in the last class session. Thus, for what Elbow calls the most ' "writerly dimensions" of writing', namely audience and response (2000: 28), project participants had multiple audiences and feedback. Their first audience was one another as readers of their co-writing efforts.

The second audience was the two of us, though we confined ourselves mainly (though not exclusively) to the editing process, giving students concrete instructions on how to improve the language of the text, not only to make it more accurate and sophisticated but also to instil confidence in the linguistic quality of the final project.

The third audience was then their fellow students who responded to the pieces as literary and cultural artefacts in the context of the entire reading done during the course. An opportunity for a further, more open audience for the pieces was provided by inclusion of the short stories produced, with the permission of the writers, in an electronic course archive that continues from course to course in fantasy and science-fiction courses, with stories of the current creative writing projects added. In the following, selected products of the project will be discussed in more detail.

The Project Results

The project resulted in eight stories, which were a broad mix of genre and theme. In terms of genre, four were pieces of young adult fiction and one, the only fantasy work among the eight, was a children's story in which the young protagonist grieved over the death of his brother by meeting him in a fantasy world. Two of the four works of young adult fiction were graphic texts, one of them wordless. Of the seven science-fiction texts, four of the stories featured robots. Two of them were mysteries, one of them based on Asimov's Three Laws of Robotics and the other, 'Mission: "Restore Lost Memory"', a sequel to Phillips's story, in which another robot reporter visits a planet populated by humans and tries to make sense of what a human being is.

The other story based on Phillips's story will be accorded a separate discussion because of the way it illustrates the suitability of the comic medium for storytelling and reveals the significance of the visual dimension to world building.

'Lost Human' puts the idea of the lone survivor who crashes on a planet into a modern context. Here is the story's prologue:

> Around 80 years earlier, especially young folks fought for climate protection. They used to go out and demonstrate each Friday and demanded actions to be taken of their governments … Governments promised to abandon plastic articles, arranged climate agreements, some have guaranteed a coal phase-out by 2030. Despite what scientists around the world said about the urgency of climate protection measurements, actions on behalf of powerful politicians were taken too late. Due to the human-caused climate change, a mass extinction occurred. In the year 3000, the human race as well as all animal species vanished completely. A few astronauts missed the extinction of life on earth because they travelled through time and space at this time … Luna, a young astronaut, could not believe her eyes when she entered earth and really saw what she had assumed would happen before she left. Since there was no living cell left on her home planet, she decided to take wings and discover other planets where there is still human life. (Dinh, Friedrichs and Karakay 2020, reprinted with permission)

The prologue takes us back eighty years in the past, to the 2020s, when humankind failed to take climate action to counter global climate change, which in the story led to the extinction of all life on Earth. In contrast to 'Lost Memory', we learn why Luna, the female pilot of the spaceship, has left earth (Figure 11.1). When Luna crashes on Planet 21, she realizes that she has run out of fuel and that the ship's systems are malfunctioning. Despite the fact that the planet is rather hostile to living creatures due to its high surface temperature and decreased atmospheric pressure, she decides to leave her spacecraft and ask the 'human-like creatures' (Dinh, Friederichs and Karakaya 2020: n.p.) that presumably

Figure 11.1 Excerpt from *Lost Human*. Courtesy of Thi Hanh Quyen Dinh, Mirjam Friedrichs and Sonay Karakaya.

live on the planet for help. The last single-page panel where she appears shows Luna looking down on the planet. The story concludes by using quotes from Phillips's short story, indicating that Luna has been found by the robots who are about to examine her. The graphic short story powerfully illustrates how the group engaged with the original short story and retold it in the form of a graphic novel. In order to do that, the authors had to deal not only with questions of storytelling and story structure but also with medium-specific questions such as page and panel layout.

As Baetens points out, the use of colours, or their absence, 'cannot be separated from the system of narrative' (2011: 111). The graphic short story 'Lost Human' is a good example of this: it is drawn entirely in black and white, adding to the gloomy atmosphere of a post-cataclysmic world in which almost all of humanity has been wiped out. In other words, the black and white functions as a graphic objective correlative (Pointner 2013) which emphasizes the protagonist's loneliness and despair. The panel is divided into two parts. The upper part shows the astronaut's small spaceship in the endless vastness of space. The lower part zooms into the spaceship. We see Luna from behind, looking down on the surface of Planet 21, her face mirroring in the ship's porthole. The quietness of the scene, evoked through the absence of speech and thought balloons, motionlines or any other stylistic devices that indicate movement or the passing of time, help the viewer to empathize with Luna, one of the last remaining survivors of humanity. It is significant that the protagonist of this modern version of the 1952 story is a woman and an African American and that climate change leads to the extinction of humanity despite the Fridays for the Future movement, a grim commentary and mirror of our present situation in the world of cataclysmic climate events. This was one of two stories based on the idea of annihilation of the human race through human hubris and thoughtlessness.

The Participants' Opinions

After the project, all students were asked to send us their individual feedback in English, reflecting on the process and the potential of collaborative creative writing activities for primary and secondary learners. The following guiding questions were given as an aid:

1. Now that it is over, what are your first thoughts about this project?
2. What specific positive and/or negative aspects come to mind?
3. In which way did you benefit from this creative writing project?

4. Did participating in the project help you to get some ideas about how to teach creative writing to children?

The responses show that the students overall enjoyed participating in the project. They used a variety of tools and platforms to organize the group work and write their stories, including, among others, Skype, WhatsApp, email and Google Docs. The use of digital collaborative writing tools was considered especially beneficial with regard to the current situation: 'It was really nice to work on a project which wasn't made more difficult by the current situation' (S1). Although some considered collaborative story writing a challenge in a digital environment, most were surprised about how smoothly the writing process went as the following quote illustrates:

> I was concerned about it being a collaborative writing project at first. I had never written a story with someone else's ideas to consider and I didn't know whether that could interfere with the creative writing process. I, at first, thought that it would be quite difficult to find a topic that everyone liked, especially as my mind started flowing with ideas, the moment I heard about the project. Then there was the question of how to write a story that was coherent, both in style of writing and content, when several people would be involved. Nevertheless, I really looked forward to starting the writing process, especially when it was clear that I could work with a group of friends with similar taste in literature as me. (S1)

Moreover, even though the collaborative aspect of the project was seen as a challenge at the beginning, most students came to appreciate their writing groups as the project progressed. As one participant puts it: 'It was nice sharing ideas with others and forming a story together' (S2). Moreover, mutual motivation and an equal distribution of the workload were considered positive. In addition, students also used the opportunities that the science-fiction genre offers to address and reflect current events and issues of global concern, such as the problematic effects of science and technology on human society, as the following quotes indicate:

> Luckily on the same day, a discussion about the SpaceX program started in my family. When I suggested the idea of using those satellites as a cause for an apocalypse, everyone was on board immediately. (S1)

> For example, we looked to Elon Musk talking about the dangers of artificial intelligence and later also used him as the inspiration for our 'genius character'. (S2)

In addition to reflecting on the project itself, students were also asked to consider the potential of collaborative creative writing for their future classrooms. Here, opinions confirmed the assumed potential of such scenarios for the secondary and even primary classroom. Some of the benefits mentioned include, among others, helping learners enjoy writing in the foreign language, inspiring creativity in learners, motivating them to explore new topics and topics which are relevant to them and providing a variety of writing activities.

Implications for Research

The findings of this specific project illustrate the significance of collaborative creative writing for the teaching of writing in EFL. With regard to future research, it would be productive to collect a corpus of L2 creative writing (cf. Iida 2019), which could, for example, be used as student-produced reading material with other classes. Having teacher support for an accurate final product as well as an appreciative audience of peers could also motivate learners to enjoy writing and develop cognitive and metacognitive skills, for example, with regard to grammar and vocabulary knowledge and fluency (see Chapter 9 of this volume for a project on teaching writing fictional narratives with beginning-level adult immigrants). During this process, it would be beneficial to investigate how students distribute tasks during collaborative writing, when the autonomous group structuring of work is successful or when it might require teacher guidance.

Moreover, the value of the use of technology in collaborative (creative) writing has not yet been sufficiently explored, in particular, the seminal role that the genre of fantasy and science fiction can play. For this, practitioner research would be a suitable approach as it encourages teachers to research their own practice, not only alone but also in collaboration with colleagues and students (Watts 1995; Pine 2009). The findings of further research beyond this project are also important for educators as creative writing needs to be recognized as a vital component of curriculum design for students at all levels and ages.

Conclusion

Finally, we see that although in-person teaching is returning to university, the pandemic has left indelible footprints along the way. It is important that in future classroom work, teachers do not overlook and ignore the many new approaches and discoveries with the help of technology which were developed out of necessity through Covid-19. Though nothing can replace in-person contact and communication, these digital alternatives have nonetheless become valuable components of our repertoire and have provided us with innovative tools that allow us to go beyond traditional curricular goals.

Teaching writing in second language contexts presents its particular challenges, often a lonely task for the foreign language learner, faced with the job of performing tasks requiring a set of competences they have not yet mastered. Collaborative creative writing can be a bridge to meeting this challenge with the aid of online technology. Fantasy and science fiction, as represented by this project, have been found to be genres particularly helpful for this. The collaborative fantasy and science-fiction creative writing project between Berlin and Karlsruhe serves as one model of how the future of teaching creative writing in EFL could look, an attempt towards writing the future.

References

Primary Literature

Asimov, I. ([1976] 1991), 'The Bicentennial Man', in *Robot Visions*, 245–90, New York: Byron Preiss Visual.

Dick, P. (1968), *Do Androids Dream of Electric Sheep?* New York: Del Rey.

Dinh, T. H. Q., M. Friedrichs and S. Karakaya (2020), 'Lost Human'. Unpublished student project, Courses at Freie Universität Berlin and Pädagogische Hochschule Karlsruhe.

Hartisch, G. (2020), 'Wumman hurt in darkness'. Unpublished student project, Courses at Freie Universität Berlin and Pädagogische Hochschule Karlsruhe.

Le Guin, U. ([1968] 2012), *A Wizard of Earthsea*, New York: Houghton Mifflin Harcourt.

Martin, G. R. R. (1996), *A Game of Thrones*, New York: Bantam Spectra.

Phillips, P. ([1952] 1986), 'Lost Memory', in I. Asimov and M. H. Greenberg (eds), *Isaac Asimov Presents the Great SF Stories 14 (1952)*, 35–47, New York: Daw.

Shelley, M. ([1818] 1994), *Frankenstein or, The Modern Prometheus*, New York: Penguin.

Shipley, J. (2016), 'Pale as the Noonday Sun', in R. Stephenson (ed.), *The Worlds of Science Fiction, Fantasy, and Horror*, vol. 1, 166–80, Adelaide: Altair Australia.

Shipley, J. (2017), 'Sanguine', in R. Stephenson (ed.), *The Worlds of Science Fiction, Fantasy, and Horror*, vol. 2, 179–225, Adelaide: Altair Australia.

Tolkien, J. R. R. (1954-5), *The Lord of the Rings*, London: George Allen & Unwin.

X-Men (2000–20), [Film series] Dirs Josh Boone, Gavin Hood, Simon Kinberg, David Leitch, James Mangold, Tim Miller, Brett Ratner, Bryan Singer and Matthew Vaughn, USA: Marvel Entertainment et al.

Secondary Literature

Atkinson, D. (2003), 'L2 Writing in the Post-Process Era: Introduction', *Journal of Second Language Writing*, 12 (1): 3–15.

Baetens, J. (2011), 'From Black & White to Color and Back: What Does It Mean (not) to Use Color?' *College Literature*, 38 (3): 111–28.

Bear, R., H. Estrem, J. E. Fredricksen and D. Shepherd (2014), 'Participation and Collaboration in Digital Spaces: Connecting High School and College Writing Experiences', in J. P. Purdy and R. McClure (eds), *The Next Digital Scholar: A Fresh Approach to the Common Core State Standards in Research and Writing*, 141–73, Medford, NJ: Information Today.

Brauweiler, P. (2021), 'Kollaboratives Schreiben im Englischunterricht in einer Kultur der Digitalität', in J. Buendgens-Kosten and P. Schildhauer (eds), *Englischunterricht in einer digitalisierten Gesellschaft*, 26–45, Weinheim: Beltz Juventa.

Buendgens-Kosten, J., and P. Schildhauer, eds (2021), *Englischunterricht in einer digitalisierten Gesellschaft*, Weinheim: Beltz Juventa.

Cornille, F., J. Buendgens-Kosten, S. Sauro and J. Van der Veken (2021), ' "There's Always an Option": Collaborative Writing of Multilingual Interactive Fan Fiction in a Foreign Language Class', *CALICO Journal*, 38 (1): 17–42.

Dürscheid, C., and K. Frick (2016), *Schreiben digital: Wie das Internet unsere Alltagskommunikation verändert*, Stuttgart: Kröner.

Ekman, S. (2018), 'Entering a Fantasy World through Its Map', *Extrapolation*, 59 (1): 71–87.

Elbow, P. (2000), *Everyone Can Write: Essays Toward a Hopeful Theory of Writing and Teaching Writing*, New York: Oxford University Press.

Furneaux, C., A. Paran and B. Fairfax (2007), 'Teacher Stance as Reflected in Feedback on Student Writing: An Empirical Study of Secondary School Teachers in Five Countries', *International Review of Applied Linguistics in Language Teaching*, 45 (1): 69–94.

Gabel, S., and J. Schmidt (2017), 'Collaborative Writing with Writing Pads in the Foreign Language Classroom – Chances and Limitations', in C. Ludwig and K. Van de Poel (eds), *Collaborative Learning and New Media: New Insights into an Evolving Field*, 189–211, Berlin: Peter Lang.

Gibson, R. H. (2021), *Paper Electronic Literature: An Archaeology of Born-Digital Materials*, Amherst: University of Massachusetts Press.

Goldberg, N. (1986), *Writing Down the Bones: Freeing the Writer Within*, Boston, MA: Shambhala.

Hanauer, D. I. (2011), 'The Scientific Study of Poetic Writing', *Scientific Study of Literature*, 1 (1): 79–87.

Harper, G. (2015), 'Creative Writing and Education: An Introduction', in G. Harper (ed.), *Creative Writing and Education*, 1–16, Bristol: Multilingual Matters.

Hayles, N. K. (2004), 'Print Is Flat, Code Is Deep: The Importance of Media-Specific Analysis', *Poetics Today*, 25 (1): 67–90.

Hyland, K. (2003), 'Genre-Based Pedagogies: A Social Response to Process', *Journal of Second Language Writing*, 12 (1): 17–29.

Iida, A. (2019), 'Haiku and Spoken Language: Corpus-Driven Analyses of Linguistic Features in English Language Haiku Writing', in C. Jones (ed.), *Literature, Spoken Language and Speaking Skills in Second Language Learning*, 96–117, Cambridge: Cambridge University Press.

Jenkins, H. (2006). *Convergence Culture: Where Old and New Media Collide*, New York: New York University Press.

Kieweg, W. (2009), 'Schreibprozesse gestalten, Schreibkompetenz entwickeln', *Der fremdsprachliche Unterricht Englisch*, 43 (97): 2–8.

Kirchhoff, P. (2018), 'Productive Competences – Speaking, Writing, Mediating', in C. Surkamp and B. Viebrock (eds), *Teaching English as a Foreign Language: An Introduction*, 109–32, Stuttgart: J.B. Metzler.

Kirchhoff, P. (2019), 'Your Story in 280 Characters Max: Twitter fiction für das kreative Schreiben nutzen', *Der Fremdsprachliche Unterricht Englisch*, 53 (160): 40–5.

Landow, G. P. (1992), *Hypertext: The Convergence of Contemporary Critical Theory and Technology*, Baltimore, MA: Johns Hopkins University Press.

Ludwig, C. (2019), *Envisioning Other Worlds: Science Fiction and Dystopias – Handreichungen für den Unterricht*, Berlin: Cornelsen.

Ludwig, C. (2021), 'Teaching Literature with Digital Media', in C. Lütge and T. Merse (eds), *Digital Teaching and Learning: Perspectives for English Language Education*, 207–30, Tübingen: Narr.

Ludwig, C., and E. Shipley, eds (2020), *Mapping the Imaginative: Teaching Fantasy and Science Fiction in the EFL Classroom*, vols I and II, Heidelberg: Universitätsverlag Winter.

Lütge, C. (2018a), 'Literature and Film – Approaching Fictional Texts and Media', in C. Surkamp and B. Viebrock (eds), *Teaching English as a Foreign Language: An Introduction*, 177–94, Stuttgart: J.B. Metzler.

Lütge, C. (2018b), 'Digital, Transcultural and Global? Reconsidering the Role of Literature in the EFL Classroom', in A.-J. Zwierlein, J. Petzold, K. Boehm and M. Decker (eds), *Anglistentag 2017 Regensburg: Proceedings*, 299–309, Trier: Wissenschaftlicher Verlag Trier.

Lütge, C., and T. Merse, eds (2021), *Digital Teaching and Learning: Perspectives for English Language Education*, Tübingen: Narr.

Matsuda, P. K. (2003), 'Process and Post-Process: A Discursive History', *Journal of Second Language Writing*, 12 (1): 65–83.

Matz, F. (2014), 'Schreiben', in C. Lütge (ed.), *Englisch Methodik: Handbuch für die Sekundarstufe I und II*, 33–50. Berlin: Cornelsen Scriptor.

Morley, D. (2007), *The Cambridge Introduction to Creative Writing*, Cambridge: Cambridge University Press.

Myers, J. (2014), 'Digital Conversations: Taking Reader Response into the 21st Century', *Journal of the Texas Council of Teachers of English Language Arts*, 44 (1): 59–65.

Neef, S. (2010), *Imprint and Trace: Handwriting in the Age of Technology*, London: Reaktion.

Ohler, J. (2007), *Digital Storytelling in the Classroom: New Media Pathways to Literacy, Learning and Creativity*, Heatherton: Hawker Brownlow Education.

Pine, G. J. (2009), *Teacher Action Research: Building Knowledge Democracies*, Thousand Oaks, CA: Sage.

Pointner, F. E. (2013), 'Teaching Comics as Comics', in C. Ludwig and F. E. Pointner (eds), *Teaching Comics in the Foreign Language Classroom*, 27–68, Trier: WVT.

Sauro, S., and B. Sundmark (2019), 'Critically Examining the Use of Blog-Based Fan Fiction in the Advanced Language Classroom', *ReCALL*, 31 (1): 40–55.

Sauro, S., and K. Zourou (2019), 'What Are the Digital Wilds?', *Language Learning & Technology*, 23 (1): 1–7.

Skorge, P. (2021), 'Poetry Writing in the Secondary EFL Classroom – Digitally Triggered and Transfigured', in J. Buendgens-Kosten and P. Schildhauer (eds), *Englischunterricht in einer digitalisierten Gesellschaft*, 57–68, Weinheim: Beltz Juventa.

Soobin, Y., and M. Warschauer (2014), 'Technology and Second Language Writing: A Framework-Based Synthesis of Research', in K. E. Pytasch and R. E. Ferdig (eds), *Exploring Technology for Writing and Writing Instruction*, 298–312, Hershey, PA: IGI Global.

Thomas, B. (2020), *Literature and Social Media*, New York: Routledge.

Tobin, L. (2001), 'Process Pedagogy', in G. Tate, A. Rupiper and K. Schick (eds), *A Guide to Composition Pedagogies*, 1–18, Oxford: Oxford University Press.

Toffler, A. (1980), *The Third Wave*, New York: William Morrow.

Tolkien, J. R. R. (1947), 'On Fairy-Stories', in C. S. Lewis (ed.), *Essays Presented to Charles Williams*, 38–89, Oxford: Oxford University Press.

Vass, E., K. Littleton, D. Miell and A. Jones (2008), 'The Discourse of Collaborative Creative Writing: Peer Collaboration as a Context for Mutual Inspiration', *Thinking Skills and Creativity*, 3 (3): 192–202.

Watts, H. (1995), 'When Teachers Are Researchers, Teaching Improves', *Journal of Staff Development*, 6 (2): 118–27.

Zamel, V. (1982), 'Writing: The Process of Discovering Meaning', *TESOL Quarterly*, 16 (2): 195–209.

Zamel, V. (1985), 'Responding to Student Writing', *TESOL Quarterly*, 19 (1): 79–101.

Afterword: Closing Reflections on the Brave New World of Literature and Language Education Online

Geoff Hall

MIRANDA
O brave new world,
That has such people in 't!
PROSPERO
    Tis new to thee.

      – William Shakespeare, *The Tempest*, V.1

Shakespeare's *The Tempest* is ultimately a romance. Thus, while our first response to Miranda's inexperienced exclamation may be closer to Prospero's world-weary cynicism, Shakespeare shows us that the truth and the future are more hopeful than this, whatever difficulties may need to be overcome, and indeed that the future is with the young and the new, not with the old. In the same way, while we should not be naive about the challenges of e-learning and e-teaching, experience since early 2020, as represented in this timely collection, still gives some cause for optimism. The rapid, unprepared and unprecedented move to online education as 'emergency remote teaching' as opposed to 'online learning' is a pithy and important formulation, so that Hodges et al. (2020) is already understandably a widely referenced position in this collection as elsewhere. Nevertheless, the enforced and speedy shift online has stimulated some valuable new practices and ideas.

    Teachers and learners teach and learn in different ways under different circumstances, and the internet offers affordances that should be taken up to expand all our repertoires and horizons. The internet is no different to traditional physical learning spaces in this respect. The best practice moves beyond unreflecting transfer of print culture materials to screens and servers, to explore the educational possibilities of sound, image and multimodality. The interest of this book is in the evidence it shows of this kind of rethinking and new thinking being done with reference to literature teaching and learning in particular, and across all levels from primary (Ellis and Mourão) to secondary (Schumm Fauster, Gardemann) and higher education (Laschinger, Abubaker and El-Badri), teacher training (Kaminski) extending to beginner immigrant ESL learners (Malard Monteiro, Wilkinson and Young-Scholten). Literature-based learning typically involves broadening of 'experience' and understanding rather than just another knowledge 'topic' to be ticked off the curriculum list (Schumm Fauster), with activities and resources developed accordingly. Here, beyond generalities and abstract ideas, we are shown numerous instances of creative innovation for literature, language and e-learning in practice which other practitioners can reflect on and learn from, including learning from mistakes that were inevitably made by all of us as we rushed or were pushed into this brave relatively new world for most of us.

The naive celebrations of the move by managers who see only apparent short-term financial savings to be made have been unfortunate if only too predictable. The requirement for training and support needs to be better recognized, including workload recognition for the efforts that have been made and will need to be made from here on. A first important conclusion from what we have learned so far is that online provision and maintenance demand resource. Most teachers and students are still saying – both in surveys and in conversations with colleagues – that they prefer face-to-face contact, that internet provision comes a poor second. More interesting than such an either-or mindset is an increasing recognition all around that intelligently designed so-called hybrid provision (Kaminski), catering for synchronous and asynchronous study, a mix of students present and students (or teachers) online, is the new norm and can benefit learning but needs to be improved much further in most cases. How do we promote and maintain participation (Summer) and engagement (Ellis and Mourão) with materials and teachers in a given group? Laschinger provides a worthwhile example of motivated collaboration by learners (see also Ludwig and Shipley). Some evidence (e.g. Schumm Fauster) suggests that once learners are engaged, the students' more public perception of a recorded online presentation or performance can prompt better quality work than is usually seen in the face-to-face classroom with the possibility of enhanced learning. What principles underlie the most effective interaction and outcomes? When and how do we interact with our student groups and individuals? These are recurrent concerns of the collection with some first tentative answers sketched.

As human beings, we have all used the internet during lockdowns and other restrictions not only to catch up on Netflix and box sets, or to 'doomscroll' down the latest increasingly depressing news, but also to interact in ways that helped keep up our spirits and to reassure us that we were not alone, and that we should appreciate what we have as well as what we may be missing. Bird song was almost as popular through the BBC as through actual daily walks through newly quiet neighbourhoods (compare Summer's chapter or that of Laschinger). Gessner in this collection reports narrative as a personal and shared supportive resource for many through this crisis.

As in wartime, poems and other literary memes circulated quickly and widely. Derek Mahon's poem 'Everything Is Going to Be Alright' was appreciated by more people online than would ever have considered it in print; I found (and used with students) some marvellous everyday haiku sites where many tried creative writing in a sustained and rewarding way for the first time. These continue to proliferate. An issue that has bothered many educators for a long time is that the kind of individualized formal writing required by the academy no longer occurs anywhere else outside the academy (Ludwig and Shipley). Creative writing (as an example of a way of learning and a skill in itself to learn) is referenced in this collection in interesting ways by Gardemann, by Ludwig and Shipley and by Malard Monteiro, Wilkinson and Young-Scholten, among others. Play generally, the root of creativity, long recognized for its value for learners, may be easier to encourage in relevant ways and more natural on the internet than in the more obviously disciplined space of the physical classroom.

It may even be argued, paradoxically, with evidence in these chapters, that internet activities can help build sensitivity to others under the right conditions. Teaching and learning for many developed a new heightened awareness of the contextual circumstances of real people's everyday lives impacting on their/ our educational activities during lockdowns and other restrictions. Can you hear me? Is anybody there? as we kept asking each other, the questions taking on a new existential resonance beyond purely technical concerns. Education is by definition about change, liminality and movement in a time of stasis (compare Gessner's chapter). The pandemic prompted reflection (as Thaler and others show), for example, on the idea of our hyperconnected world – and our vulnerability as human beings – which took on new and less positive meanings than many entertained before.

Most chapters here refer to multimodal affordances of the internet and other media. And still, how little research has been previously reported, for example, on use of 'read-alouds' (Ellis and Mourão) and on picturebooks, audiobooks, podcasts and mixes of sound, music, images, including moving images (Summer), in language education, despite the length of time they were with us long before Covid-19. More active participation from learners can include preparation and performance followed by shared recordings and discussion of their own input, beyond the usual one-word answers to the teacher of a traditional classroom. For some, undoubtedly including many literature teachers, the position regarding online learning and the internet hitherto seems to have been something like 'ignore it and it might go away'; screen reading and hyperlinks often on commercial sites with cookies certainly offer real challenges to concentration and traditional ideas of reading and thinking. Interactions with text and with others are crucial to all learning but again research till now has largely been in textual and verbal interaction only and normally under face-to-face conditions. The internet reminds us that the world is larger and more multimodal than that.

And what is the teacher's role in all this? Most of us did not join the profession to become technical managers facilitating meetings on Teams or Zoom (Kaminski). 'Please turn your camera on.' We are not so good at that yet; more important, we feel we have other skills and strengths to offer our learners that interest us more. One such strength which this collection can prompt is to critically interrogate innovations to see what is added and what may be lost, to balance disruption against continuity (Gardemann). What support and professional development do teachers require to make the most of these new possibilities? Teachers must input into that discussion, based on their experiences to date. Note also (e.g. the differences between Kaminski's first and second cohorts and changing teacher strategies) that the situation changes as learners and teachers get used to the idea of working with and making more of IT in their learning and in changing circumstances. The picture is not static or one-dimensional (Laschinger). The basic truth remains that technology should be used to promote better learning, probably in hybrid and flipped learning combinations, not for its own sake or simply as a temporary measure when there is no choice (Abubaker and El-Badri). Indeed Abubaker and El-Badri do well to remind us that in many parts of the world assumptions about availability of hardware and software will need to be localized and adapted.

In conclusion, three simple but related important questions consistently emerge for me from this collection as well as from wider reading and my own pedagogical experience:

1. What did you do/can you do that could only have been done online or would not be likely to happen in classrooms as we knew them 'before Covid-19'?
2. What is/was better about doing it online (e.g. presentations or enhanced student autonomy and agency)?
3. What needs to be done differently or with new awareness of interacting through remote media?

Necessity has undoubtedly been the mother of invention in these new times. The challenge now is to evaluate, then retain and develop worthwhile innovations in times of ongoing change and uncertainty, and this requires in most cases so far reported enhanced ongoing support from institutions, including increased preparation time as well as training sessions, ongoing support for the development of fit and relevant materials, and continued financial support through IT budgets. Additional workload issues have not begun to be tackled in situations I am aware of or have read about (see also Richards 2021). Rightly, the experienced contributors to this collection use a cautious language of 'potential' and possibility, informed judgement and data-based evaluation, context and contingency, people and participation, in an important first sustained intervention to explore applications of e-learning for literature teaching in their own circumstances. These valuable contributions should be taken in this critical and provisional spirit in which they were offered. Continuing flexibility and resilience are incumbent upon all of us. Let us consider and adapt these opportunities constructively and positively as a mark of faith in the future brave new world in these often dark and difficult present conditions in which we are working. Education has always been defined by its concern with change and futurity. Real change is afoot, but change for the better is central to what we do and who we are as educators and requires the active participation of all.

References

Primary Literature

Shakespeare, W. (1998), *The Tempest*, Project Gutenberg. https://gutenberg.org/ebo oks/1540 (accessed 6 December 2021).

Secondary Literature

Hodges, C., S. Moore, B. Lockee, T. Trust and A. Bond (2020), 'The Difference between Emergency Remote Teaching and Online Learning', *EDUCAUSE Review*, 27 March.

https://er.educause.edu/articles/2020/3/the-difference-between-emergency-remote-teachingand-online-learning (accessed 28 November 2021).

Mahon, D. (2012), 'Everything Is Going to Be Alright'. https://anthonywilsonpoetry.com/2012/10/06/lifesaving-poems-derek-mahons-everything-is-going-to-be-all-right/ (accessed 1 December 2021).

Richards, J. (2021), 'Message from the Outgoing Editor', *RELC Journal*, 52 (3): 356–8. https://doi.org/10.1177/00336882211061885.

Index

Lightning Source UK Ltd.
Milton Keynes UK
UKHW021456040123
414802UK00004B/94